THE VICE OF KINGS

THE VICE OF KINGS
How Socialism, Occultism, and the Sexual Revolution Engineered a Culture of Abuse

Jasun Horsley

AEON

First published in 2019 by
Aeon Books Ltd
12 New College Parade
Finchley Road
London NW3 5EP

British Library Cataloguing in Publication Data

A C.I.P. for this book is available from the British Library

ISBN-13: 978-1-91159-704-9

Typeset by Medlar Publishing Solutions Pvt Ltd, India

www.aeonbooks.co.uk

"In every cry of every Man,
In every Infant's cry of fear,
In every voice: in every ban,
The mind-forg'd manacles I hear."
—William Blake, "London"

"One resists the invasion of armies; one does not resist the invasion of ideas."
—Victor Hugo, *History of a Crime*

To
my brother
and
my father.

And
to those who
came before.

CONTENTS

A word of caution: *The book you are about to read is an exploration into (among others things) systematized child sexual abuse, in some cases of the most extreme kind, as well as the philosophies and rationales behind it. It includes some of the author's own possible experiences of the same. As such, it may be disturbing—and even potentially destabilizing—to readers with experiences of sexual abuse in their own past.*

COCK-UP OR CONSPIRACY?
(AUTHOR'S NOTE)

Theodore Dalrymple once said that we are more attached to our worldviews than we are to the world. The book you are about to read presents a challenge to *my* worldview, and I wrote it, so I fully anticipate that some readers will have objections to what I have written. *The Vice of Kings* is the third in a loose-knit trilogy, with *Seen and Not Seen: Confessions of a Movie Autist* and *Prisoner of Infinity: UFOs, Social Engineering, and the Psychology of Fragmentation* as the first installments. Familiarity with these other works is helpful but not essential. While these books' thesis—that of cultural engineering—may appear to have much in common with the (increasingly mainstream) conspiratorial view of history, I have made every effort throughout to keep my own interpretations, speculations, and theories to the minimum, and let the facts speak for themselves. As independent researcher Ty Brown once put it, "Observe more, interpret less." Of course, what constitutes a fact is itself open to interpretation, especially when it comes to the kind of controversial subject matter that this book covers. For this reason, I have done my best with this present work to only cite books from reputable publishers and authors, articles from mainstream papers, magazines, and websites (mostly British), and, whenever straying of necessity into the murky

xvi   COCK-UP OR CONSPIRACY? (AUTHOR'S NOTE)

waters of independent online research, to stick to responsible and fully cited articles (such as appear at *The Needle* or Ian Pace's site).

It may be argued that mainstream media itself is hardly a trustworthy source when it comes to reporting high-level crimes and institutional corruption (and I admit to resorting to *The Daily Mail* whenever more respected papers have stayed away from a given subject). But even the British popular press is at least subject to reprisals for irresponsible journalism, so I have trusted that, as long as information printed has not been contested, it now belongs in the category of "official" history.

Regarding Part II of the book, which focuses on the infamous occultist Aleister Crowley, I relied more on existing literature (Crowley's books, various biographies, and various books on the occult). It might be argued (by some) that I have merely cherry-picked the data that supports my case against Crowley. This would rather miss the point, however, since my aim is not to present a rounded picture of Crowley but to address the omissions, obfuscations, and distortions from and in the dominant narrative of his life, specifically by presenting the evidence for his involvement in criminal acts and covert programs of abuse. One might as well argue that a portrait of Jimmy Savile that zeros in on his crimes is "unbalanced." We all know that a single heinous act, once established, is enough to cancel out a thousand good deeds in our minds, while it certainly doesn't work the other way. I think this is a reasonable enough perspective. As C. S. Lewis's demon Screwtape observed, "To be greatly and effectively wicked a man needs some virtue" (2002, p. 159). I do not think it goes the other way, that to be an effectively virtuous person one needs some wickedness—though Crowley and his many followers would doubtless disagree.

This book is about the vices of our kings (our cultural heroes and political leaders), not their charms, talents, or occasionally genuine virtues, since, as Lewis well knew, these latter are often but cloaks that facilitate the former rather than positive attributes unto themselves. The same might be said for government (and even society) in general, as seen in the present work at least. But this latter is only my opinion, and I trust the reader will do his or her part to keep their attention on the facts being presented, no matter how challenging they may be to their worldview, and try not to blame the messenger, bearing in mind that I am not a historian and this book is not a history book, unless it be one of personal history. For the most part, these facts were already "out there" and available to everyone: All I have done is arrange them into some sort of coherence between two covers. Correlation is not causation, however, and there is always the danger that, by placing related facts side by side (which inevitably means leaving out other related facts), a premature assumption of conspiracy may arise, or—since conspiracy is *almost* as *verboten* a word as there is these days—let us call it *conscious complicity of intent.*

My father used to say, "There's the conspiracy theory of history, and then there's the *cock-up* theory of history. I believe in the cock-up theory." In a similar spirit, Theodore Dalrymple joked recently that every policy implemented by the British government creates the exact opposite result to the one intended. This is a well-observed fact of unconscious behavior: that we tend to bring about results according to our unconscious drives, not to our conscious aims. I have no doubt at all as to the existence of an unconscious conspiracy (or "conspiracy") at the heart of Western society. Nor do I have any doubt that there exist—at any given time in history—a bevy of conscious conspiracies embedded into this larger, unconscious one. (And let's be honest at the start, anyone who doubts that conscious conspiracies are *at least sometimes* a driving force in human history is either ill-informed or ill-intended.) Regarding the degree to which they might all be stitched together by the principle of "cock-up," namely, by a force both more and less than human, I would rather not venture an opinion. I will let the reader decide: cock-up, conspiracy, or a diabolic confluence and collaboration of the two?

My thanks to the many researchers in this particular ontological minefield who have courageously attempted to uncover the true nature of our society and the "principles of darkness" that characterize it. Credit is due to the forum Rigorous Intuition, where the "Occult Yorkshire" investigation first began, and to my longtime readers and listeners for sticking with me through this arduous and often exhausting process. Thanks to Ann Diamond, Cathy Morgan, Wendy Hoffman, Chris (Anonymous Italian), Gary Heidt, and Alison Miller, as well as any other survivors of extreme trauma who have reached out to me. Your input has helped ground my investigations in the realm of the real, like a phosphorescent compass in sometimes overwhelming darkness. More personally, my thanks to my sister and cousin, the only two Horsleys willing to pay a visit to the family excavation site while it was ongoing.

Also thanks to Tuco and Garbanzo and all the cats who have accompanied me through life and kept me on the straight and narrow.

Lastly, thanks must go to my wife, for her endless patience, interest, and invaluable intuitive gift for finding the most recondite material in the almost infinite recesses of cyberspace. Perhaps more than any other factor—besides my own stubbornness—her input made this book what it is.

Jasun Horsley, March 2018

Glamor vice

> "I too found my inner child some years ago—and had an abortion."
>
> —Sebastian Horsley, 2004, private correspondence

My brother, self-proclaimed "dandy in the underworld" Sebastian Horsley, was an artist most celebrated for his potentially (and in the end actually) self-destructive pursuits. As one reviewer of his "unauthorized autobiography" *Dandy in the Underworld* wrote, "Unless he is experiencing extreme sensations, Horsley doesn't seem to feel he exists" (Lewis, 2007). A recent *Time Out* article listed him as one of London's top ten drug-users; another 2014 piece about the Hollywood actor Shia LeBeouf wrote that my brother "convincingly made his own fatal self-destruction a work of art." That sentence speaks volumes. Who exactly did my brother's artistic self-destruction convince, and of what? That suicide is a worthy artistic pursuit? Or that artistic expression (or fame) is worth destroying oneself for? What sort of legacy does such a "work of art" leave? How can someone compulsively driven to destroy themselves be turned into a cause for celebration?

I am one of two people still living (along with my sister, a psychotherapist) with close inside knowledge of the forces that drove my brother to self-destruct. As such, one thing is painfully clear to me: Whatever "message" my brother conveyed, via his life and death, it is not a true message but a fiction, a cover story that covers a legion of sins. Ironically, it covers them not so much with an illusion of virtue, as in the much more famous case of Jimmy Savile (though Savile also paraded his vices). More akin to the magician Aleister Crowley (the subject of Part II of this work), my brother's cover was a dandy's cloak of glamorized vice, the art of which can be summed up (in a phrase he plagiarized from Quentin Crisp) as: "[T]hat which cannot be wholly concealed should be deliberately displayed" (S. Horsley, 2007, p. 184). It's my belief that Sebastian Horsley's "art" was not self-destruction, *per se* (though that was certainly a consequence of it), but the elaborate concealment of the social, cultural, and domestic forces that made his destruction inevitable. I think it shows how the abused is *engineered*, not only to protect his abusers, but to perpetuate the abuse.

Nor is my comparison to Savile entirely random. As I wrote in *Seen and Not Seen*, with his flamboyant outfits, bleached hair, jingle-jangling jewelry, and bizarre persona, Savile was also a dandy. Like my brother, and like the Child Catcher in *Chitty Chitty Bang Bang*, Savile was known to wear a top hat once in a while. For those (non-British) readers who are unfamiliar with Savile, he was an English DJ, television and radio personality, dance hall manager, and charity fundraiser who hosted the BBC television show *Jim'll Fix It*, was the first and last presenter of the long-running BBC music chart show *Top of the Pops*, and who raised an estimated £40 million for charities. At the time of his death, he was admired by millions. After his death, however, hundreds of allegations of sexual abuse were made against him, indicating that Savile was possibly Britain's most prolific predatory sex offender. There were allegations during his lifetime, and rumors circulating for decades, but the accusers were ignored or disbelieved (Savile took legal action against some of them), and the rumors were dismissed. Savile's predations covered at least five decades and included hundreds, if not thousands, of victims, both male and female, ranging in age from five to seventy-five. Yet what is perhaps just as remarkable is the degree to which Savile's activities were facilitated, indicating that he was part of a larger criminal network that included the highest levels, not just of mass media and entertainment, but of government, law enforcement, and the intelligence community. Of the many honors he received, only some were removed after the truth came out. As discussed in *Prisoner of Infinity*, Jimmy Savile was a Catholic and belonged to the religious order of the Knights of Malta. He was given an OBE (Officer of the Most Excellent Order of the British Empire) in 1972, was made a Knight Bachelor "for charitable services," and awarded a papal knighthood (Knight Commander of the Pontifical Equestrian Order of Saint Gregory the Great (KCSG)) from Pope John Paul II, in 1990. He held an honorary doctorate of law (LLD) from the University of Leeds, was an honorary fellow of the Royal College of Radiologists (FRCR), had the Cross of Merit of the Order pro merito Melitensi, an honorary green beret from the Royal Marines, an honorary doctorate from the University of Bedfordshire, and he was a Freeman of the Borough of Scarborough. In short, he was a national institution, and tearing that institution down after his death has not obscured the fact that it was the nation that made him thus.

I doubt my brother ever emulated Savile, but at the same time it's difficult to calculate the extent of Savile's influence on us, growing up during the Sixties and Seventies. During that period, Savile was considered the most influential man in British rock and roll, and my brother and I watched *Top of the Pops* every week, you might say religiously. My brother's first, and most lasting, role model was glam-rocker Marc Bolan, and in some ways Savile was an avatar of glam rock. Is it possible my brother could have learned some of his dandy-tricks from Savile? One of the most disturbing things about Savile was how open he was about his proclivities. He joked about them on TV and the radio (sometimes even with his victims present). He admitted to some in his autobiography, *As It Happens*. Yet nobody said anything.

The ongoing, seemingly unending revelations in the UK (which I suspect are just beginning in the US) around the institutionalized sexual abuse of children have forced people to reevaluate what they know about how corruption works and what it looks like. Once upon a time, we looked for sexual predators lurking on street corners and outside schoolyards: shady, shifty characters malingering on the margins of society, easy to identify and even easier to scapegoat. In post-Savile Britain, such a simple view is a luxury of ignorance. The real predators are in positions of power and access; they aren't marginal characters or outsiders, but the pillars of our community. Far from unwittingly exposing themselves by their shifty looks and guilty demeanors, they seem devoid of the self-awareness necessary for guilt. They don't give any of the "tells" we count on to alert us that someone is up to no good.

In their own eyes, they are *entitled* to act the way they do. It is the power of privilege, and the privilege of power.

It's my view that the qualities for which my brother's self-destructive life and art (his artful self-destruction) being celebrated were not the unique expressions of a creative soul, but symptoms of a fatally traumatized psyche. They were his desperate public attempt to get free of a cultural and familial morass, a struggle that, ironically and tragically, was embraced by that same culture as "art." In *Dandy in the Underworld*, he even described that morass in terms of art: "If someone were to set up a production in which Bette Davis was directed by Roman Polanski," he wrote, "it could not express to the full the pent-up violence and depravity of a single day in the life of my family. It was a foul octopus from whose tentacles I would never quite escape."

*

> "'Sensation' is deeply conventional, but it obeys a wicked and socially destructive convention."
> —Theodore Dalrymple, *Our Culture, What's Left of It*

My brother and I were born into the same tentacles of privilege. Our grandfather, Alec Horsley, went to Oxford, was assistant district officer in Nigeria from 1925 to 1932, and founded his own business, Northern Dairies, in 1937. He was also a founding member of the Hull Fabian Society, whose logo was and is a wolf in sheep's clothing. The Fabian Society laid the foundations for the UK Labour party, and Russell Brand has recently been advocating their ideas to the masses: a curious detail because my brother saw Brand as a rival. (Besides a penchant for top hats, sex, and drugs, and a camp messiah complex, there are other striking parallels between them.) In my grandfather's day, Fabian Society members advocated the ideal of "a scientifically planned society" which included "eugenics by way of sterilization." The Hull branch of the Fabians was established in 1943, with sixteen members including a committee chaired by my grandfather. Apparently my grandfather followed closely in Bertrand Russell's footsteps, being a (closet) aristocrat who spoke out for the common man yet had little in common with him. (As far as I know, and apart from visiting prisons, he rarely if ever mixed with the lower classes.)

My father, Nicholas Horsley, joined Northern Dairies in the late 1950s, shortly after meeting my mother. Eventually, he took over as chairman and Northern Dairies became Northern Foods, a massive conglomerate most famously affiliated with Marks & Spencer (along with M&S, Northern Foods is credited with creating the chilled food industry). I was only dimly aware of any of this while growing up. The most significant development for me as a child was probably when Northern Foods forged an alliance with Rowntree Mackintosh, which meant our house was always full of chocolates. I *was* aware of the many parties, at both our own house and that of our grandparents, and of the many strangers who came and went, the general atmosphere of drunkenness, social and intellectual idealism, sexual license, and my grandfather's peculiar interest, not just in celebrity but in criminality.

In *Seen and Not Seen*, I quoted a passage in *Dandy in the Underworld* that describes a "pedophile friend of Grandfather's" who took a shine to me as a child. The book describes me as having "one of those faces of marvelous beauty which stopped strangers in the streets," then adds that "a pedophile invited into the family circle could hardly have been expected to be indifferent." I have no memory of this man, but I do recall how stories of his clumsy attempt at fondling me under the dinner table were told with amusement by my parents. The incident is equally lost to memory, but apparently it was never seen as a cause for alarm.

Another odd detail is that my sister had Jimmy Savile's autograph when she was a teenager. Allegedly my father had a chance meeting with Savile on an airplane (though interestingly enough, Savile claimed he never flew). As the head of Northern Foods, my father was a highly respected businessman with political connections, and he might well have run into Savile in, shall we say, less neutral circumstances. In Savile's surprisingly revealing autobiography, *As It Happens*, Savile mentions that, on his famous John o'Groats to Land's End charity run, he was accompanied by an executive from Northern Foods, the company that supplied him with food and drink for the run. So you could say that my family's business literally fueled Jimmy Savile's "run."

What's in a metaphor?

*

> "[I]f all art is the breaking of taboos, all breaking of taboos soon
> comes to be regarded as art .... and what is broken symbolically
> in art will soon enough be broken in reality."
>
> —Theodore Dalrymple, *Our Culture, What's Left of It*

In *Dandy in the Underworld*, Sebastian wrote: "A lifetime of neglect had left me seething with a lust for revenge."

It was our grandfather who introduced my brother to the Glaswegian ex-gangster Jimmy Boyle. Alec had arranged for some of Boyle's sculptures to be exhibited in Hull. With his staunch liberal values about reform, he was impressed by Boyle, a celebrity after his book *A Sense of Freedom* was turned into a BBC film. Boyle was first imprisoned for murder in 1967, and was released in 1982. In his heyday, he was an enforcer and debt collector for the Glasgow mafia, known as "Scotland's most violent man." Despite this, his sentence was reduced, and it seems reasonable to suppose my grandfather's support had something to do with it.

In 1983, Boyle and his wife Sarah Trevelyan teamed up with my brother and his partner and started the Gateway Exchange, a reform center for drug addicts, sex offenders, and ex-convicts in which my brother professed to be "well-camouflaged." In his memoir, he writes how Boyle "allowed [him] to express forbidden impulses, secret wishes and fantasies" (S. Horsley, 2007, p. 119).[1] My brother's fascination for criminality was something he shared with Alec and that included writing letters to the Kray twins and the notorious Moors murderer, Myra Hindley. A 1999 *Guardian* article about Jimmy Boyle mentions how, in 1967 (just before he was arrested), Boyle "was on the run in London and under the protection of the Krays". According to my brother, Boyle worked with the Krays during the Sixties and possibly earlier. Jimmy Savile was connected to the Krays, and Savile was from Yorkshire, where my brother and I grew up and where Peter Sutcliffe, the Yorkshire Ripper (whom Savile also knew), allegedly stalked his victims during my teen years. (During that period, Savile was questioned by police about the murders and briefly considered to be a suspect.)

As described in *Seen and Not Seen*, Savile's early days as a dance-club manager meant rubbing shoulders with gangsters, maybe even as a teenager. He and the Krays worked and played together in the Sixties, and were likely involved with the sex trafficking of children to members of the British elite, including via care homes where children were allegedly tortured, even killed (see Chapter 14). Myra Hindley and Ian Brady frequented the same dance halls where Savile DJ-ed, in Manchester in the 1960s, and Savile talked about being friends with Ian Brady. Brady (who grew up in Glasgow before moving to Manchester), bragged about his associations with the Glasgow mafia and the Kray twins. Glasgow was also where the Paedophile Information Exchange (PIE) was founded, in 1975. It was affiliated with the National Council for Civil Liberties, a cause my family would almost certainly have actively supported. PIE's aim was to lower the age of consent to four, or to abolish it altogether.

It wasn't until I was writing *Seen and Not Seen* that I began to try to put all of these pieces together. It was like a first flyover of the scorched earth of my childhood. Since then I have touched down and begun to explore it more directly. The present work is like the first draft of a charred map.

*

> "It is a tragic paradox that the very qualities that lead to a man's extraordinary capacity for success are also those most likely to destroy him."
> —Sebastian Horsley, private correspondence with the author

My brother's life-path combined worldly success with self-destruction and showed that the two were inseparable for him. When I first quoted the above line in *Seen and Not Seen* (a line my brother inscribed to me, though he probably stole it from somewhere), I understood it differently. I understood it to mean that the unconscious forces within a person's soul that drive them to create can also drive them to self-destruct. I am fairly sure that was how my brother meant it. Yet he chose the word "success," not creativity or genius, and success has a distinctly worldly flavor to it. The way I read that quote now (at the end of the investigation you are about to read, if you do), is that the acts a man must commit in order to succeed, and the forces he must align himself with, are also those most likely to destroy him. This has nothing to do with creative self-expression, and everything to do with the will to *power*.

The tragic paradox of the artist is that the desire for worldly status is completely at odds with the deeper need of the soul to express what is within it to express. Yet both my brother and I were raised with the notion that worldly success was the final measure of how true or valuable one's expression (one's soul) was. To become a cultural leader was bred into us as the supreme social and personal goal, and as something we were entitled to *by birthright*. Despite Alec's Quakerism, which he only adopted later on and which my father probably rejected as hypocrisy, we had no religion in our family. My father's highest regard, like his father's, was for the *intelligentsia*. He made fun of my brother (a dyslexic) for being stupid, thereby delivering an axe blow to my brother's soul from which he never recovered. He gave us money in place of love, a value-set he inherited from his father, who once said, "To show you how much my father loved me, he left all his money to my brother." (Alec had a lifelong rivalry with his older brother—just as I did.) We were all given snakes in place of fish.

My brother was a lousy Fabian. He tore off the sheep clothes and openly embodied the wolf. He didn't want to please but to offend—to please *by* offending. My grandfather posed as the soul of virtue and community values but behind the scenes he was a ruthless businessman and something much more than that (as I think this work will show). Sebastian brought the hidden, criminal aspect of our family heirloom to the fore. He strove to take moral turpitude as far as it could be taken, "to turn decadence into a virtue [and] make the soul monstrous" (2007, p. 291). As I realized while writing *Seen and Not Seen*, for all his proud defiance of conventional morality and social conscience, there were almost certainly acts which my brother was involved in that he *couldn't* talk about, not only because of legal consequences but also for fear of reprisals from those involved. So while our father and grandfather hid their secret lives behind a cloak of virtue, my brother hid his behind a cloak of vice. In many ways, it is an even better disguise.

Were there things my brother, father, and grandfather were sworn not to tell? If so, what were they? What follows is an attempt to answer this maddening question, using a combination of investigation, deduction, and imagination—all of which are equally required when dealing with generational secrets.

My brother described himself as a "failed suicide" and "a futile blast of color in a colorless world" (2007, p. 323). Privately, he told me that he considered suicide the only honorable path for a nihilist, implying that at a certain point he planned to take his own life in order to cheat death, or God, of that pleasure. More poetically, he wrote in *Dandy* that the most important thing about facing the firing squad was to give the order oneself. Much of my brother's self-mythologizing was effective. It was *believed*, even, perhaps especially, by the people he kept close to him (which did not include his family). It was then picked up by the mainstream media, and today his death is seen by many as less tragic than heroic, as proof of a life lived on its own terms. Live by the needle, die by the needle. Such a view conveniently ignores—banishes—the question of what caused the suicidal addiction to begin with.

My brother and I were born and raised in an environment that glamorized vice and normalized corruption—in which corruption disguised itself as virtue. How else was he to feel safe in such an environment except by matching it, rejecting all virtue as a lie, and becoming *as* corrupt—openly so—as the world around him?

Children imitate not what they are told but what they are shown. Thinking of everyone who grew up during this period in Britain, watching Jimmy Savile cracking jokes about his crimes on national TV, going to schools and care homes run by sexual predators, unable to talk about it or even consciously acknowledge it, the question arises, what sort of long-term effect does this have on generations of children? My brother's case may just be one, particularly extreme case among legion.

There's no hard evidence my brother was sexually abused as a child. But then, there almost never is. Often the incident or incidents that traumatize a person's psyche are pushed into unconsciousness, shrouded by a protective veil of amnesia; and the deeper the trauma, the darker the veil. But the trauma shows through anyway: it shows through *as behaviors*. There is very little about my brother's public life, his persona, and his interest-obsessions, that doesn't point to a hidden history of abuse. Add to that the countless pieces of circumstantial evidence that our family circle overlapped, at multiple points—if it wasn't entirely at one with—the circles of systematized sexual abuse currently coming to light in the UK, and what does that leave?

Glamorized vice. If you can't beat them, join them.

*

The only reason you are reading this work is because my own efforts to join the culture that abused me have proven as futile as my efforts to beat it. All that leaves is to make official my refusal to participate, to testify, to defy my programming, to be the voice that was strangled, the voice that says no in thunder, even if the storm goes no further than my teacup.

It has to start somewhere.

PART I

OCCULT YORKSHIRE: FABIAN FAMILY SECRETS AND JIMMY SAVILE'S BRITAIN

"There is in society a parallel universe that is very close. All of us, whether knowingly or unknowingly, have frequent contact with it. It is populated by individuals who outwardly appear to be respectable, law abiding and not infrequently influential, and even popular members of society. They are found in all professions and they sexually abuse children, some in ways that are almost unimaginably extreme."

—"Institutional abuse and societal silence: An emerging global problem" (*Australian & New Zealand Journal of Psychiatry*, January 2014)

"If a son shall ask bread of any of you that is a father, will he give him a stone? or if he ask a fish, will he for a fish give him a serpent?"

—Luke, 11:11

The Grandfather: Alec Horsley, Northern Dairies, the Fabian Society

"Even though meritocracy is their reliable cover, social stratification was always the Fabians' real trump suit. Entitlements are another Fabian insertion into the social fabric, even though the idea antedates them, of course."
—John Taylor Gatto, *Underground History of American Education*

The first thing that stood out about my family history was my brother's relationship to Jimmy Boyle. My brother first met Boyle at Stevenson College, Edinburgh where Boyle was doing a "Training for Freedom" course, working two days a week at the local community center then returning to Saughton Prison at night. I knew he'd met Boyle via our paternal grandfather, so that was the next logical place to focus, in terms of seeking the beginning of the rot that eventually felled the tree. My brother was the eldest son of the eldest son of my grandfather, so back to the paternal ancestors I would go.

There isn't much online about Alec Horsley; fortunately, a cousin, who was also interested in our family background, sent me a PDF of a short memoir Alec wrote in 1987, as a foreword to a collection of poems by a prisoner he'd befriended in his seventies, *Joy and Woe* by Trevor Ounsworth. Ounsworth was a convicted rapist and one of the poems is allegedly about rape. I wasn't able to read the poems, but Alec's short introduction-memoir provided me with some names and dates that allowed for a whole latticework of associations to emerge.

My grandfather was born in 1902 and went to Oxford, Worcester College, probably in 1922. By his own account, he won a scholarship that almost entirely paid his way there. Who did he meet there and what was his involvement, if any, in the arcane Oxford secret societies and hazing rituals? My initial guess is that, since my grandfather (apparently) wasn't from the aristocracy, it was here he made the connections that sent him on the road to "Bilderberg" thereafter. As he writes: "My family progressed from working class to lower middle. And as for me, thanks to Oxford, country sport, and colonial appoint-ment, I was busy scaling the class ladder, *without being aware of my own drives*" (Ounsworth, 1987, p. 5, emphasis added). There is some reason to question Alec's account of things, however. His father, George Horsley, drove a Rolls-Royce *some* of the time (a habit my brother unconsciously copied in his early twenties), apparently alternating between wealth and poverty depending how well his enterprises were going. A Rolls-Royce is not a well-known perk for the "lower middle."

After Oxford, Alec worked in Nigeria from 1925 to 1932, either as assistant to the district officer or *as* district officer, depending on the source (Alec himself claimed the former, so it's most likely accurate). After he returned to the UK, got married, had children, and founded Northern Dairies, World War II broke out and my grandparents estab-lished their family home Talbot Lodge, in Hessle. "From the start," he writes, "we gained a reputation for holding 'open house' and encour-aged and of course enjoyed the visits of our many friends ... They came from all over Britain and several far off and sometimes exotic places abroad" (Ounsworth, 1987, p. 8).

As I wrote in *Seen and Not Seen*, among Alec's lifelong pals were

> Jacob Bronowski (*The Ascent of Man*), who worked for the Ministry of Home Security during World War Two (i.e., he was a spy), and Baron Eric Roll. Roll was appointed Professor of Economics and Commerce at University College, Hull, with the backing of John Maynard Keynes, the famous economist and (not so famous) ped-erast. This would have been around the time my grandfather met Roll. Roll worked for the Ministry of Food, went on to become

director of the Bank of England, and between 1986 and 1989 acted as chairman of the notorious (among conspirologists) Bilderberg meetings. (p. 274)

In 1954, Alec held the office of sheriff of Hull. The position was abolished in 1974 for whatever reason, and then reestablished in 2013. Since then it has been held by Virginia Bottomley, who was a governor of the London School of Economics for thirty-one years![1] The closely-related office of high steward of Kingston upon Hull has been occupied by the infamous Peter Mandelson since the same year, 2013, having also been abolished for the same period. Mandelson is accused of being a high-level "Satanist" at some of the more extreme conspiracy theory internet sites (e.g., Henry Makow), as well as, jokingly, of making a "satanic pact" for immortality by *The Independent*.[2] Leaving such lurid claims aside, he has also been more legitimately accused of involvement in child sexual abuse cover-ups, as reported in "Blair Paedophile Minister? Ask Peter Mandelson" (*The Needle*, 2014). Like Roll, Mandelson has chaired the mysterious Bilderberg meetings, and is, or was, closely tied to my uncle Chris Haskins, since they belong to some of the same think tanks (social engineering groups), as described in Chapter XVI.

I also found an interesting ancestral lead via the man who is listed at Wikipedia as sheriff of Hull for 1949:

> Rupert Alexander Alec-Smith, TD (5 September 1913, Beverley, Yorkshire—23 December 1983, Hull, Yorkshire) was an Englishman with an abiding interest in local history and founded the Georgian Society for East Yorkshire in 1937 [Northern Foods' start date, again] …. He was Lord Mayor of Hull in 1970–71 and made Lord Lieutenant of Humberside in 1980 …. Personal papers include over 500 letters of his parents, Alexander Alec-Smith and *Adelaide Alec-Smith (née Horsley)*, largely sent during the First World War, and about 300 letters Rupert Alec-Smith sent during the Second World War.[3]

Since Alec-Smith is a double-barreled combination of the names Alec and Smith, that means both the surnames Alec and Horsley are linked to someone who was the sheriff of Hull five years before Alec took the title. This can hardly be dismissed as a coincidence; yet if it is not, the suggestion is that Alec belonged to the same line as Robert Alec-Smith and is descended from Adelaide Horsley. If so, why has this part of my family history been so thoroughly buried?

In the early 1950s, Alec was invited to visit the USSR as part of a British team for an "East-West trade conference." In Moscow he met Lord Boyd Orr, who became president of Northern Foods. Alec then traveled to Siberia, Outer Mongolia, and China on unspecified business. What was he doing there? These were not the sorts of places one went for holidays back then (or even now), nor is it obvious how or why running a dairy would require visiting communist countries. I am not sure how easy it was to get into these countries at that time either.

Orr is an interesting character. He was born in Scotland and studied at Glasgow University. Like Alec's slightly spurious claim for himself, Orr *apparently* worked his way up from working class roots to the pinnacle of wealth and power.

> In the years following the Second World War, Boyd Orr was associated with virtually every organization that has agitated for world government, in many instances devoting his considerable administrative and propagandistic skills to the cause. "The most important question today," he says in his autobiography, "is whether man has attained the wisdom to adjust the old systems to suit the new powers of science and to realize that we are now one world in which all nations will ultimately share the same fate." (*Nobel Media*, 2007)

Soon after Alec's various sojourns, at the very start of the Suez Crisis, Lord Piercy and John Kinross of Industrial & Commercial Finance Corporation (formed by the Bank of England) approved Northern Dairies as a public firm. Then, in 1954, my grandfather was "approached by the Orthodox Church of Russia to organize a group of British churchmen to go to the USSR to visit their churches, without any strings. The visit proved most useful" (Ounsworth, 1987, p. 10. He wrote a booklet about it[4]).

In passing, I note that Lord Piercy became a full-time undergraduate student at the Fabian-created London School of Economics in 1910. He worked for the Inland Revenue during World War One, as well as being a minister of food. During World War Two, he was head of the British Petroleum mission in Washington D.C., principal assistant secretary in the Ministry of Supply and the Ministry of Aircraft Production, and personal assistant to the deputy prime minister, Clement Attlee. From 1945 to 1964, Piercy served as chairman of the Industrial & Commercial Finance Corporation which was set up to provide means to smaller businesses in the United Kingdom. He was also a director of the Bank of England from 1946 to 1956. That's a total of two directors of the Bank of England (the B of E helped found the National Socialist Party in Germany during the 1930s) whom my "socialist" grandfather chose to single out in his seven-page memoir.

During this same period (the mid- to late 1950s), Northern Dairies became affiliated with Mackintosh (Quality Street) and Terry's chocolate companies. My grandfather also mentions a trip to Dublin—Northern Ireland being the first place which Alec's company extended its business to: "The Irish gave me ... a better understanding of the men of history and conviction who will fight to the end and achieve little. So often such men are better at dying than living. They will not even consider that it is possible to be good at both" (Ounsworth, 1987, p. 10).

In 1962, the year my brother was born, Alec received a letter from Errol Barrow, the premier of Barbados, inviting him to bring dairy trade there. As it happens, Barrow also studied at the London School of Economics. Jumping ahead several decades, my father spent the last years of his life in Barbados, having moved there after he left Northern Foods. He ran an ice cream business during his retirement years: a return to his roots, since his first major success as a director of Northern Dairies was to acquire a stake in the Mr. Whippy ice cream company and then sell it at a large profit two years later.

In the 1980s, while my father was going from success to success as the chairman of Northern Foods, my grandfather, in his late seventies, entered into "very active voluntary work both with Hull's top security prison and Age Concern" (Ounsworth, 1987, p. 8.) (Age Concern was the banner title used by a number of charitable organizations concerned with the needs of older people and based chiefly in the four countries of the United Kingdom.) It was presumably the former activity that led to Alec's involvement with Jimmy Boyle. I don't know much about his work with Age Concern, but I do know that he was involved with some sort of scandal in his later years concerning a bicycle business by which he allegedly embezzled money by stealing old people's pensions.

I also know that my father disliked Alec for his entire life. Even after Alec had died, he appeared to bear ill feelings for him. Yet beyond indicating that Alec was a bully, I never really knew why.

CHAPTER II

A brief history of Fabianism: co-opting the left and right

"To speak of scientific management in school and society without crediting the influence of the Fabians would do great disservice to truth, but the nature of Fabianism is so complex it raises questions this essay cannot answer. To deal with the Fabians in a brief compass as I'm going to do is to deal necessarily in simplifications in order to see a little how this charming group of scholars, writers, heirs, heiresses, scientists, philosophers, bombazines, gazebos, trust-fund babies, and successful men and women of affairs became the most potent force in the creation of the modern welfare state, distributors of its characteristically dumbed-down version of schooling."

—John Taylor Gatto, *Underground History of American Education*

As a child and teenager attending private school, I never had any time for history. I hated school with a passion and experienced its regimentations as suffocating and oppressive. Every class was an ordeal to be endured, and my overall ambition was simply to avoid as much as possible being in any way influenced, shaped, or informed by the "masters" and their regimens. In terms of historical facts, I retained almost nothing of what we were taught in history (just a bit about Mussolini getting the trains to run on time). So for me to be writing a historical work overflowing with names, dates, and events, all of which I fear may be numbing to the reader, and to find my own interest so keen, is ironic, to say the least. But then, a large part of my ennui at school related to my felt sense that what I was being taught was *not the real truth*.

Another, even deeper reason for my ennui at school was that the methods of teaching—which as we'll see directly relate to Fabian methods of social engineering—were very much *meant* to be soul-deadening and mind-crushing. It was only that I would not, or could not, submit to them. As it happens, the first thing that really tipped me off that something was missing from my family's "official" history was the Fabian link to my grandfather. And one of the first really shocking discoveries was that two of the schools which my siblings and I had attended also had Fabian affiliations, even though there was no reason to think my grandfather had anything to do with our being sent there. In fact, in all the time I spent with my family, I don't remember ever once hearing anyone mention the Fabian Society.

Yet once I began to follow that lead, I quickly found out that the Fabians are the conspiracy bugaboo of the right. This presented a problem so far as finding reliable information about them, because a great deal of the unofficial history of the Society seems to be confined to websites with axes to grind. Actually, what I was initially looking for was some sort of concrete evidence of sexual abuse in my family history, since all the signs seemed to point that way. The Jimmy Boyle/ Kray connection certainly did, and I began to wonder: Did the Fabian octopus share a tentacle or two with that of organized crime and child sexual abuse?

Early Fabians tended to downplay their interest in—or debt to—Karl Marx but there can be little doubt that they were inspired by his work, directly or otherwise. I say directly because Marx lived in London from 1849 up to his death in 1883, and spent countless hours working on his *Das Kapital* in the reading room of the British Museum (which then housed the British Library collection). George Bernard Shaw was introduced to Marx's work by Henry Hyndman, who discovered *The Communist Manifesto* in 1864 and formed Britain's first socialist political party, The Social Democratic Federation, in 1881. He was the first author to popularize Marx's works in English and introduced them to Shaw around 1882. The Fellowship of the New Life (which later became the Fabian Society) was founded the following year, in 1883, the year of Marx's death.[1]

Shaw described Marx's *Kapital* as

> not a treatise on Socialism: it is a jeremiad against the bourgeoisie .... It was addressed to the working classes; but the working man respects the bourgeoisie, and wants to be a bourgeois. Marx never got a hold of him for a moment. It was the revolting sons of the bourgeoisie itself ... like myself, bourgeois, who painted the flag red. The professional and penniless younger son classes are the revolutionary element in society: the proletariat is the Conservative element .... Marx made me a Socialist and saved me from becoming a literary man. (1949, pp. 49–50)

The Fellowship of the New Life dissolved in 1898, after which the Fabian Society grew to become a preeminent academic society in the UK. Many Fabians participated in the formation of England's Labour Party in 1900. The party's constitution, written by Sidney Webb, borrowed heavily from the founding documents of the Fabian Society. As seen in the Labour Party Foundation Conference in 1900, the Fabian Society claimed 861 members and sent one delegate. (See *World Heritage Encyclopedia*, no date given.) The Society grew throughout 1930–1940 over many countries under the British rule, and many future leaders of these countries were influenced by the Fabians during their struggles for independence from the British. These leaders included India's Prime Minister Jawaharlal Nehru (whose fashion sense—"the Nehru jacket"—influenced the counterculture[2]), Obafemi Awolowo, who later became the premier of Nigeria's defunct Western Region, and the founder of Pakistan, barrister Muhammad Ali Jinnah. Lee Kuan Yew, the first prime minister of Singapore, had a political philosophy strongly influenced by the Fabian Society. In the twenty-first century, the Fabian Society's influence is felt through Labour Party leaders and former prime ministers of Great Britain, such as Tony Blair and Gordon Brown.

The name Fabian was apparently suggested by the spiritualist Frank Podmore, after the brilliant third century Roman general, Quintus Fabius (Maximus Verrucosus, 303-203 BC). Fabius was made a dictator in 221-217 BC, and, with a small band of fighting guerrillas and superior cunning, successfully defended Rome from Hannibal's mighty

Carthaginian army. Fabius's tactics involved "gradualism" and "terrorism," delaying tactics which were greatly disapproved of by his soldiers and the civilians, and which earned him the name of "the Delayer." After these tactics triumphed, however, his skill and wisdom was more appreciated.

Moving past the more or less established history of Fabianism, I found a compelling, and damning, description of the Fabian plan as central to the whole "New World Order" millennia-long Conspiracy (big "C"), in an archived essay called "Fabian Influence on Council Developments in New Zealand" (Christian, 2006). One premise of the information was that the Fabian Society was behind the various Labour movements in Britain and that it concealed elitist, and even capitalist, interests. This was something I could vouch for from direct experience, having grown up in a wealthy socialist family (we were called "champagne socialists") who were above all business people but also actively involved in local (and, I was slowly discovering, global) politics, in *seemingly* reformist and New Left movements such as the Campaign for Nuclear Disarmament (CND), all having, sometimes obvious sometimes less so, ties to the Fabian Society.

According to another online source (Cassivellaunus, 2013), the Fabian Society has 7000 members, 80 percent (5,600) of whom are members of the Labour Party, amounting to about three percent of the general Labour Party membership (about 190,000 in 2010). The Fabian percentage increases dramatically in the higher reaches of the Labour Party.[3] George Bernard Shaw declared the aim of Fabian educational reform as entailing the creation of a minister for education, with "control over the whole educational system, from the elementary school to the University, and over all educational endowments" (S. Webb, 1889, p. 55). This allegedly led to the creation of a wide range of interconnected organizations, societies, and movements. In education, councils like the London County Council, university societies, and schools like the London School of Economics, Imperial College, and London University. In culture, the New Age movement (Annie Besant was a founding Fabian), the Central School of Arts and Crafts, the Leeds Arts Club, the Fabian Arts Group, and the Stage Society. In economics, the LSE again, the Royal Economic Society, the National Institute of Economic and Social Research (NIESR). In law, the Haldane Society (named after Fabian Society member Lord Haldane). In medicine: the Socialist

Medical League. In religion, the Labour (later Socialist) Church movement, the Christian Socialist Crusade, the Christian Socialist League, the Christian Socialist Movement. And so on (you get the picture).

Shaw expressed a desire to make the Fabians "the Jesuits of Socialism," while H. G. Wells (number four on the Fabian executive after Webb, Pease, and Shaw) proposed to turn the whole Society into a ruling order, similar to the "Samurai" in his *A Modern Utopia*. That the Fabians consciously sought the company, collaboration, and support of the wealthy and powerful is evident from Fabian writings such as Beatrice Webb's *Our Partnership*, which abound in references to "catching millionaires," "wire-pulling," "moving all the forces we have control over," while at the same time taking care to "appear disinterested" and claiming to be "humble folk whom nobody suspects of power" (B. Webb, 1948, p. 196).

The reliable John Taylor Gatto affirms this view in *Underground History of American Education*:

> As the movement developed, Fabians became aristocratic friends of other social-efficiency vanguards like Taylorism or allies of the Methodist social gospel crowd of liberal Christian religionists busy substituting Works for Faith in one of the most noteworthy religious reversals of all time. Especially, they became friends and advisors of industrialists and financiers, travelers in the same direction. This cross-fertilization occurred naturally, not out of petty motives of profit, but because by Fabian lights evolution had progressed furthest among the international business and banking classes! ... Fabian practitioners developed Hegelian principles which they co-taught alongside Morgan bankers and other important financial allies over the first half of the twentieth century. (2006, p. 182)

Gatto trumps and essentially invalidates a large subculture of conspiracy theorists and right-wing, anti-socialist writers, by pointing out:

> One insightful Hegelianism was that to push ideas efficiently it was necessary first to co-opt both political Left *and* political Right. Adversarial politics—competition—was a loser's game. By infiltrating all major media, by continual low-intensity propaganda, by massive changes in group orientations (accomplished through

principles developed in the psychological-warfare bureaus of the military), and with the ability, using government intelligence agents and press contacts, to induce a succession of crises, they accomplished that astonishing feat. (2006, pp. 182–183)

*

> "When I was young, my friends at Oxford consisted largely of Fabian Socialists, and not a few of the dons were themselves Socialists. Today, of course, they would not call themselves Fabian Socialists, but Marxian Communists."
>
> —G. K. Chesterton

A few more suggestive facts: Hubert Bland, cofounder of the Fabian Society and a bank employee-turned-journalist, worked for the London *Sunday Chronicle*, a paper owned by newspaper magnate Edward Hulton. It was allegedly Bland who recruited his friend and fellow journalist George Bernard Shaw to the Fabian Society (Cassivellaunus, 2013). Hulton's son, Edward G. Hulton, was the owner of *Picture Post* and "almost certainly a loyal agent of MI6's Section D" (Dorril & Ramsay, 1990).[4] He was also the founder of the 1941 Committee, a think tank that recruited "star" writers J. B. Priestley and Tom Wintringham, and that also included David Astor (more on him soon), Sir Richard Acland, and my grandfather. Alec mentions Acland in his short memoir in reference to Acland and Priestley's Common Wealth, in which Alec "took a very active part." Acland was also a Quaker, which Alec later became.

G. B. Shaw's friend, Fabian Society leader Sidney Webb, married Beatrice, daughter of Richard Potter, a wealthy financier with international connections who was chairman of the Great Western and Grand Trunk railways of England and Canada. Beatrice was also a close friend of Rothschild associate and Conservative Prime Minister Arthur Balfour. Rothschild and Balfour were founding members of the Round Table. When I first wrote this chapter I included the data point that my grandfather was one of the two "Round Table's main British backers" during the 1930s, 1940s, and 1950s.[5] I found this startling, to say the least, since I understood the Round Table to be a massive, multinational organization and though my grandfather was rich, I didn't think he was that rich. Eventually I got ahold of the book that contained this quote, *Zilliacus: A Life for Peace and Socialism*, by Archie Potts, and discovered that Potts was referring to the East-West Round Table, an organization about which there is very little information but which had to do with peace negotiations between the Soviet Union and the United Kingdom, something my grandfather was apparently deeply involved in. Whether there was any connection between this Round Table and the Round Table of Rothschild and Balfour is something I have been unable to find out. At the very least, with my grandfather as the *vesica piscis* between the two, some of the same names and causes seem to crop up around both.

For example, the aforementioned David Astor, alleged MI6 agent and editor of the UK paper *The Observer*, was the grandson of William Waldorf (the first). He lobbied for the release of Myra Hindley in the 1970s along with Lord Longford. My grandfather visited Hindley in jail and my brother wrote letters to her. Astor was also affiliated with the Round Table Group. According to author and *Lobster* editor Stephen Dorril, Astor

> created the Europe Study Group to look at the problems of Europe and the prospects for a non-nationalist Germany. At the core of the group were a number of emigré Germans destined to play a role in the European Movement, such as the future leader writer on the *Observer*, Richard "Rix" Lowenthal. Interviewed for recruitment by MI6, Astor was turned down for a full-time post but was subsequently used by MI6 officer Lionel Loewe to establish contact with the German opposition. Employed as the press officer in Lord Mountbatten's Combined Operations Headquarters in London, Astor continued with his group, which drew on the ideas of the Cecil Rhodes-inspired Round Table Group and its belief that "the British Empire should federate." (Dorril, 2002, p. 456)

This places my grandfather squarely in the circles of the *other* Round Table Group—the one laying the groundwork for the European Union and a one world government—and, by inevitable extension, MI6. The shared interests alone (leaving aside the uses Alec was putting his money to) make it inevitable their paths would have crossed. Yet these interests appear to have little to do with socialism, at least as I grew up understanding it.

Meanwhile, Round Table founding member Lord Rothschild "was personally involved, with Sidney Webb, in the restructuring of the University of London into which the Fabians' London School of Economics (LSE) was incorporated in 1898" (Cassivellaunus, 2013) (LSE was founded by the original Fabians, Sidney and Beatrice Webb, Graham Wallas, and George Bernard Shaw; Annie Besant and Bertrand Russell were early participants). Rothschild also provided funds for the LSE and served as its third president, "after his relative Lord Rosebery" (B. Webb, 1948, pp. 182, 214). LSE is connected, not just to the various Fabian groups, but also to Gay Liberation and PIE, the Paedophile Information Exchange, a faction within the Labour government in the 1970s, more on which later. (Economist John Maynard Keynes was a key figure at LSE. The school's alumni include my grandfather's pal John Saville, Harold Laski—cofounder of the New School for Social Research, Nicholas Humphrey, Edwina Currie, David Rockefeller, Mick Jagger, Zecharia Sitchin, Naomi Klein, John F. Kennedy, and—the subject of my last book, *Prisoner of Infinity*—Whitley Strieber.)

In *Fabian Freeway*, Rose L. Martin describes Keynes as the "Spiritual heir and latter-day facsimile" of the occultist Count Cagliostro. Rather like my brother, Keynes cut

> a magnificent figure: six feet three, and superbly tailored; an authority on wines, fine foods and beautiful women; patron of the arts, and master of the English language which he only distorted by design. He, too, posed as the possessor of elusive secrets, key to the Higher Mysteries of economics and public finance .... An alchemist who succeeded in substituting paper for gold, a mystifier who claimed that money multiplied itself in the spending, Keynes compelled bankers to do his bidding and imposed his schemes on the highest personages in an age of political unreason. (Martin, 1966, p. 323)

Keynes is known today as the father of deficit spending:

> The system promulgated by Keynes, as even his most loyal disciples admit, was in reality no system at all. It was a rationale and a tool for achieving total political control, at a gradually increased tempo, over the economic life of a nation .... It is generally agreed today that there is hardly a political economist of prominence in America who—even when he appears critical of Keynes—has not been influenced by the Keynesian method. If he had resisted seriously, it is safe to say he would not be prominent.[6]

Another Fabian line of connection with industrial interests was apparently the chocolate manufacturers Rowntree's, which funded many Fabian projects (Cassivellaunus, 2013). The alliance between Northern Dairies and Rowntree Macintosh meant that (until our parents split) our house was always full of chocolates, and we even got to visit the Rowntree Macintosh factory as kids. One of my favorite books as a child was *Charlie and the Chocolate Factory*, by Roald Dahl (with whom I corresponded briefly when I was young, though I don't think I ever met him; Dahl did propaganda work for British Intelligence in World War II[7]). Willy Wonka, as illustrated in the book and later depicted in the movies, wears a top hat and a purple jacket, like the infamous Child Catcher from *Chitty Chitty Bang Bang* (and like my brother in his last years, though he preferred red). *Chitty Chitty Bang Bang* was based on the book by MI5 agent Ian Fleming and it was probably the movie that was most beloved in my early childhood. More recently, the Child Catcher has been compared to Jimmy Savile.

Savile's predations have been linked to those of an ice cream manufacturer and retailer, Peter Jaconelli (*BBC News*, 2014b), in Scarborough, Yorkshire, a town I visited as a child. Northern Dairies had its own ice cream products and also provided milk to other companies. (When I was an adolescent, we lived opposite a famous ice cream shop called Burgess's.) The link between ice cream, chocolate, and predatory child molestation rings would seem to pertain not only to works of children's fiction.

The Fabian Society has also apparently been of particular interest to the Rockefellers—David Rockefeller did his senior thesis on Fabian Socialism at Harvard ("Destitution Through Fabian Eyes," 1936), and studied left-wing economics at LSE. The Rockefellers have allegedly funded many Fabian projects, including the LSE, which "in the late 1920s and 1930s received millions of dollars from the Rockefeller and Laura Spelman Foundations, becoming known as 'Rockefellers baby.'" The International Monetary Fund (IMF), established in 1944 along with the World Bank, was also reputedly a Rockefellers project, and the IMF provided several loans to Labour governments, in 1947, 1969, and 1976.

> Another important loan of $4.34 billion was negotiated in 1946 by Fabian economist John Maynard Keynes and facilitated by his friend and collaborator Harry Dexter White who operated within

> the US Treasury as well as the IMF. All these loans were organised
> under successive Fabian Chancellors Hugh Dalton, Roy Jenkins
> and Denis Healey. (Cassivellaunus, 2013)

$4.34 billion was an astronomical amount in 1946, and if these facts are accurate, it's easy to imagine how far-reaching and pervasive the Fabian influence might have become, via the organizations and agendas fueled by such monies.

Hugh Dalton is mentioned in *The Dust Has Never Settled* by Robin Bryans (a very oblique exposé on government corruption, occult secret societies, and child abuse), with reference to his title as "the Minister of Economic Warfare," as a possible procurer of children for sexual use (it's hard to tell with Bryans's cryptic phrasings). Roy Jenkins is a lot easier to nail down, but we'll get to him later. John Maynard Keynes is linked directly to two close associates of my grandfather, including John Boyd Orr, who my grandfather met in the USSR in the 1950s. Boyd Orr was the first director-general of the United Nations Food and Agriculture Organization and the cofounder and first president (1960–1971) of the World Academy of Art and Science. He gave an address to the Fabian Society on "food policy" in 1940, three years after my grandfather founded his own company. In the 1950s, he became president of Northern Dairies.

According to the aforementioned anti-Fabian site, the Fabian Society "developed an obsession with economics" early on and "its members met regularly to study and discuss Karl Marx and his economic theories".[8] Literally dozens of different organizations sprung up over the decades prior to the Sixties, including the Social Science Research Council, some of whose documents are held at the London School of Economics library, under such titles as "Outline proposals for development of Albany Trust, 1967–1978" and "Study of Human Sexuality in Britain: proposals for establishing an institute of social behaviour." The Albany Trust was founded, the same year homosexuality was legalized, in the apartment of one of my grandfather's (seemingly) close associates, J. B. Priestley, the chairman of the aforementioned 1941 Committee, with whom my grandfather started the CND. The Albany Trust is generally associated with civil liberties and gay rights, hence is seen as being left-leaning. Yet there's evidence to suggest it may have been funding the right too, such as its involvement with the *Conservative* Group for Homosexual Equality (CGHE).

The abuse research blog *The Needle* (2013) implies that the CGHE was implicated in the promotion of Elm Guest House, a now-notorious child brothel in Barnes, London. The CGHE was founded in 1975 by Professor Peter Campbell, of Reading University, who was chairman or vice-president through most of the Thatcher years. Campbell also edited the newsletter and has been named as a visitor to the Elm Guest House. According to *The Needle*, "The minutes from the founding meeting clearly show that, despite being labelled as an organization that promoted gay equality, it was from inception a 'pro-pedophile organization.'"

CHAPTER III

Havelock Ellis, *Lolita*, and the sexual child

> "Once again, you need to remember we aren't conspiracy hunt-
> ing but tracking an idea, like microchipping an eel to see what
> holes it swims into in case we want to catch it later on."
> —John Taylor Gatto, *Underground History of American Education*

The link between the Fabian Society and the Paedophile Information
Exchange, while unmistakable, is also inconclusive. It's necessary to go
further back, to the founding Fabians, to get a better sense of the philosophy which my grandfather embraced.

As far as I can trace it, the Fabian Society (originally the Fellowship
of New Life) began with the sexologist Henry Havelock Ellis (some
accounts have spiritualist Frank Podmore as the originator). The son of
a sea captain, born in Croydon in 1859, Ellis traveled widely in Australia
and South America before studying medicine at St. Thomas' Hospital
in London. In 1883, he joined a socialist debating group established by
Edith Nesbit and Hubert Bland, and in 1884 the group became known as
the Fabian Society. At these meetings, Ellis met Annie Besant, Graham
Wallas, George Bernard Shaw, Edward Carpenter, Walter Crane, H. G.
Wells, and Sidney and Beatrice Webb.

21

Havelock Ellis is attributed with coining the word "homosexual" and was one of the first people in history to show an academic interest in pedophilia. (The term did not become widespread until the 1950s.)[1] This is hardly surprising, since Ellis compiled a six-volume work entitled *Studies In The Psychology of Sex*, between 1897 and 1928. Ellis was reputedly a sexual experimenter as well as a drug user, and allegedly even combined the two (hallucinogens and private group sex sessions). The writings of Ellis were among the key texts that formed the basis for sex education in British colleges and, later, schools. Ellis is sometimes known today as "the father of social psychology." From *Science in the Bedroom: A History of Sexual Research*:

> Essentially, Ellis' work was a plea for tolerance and for accepting the idea that deviations from the norm were harmless and occasionally perhaps even valuable. He, like [Magnus] Hirschfeld [who founded the Scientific Humanitarian Committee, perhaps the first organization to advocate for homosexual and transgender rights], was a reformer who encouraged society to recognize and accept sexual manifestations in infants and realize that sexual experimentation was part of adolescence. Ellis held that it was important to repeal bans on contraception as well as laws prohibiting sexual activity between consenting adults in private. (Bullough, 1996, p. 76)

This sounds reasonable enough, and it was entirely in accord with the value-set I was raised with. Yet, in the context of other less openly-discussed areas of "sexual exploration" which seemed to sprout quite organically from the Fabian tree (such as PIE), it also reads like a recipe for disaster.

One of Ellis's best known followers appears to have been the aforementioned economist, John Maynard Keynes. Keynes, the attentive reader may recall, backed my grandfather's friend and future Bilderberger, Eric Roll, as professor at Hull University. One of Alec's other associates was the psychologist Nick Humphrey, who was Keynes's grandnephew. Keynes is known to have been a pederast and probably a child molester too. Unfortunately, the most explicit source of information for Keynes's sexual proclivities, his adherence to Ellis's teachings, and his Fabian associations, "Keynes at Harvard: Economic Deception as a Political Credo," is by Zygmund Dobbs, who rails against all things Fabian. According to Dobbs, "The Fabian perverts used the areas mentioned by Ellis [in his *Studies in the Psychology of Sex*] practically as a guide book. Keynes visited all of the Mediterranean areas mentioned, usually in the company of another English homosexual (Tunis, Algeria, Constantinople, Sicily, Capri, Cairo, Greece and Salerno) [areas] where little boys were sold by their parents to bordellos catering to homosexual appetites" (Dobbs, 1962, p. 118n.).

Ellis's influence extended beyond his fellow Fabians, however, all the way to Freud, and later, to Vladimir Nabokov.

> The only psychiatrist Nabokov could tolerate was Havelock Ellis, for whom "the individuality of each case is respected and cata- logued in the same way that butterflies are carefully classified," as one of Nabokov's biographers has explained. (Nabokov was a famous lepidopterist.) Conversely, Nabokov detested "Freudian voodooism," as he once put it, because he saw in Freud an attempt by psychiatry to corner, appropriate, and submit to generalized principles people's inner lives. And submitting one's inner life— the unique hazard of one's personality, the camera obscura of one's own personal store of memories—to a set of deterministic explana- tions was for Nabokov an indignity on par with the expropriations of the Bolsheviks. (Metcalf, 2005)

A collection of letters between the novelist and social critic Edmund Wilson makes it clear that Ellis's research was a direct inspiration for *Lolita*. In 1948, Wilson sent Nabokov a copy of "Havelock Ellis's Russian sex masterpiece," and nine days later, Nabokov responded by writ- ing: "I enjoyed the Russian's love-life hugely. It is wonderfully funny" (Karlinsky, 2001, p. 230). The 106-page "sex masterpiece" is an account of a young man, sexually initiated at the age of twelve, who in his thir- ties begins to seek out the favors of child prostitutes (from age eleven on up) in the Ukraine. Nabokov shares his fascination for Havelock's "tiny tots" in his memoir *Speak, Memory*, most explicitly in the Russian version, *Drugie Berega*:

> Our innocence seems to me almost monstrous in the light of vari- ous confessions dating from the same years and cited by Have- lock Ellis, which speak of tiny tots of every imaginable sex, who practice every Graeco-Roman sin, constantly and everywhere, from the Anglo-Saxon industrial centers to the Ukraine (from

where an especially lascivious report by a land-owner is available).
(Karlinsky, 2001, p. 229)[2]

One thing of note about Nabokov's *Lolita*, in the context of Ellis, PIE, and the steady propagation of the idea of children as sexual beings, is that Lolita was the sexual *aggressor* in the relationship, and Humbert Humbert, for all his unpleasantness, more of a hapless victim of her seductions than an actual predator.

To get a sense of how far-reaching Ellis's influence is—not apart from but congruent with his influence on literature—there was a syllabus in the 1990s at Cornell University called "The Sexual Child," described as follows:

> With respect to children, the American imagination today is defined by what we might call pedophile gothic. The sexual child, as a volatile emblem of trauma, has become the focus of moral panics from every point on the political spectrum—panics about cultural phenomena as various as pornography, psychotherapy, day care, parenting, the women's movement, the Roman Catholic priesthood, access to the Internet, and every level of school curricula. But what do we think a child is or ought to be? What does it mean to love or desire a child? Who promotes the idea of child sexuality and why? (*Free Republic*, 2002)

Havelock Ellis was included in the course, and lectures had titles such as "The Child as Sexual Object and Sexual Subject," "Big Bad Wolves," "Loving Children," and "Having Children" (for which one of the readings was Nabokov's *Lolita*). English professor Ellis Hanson, the course instructor, defended the course's content by stating, "The erotic fascination with children is ubiquitous. One could hardly read a newspaper or turn on a television without feeling obliged to accept, study, and celebrate it." In his own words, the course was designed to "undermine preconceived notions about what a child is, what sexuality is, and what it means to love or desire a child" (Capel, 1998).

The bisexual "trans man" Pat Califia also contributed to the course. At the Ipce (International Pedophile and Child Emancipation) site, Califia wrote:

> Culturally induced schizophrenia allows parents to make sentimental speeches about the fleeting innocence of childhood and the

happiness of years unbroken by carnal lust—and exhaust themselves policing the sex lives of their children. Children are celibate
because their parents prevent them from playing with other little
kids or adults .... They are not innocent; they are ignorant, and that
ignorance is deliberately created and maintained by parents ....
Even though many prominent sex researchers have documented the
existence of sexual capacity in children (for instance Kinsey verified
the occurrence of orgasm in girls and boys at less than six months of
age), our society is fanatically determined to deny it. (2003)

As I'll get to in a later chapter, Kinsey's "researches" didn't verify anything because he used child sexual abusers to get his data; oblivious
or indifferent to the children's suffering, he almost certainly misrepre-
sented it as pleasure—just as child abusers often do. Califia's piece cites
how "very often, these children are consenting partners in the sexual
activity [and even] initiate the sexual activity with direct propositions
or with seductive behavior." S/he argues that "[T]he claim that sex with
a parent is more damaging than being beaten [is] ludicrous"—without
saying why this is the case. In reference to the sexual exploitation of
children for profit, Califia writes: "Closing down this industry without
providing alternative employment is equivalent to sentencing young
people to frustration, abuse, or suicide in cozy little suburban ranch-
style prisons" (2003).

Califia was somewhat ahead of his/her time with such arguments;
or perhaps, considering that they formed a central part of the Cornell
University course in the 1970s, s/he was instrumental (like my brother)
in normalizing prostitution, child or otherwise. In March 2015, *The
Daily Telegraph* ran a piece about how British university students are
now making extra money in the sex industry. The piece reads more like
an advertisement:

Researchers surveyed 6,750 students, of whom 5 per cent said
they'd worked in the sex industry. Almost a quarter admitted they
had considered it. The reasons they gave were to fund their lifestyle, pay basic living costs, reduce debt at the end of university,
sexual pleasure and curiosity. One in 20 sounds like a lot, hence a
general shock at the findings. But frankly, given the relative ease of
sex work—and the fact that it's so lucrative—I'm surprised more
undergrads aren't giving it a go .... There are, of course, less than
pleasurable elements of sex work. But aren't there in every job? ...

> Student sex workers aren't victims; they're making a choice. And
> after all: they're running a business; handling the accounts, brand-
> ing, marketing and sales. How many other undergraduates can
> claim that? (Reid, 2015)

In Germany, prostitution has been legal since 2002, and there has been
a recurring debate ever since over whether the government can legally
oblige women receiving unemployment benefit to become "sex workers" (Chapman, 2005). So much for freedom of choice.

My brother did his own stint as a sex worker, and in *Dandy in the
Underworld* he called prostitutes "the most open and honest creatures
on God's earth." "The whore fuck," he wrote, "is the purest fuck of
them all" (S. Horsley, 2007, pp. 197, 199). I am sure he would have
applauded the *Telegraph's* view of sexual self-exploitation as social liberation, though he might have been disturbed and disappointed to discover how fashionable his supposedly subversive views had become.

CHAPTER IV

Progressive politics and witchcraft: Brazier's Park, order of Woodcraft, Common Wealth

> "Under Socialism, you would not be allowed to be poor. You would be forcibly fed, clothed, lodged, taught, and employed whether you liked it or not. If it were discovered that you had not character and industry enough to be worth all this trouble, you might possibly be executed in a kindly manner; but whilst you were permitted to live, you would have to live well."
> —George Bernard Shaw, *The Intelligent Woman's Guide to Socialism and Capitalism*

It would be nice if, somehow, I could lay all of this information out as a straightforward, linear narrative; but that would be a little like hoping to put a leash on an octopus. If the connections I am attempting to map were simple, straightforward, and linear, they would already be obvious for all to see. Octopi do not come to heel when called. Of course, there is a danger that, since I am selecting the material in order to show how it *is* all interconnected, I will create a picture that exists only in my own mind due to my perceptual bias. The only remedy I know of for this is to resist the temptation to emphasize the connections, and focus primarily on the facts that appear to be connected.

27

I have briefly mentioned Common Wealth, the organization set up by my grandfather's friends, Sir Richard Acland and J. B. Priestley, to which Alec Horsley belonged. Another member was Norman Glaister, a Fabian. In 1950, Glaister set up something called Braziers Park, a country house in Oxfordshire, England, owned and operated by a charitable trust as a residential adult education college, and center for the School of Integrative Social Research. The following is from its website.

> Norman Glaister was a medical student during the period when Wilfred Trotter was Professor of Surgery at University College Hospital, although he was unaware of Trotter's interest in sociology. However, when Glaister was serving as a Captain in the RAMC [Royal Army Medical Corps] in Palestine and heard that his wife (neé Irene Sowerbutts) had died in the flu epidemic of 1918, he felt that he could only face the future if he could find some meaningful research and activity that would improve the human condition. The chance finding of Trotter's *The Instincts of the Herd in Peace and War* gave him his inspiration. Back in England, he studied psychiatry, worked for the Ministry of Pensions, the Tavistock Clinic and the Royal Free Hospital.[1] He built up his own practice. Glaister became interested in the Order of Woodcraft Chivalry, a pacifist, camping movement that encouraged children and adults to work together learning woodcraft skills and fostering new educational ideas coming from the study of evolution and psychology. He took his three young children to the annual camp in 1924. (*Braziers Park*, 2017)

Glaister had initially wanted to open a school where "the adults in charge … would offer the children experiences which would enable them to make positive and balanced choices at the time, and in later life." When this plan was frustrated, "Glaister settled for general practice and psychological work for the Clinic" (Braziers Park, 2016; presumably the clinic is Tavistock). It was not until 1950 that Glaister set up the School of Integrative Social Research, the same year Braziers Park was established. The School is partly a commune; its aim was and is "to explore the dynamics of people living in groups" (*Catalyst*, 2008).

Glaister was inspired by Trotter, who was known as "the biological father of British psychoanalysis" (Torres, 2003, p. 104). It was under Trotter that another Wilfred, Wilfred Bion (who graduated from Oxford

PROGRESSIVE POLITICS AND WITCHCRAFT   29

in 1922) worked in his own medical training, before going on to study group psychology and train as a psychoanalyst at the Tavistock Institute. In her account of his life "The Days of Our Years," Bion's wife writes that Trotter greatly influenced the direction of Bion's work on group relations. Edward Bernays, the now-notorious (thanks to Adam Curtis's documentary, *Century of the Self*) social engineer, author of *Propaganda*, and nephew to Freud, also cites Trotter in his writings.

One of Trotter's primary ideas, besides that of the herd instinct (which Freud rejected), was that of two types of human being, the "resistive" type (making up the majority) and the "unstable" type (the minority who bring about, or at least are open to, change). Glaister later replaced "unstable" with "sensitive," and later still, "sensory." This basic psychological premise of a dichotomy within the human species was adopted by The Order of Woodcraft Chivalry, founded in 1916 by Ernest Westlake, which included a "Sensory Advisory Committee." Glaister joined the Order—described by Derek Edgell (1992) as "a New Age Alternative to the Boy Scouts"—in 1924, and there met Dorothy Revel, who became his second wife.

The Order is said to have provided the basis for the New Forest coven, and through that the Neopagan religion of Wicca. Westlake was a naturalist, anthropologist, and traveler *of Quaker upbringing*, who moved away from Quakerism to extol the "old gods" of paganism. Inspired by authors such as Edward Carpenter, Nietzsche, Havelock Ellis, and J. G. Frazer, he created the Order as a means to escape "the *cul-de-sac* of intellectualized religion" and "revive the greater Hellas of modern civilization" (Hutton, 2001, p. 165). He saw women as incarnations of God, to be "worshipped in spirit and in truth," revered the Jack-in-the-Green as the English equivalent of Dionysus, and proposed a "Trinity of Woodcraft" consisting of Pan, Artemis, and Dionysus (ibid.). After Westlake's death in a motoring accident in 1922, the role of British chief of the Order fell to Harry Byngham, who subsequently changed his name to Dion, short for Dionysus. Byngham promoted phallic worship as a means of venerating the life force. He introduced an Order periodical called *The Pinecone*, which included nudity (rare at that time) and published work by Victor Benjamin Neuburg. It was Neuburg who introduced Byngham to the ideas of Aleister Crowley, under whom Neuburg discipled (he was also his lover, or abuse-victim, depending on how you read it). The Order was primarily aimed at children and, by its pacifist stance, *particularly appealed to Quaker families* as an alternative to Scouting (ibid., p. 167). Even more directly linked to the Order than Crowley was Gerald Gardner, the leading figure in the Wiccan revival of twentieth century Britain.[2]

If we seem to have strayed very far from my grandfather's leftist interests or from Fabianism, we haven't. The Order of Woodcraft Chivalry was directly affiliated with Richard Acland's party, Common Wealth, of which Alec was a member. Common Wealth also incorporated Trotter's and Glaister's philosophy of human dichotomy (resistives and sensitives) into its programs for social reform, with its peculiar emphasis on the "sensory":

> It is the opening gambit in Norman's ambitious drive towards instituting a Sensory Committee in Common Wealth and it was to be five years before the first Sensory Committee meeting proper took place .... It points out the need for men of ideas (as opposed to men of action) who could function as a "sensory body" rather than an "advisory committee" since the word "advisory" might suggest claims to superior wisdom for its members. The Sensory Committee "might be a nervous system for the Governing Body. The sensory system constantly brings to the brain up-to-the-minute information of the local conditions in every part of the body so that the motor action may be perfectly coordinated." (*Braziers Park*, 2016)

Regarding the emphasis on human dichotomy:

> [F]or the first time as far as our records suggest, the full panoply of Trotter's ideas, the gregarious habit and the Resistive/Sensitive concept were covered extensively as if laying down the framework for future development. There is a new sense of confidence, determination and an ambition to make progress from first principles— and to many, much of this would be new. I think 44 people passed through the Summer School during the fortnight. Reference was made to the Resistive/Sensory team to stress the idea that it was the creative balance of the two functions that would improve action. Their main task was to increase the positive and reduce the negative element in all situations, to try to see issues not in dualistic terms but to find a unitary approach. (*Braziers Park*, 2016)

The overlap is surprisingly clear, then, not only between leftist politics and social psychology, but between social psychology and "witchcraft."

Nor does this overlap need to be inferred: Wilfred Bion's research into group psychology included what would now be classified as a distinctly "parapsychological" angle:

> Bion's description of group phenomenology is vivid and is sug- gestive of what might be called ESP (extrasensory perception) ele- ments. He states that there is such a thing as the psychology of the group but that the origins of this psychology lie solely within the individuals comprising the group, but he also seems to believe that the potential group-relating aspect within the individuals is acti- vated by the group, i.e., the existence of the group *evokes* what we call "group psychology." How does this happen? Bion describes how individuals become caught up in different strands of the group process as if they were puppets being controlled and manipulated by an invisible puppeteer. Yet Bion did not believe that the group itself had an independent agency. Agency in the group became prime cause but remained ineffable and inscrutable—as a myste- rious, potentiating, synergistic summation and transformation of the combined agencies of the individuals in the group. (Grotstein, 2003, p. 14)

Returning to Common Wealth: "In 1941, during World War II, Sir Richard Acland founded a new political party, Common Wealth, which Norman Glaister joined" (*Braziers Park*, 2016). The Order of Woodcraft Chivalry had been proposed for affiliation with Common Wealth, but for whatever reason this did not happen. "Instead, another group had been set up, called 'Our Struggle,' in the late 1930s and it was this group that became part of Common Wealth" (ibid.). Nonetheless, Common Wealth adopted some of the same organizational/psychological principles and methods as the Order, including the meta-biological approach to human organization. (In 1940, Richard Acland's *Unser Kampf (Our Struggle)* was published by Penguin Books. Why the German title and the clear *homage* to Hitler's *Mein Kampf*? It seems especially curious in light of how Nazis and Fabians both advocated eugenics. And both were socialist movements.)

> Common Wealth's first Sensory Committee meeting took place in April 1947. Olaf Stapleton the novelist and John MacMurray were to be invited to join later. The first Common Wealth Sensory Summer School took place only 4 months after that. That Sensory

Summer School took place within three years of the founding of Braziers, which occurred as a result of this and two subsequent Summer Schools. (ibid.)

Olaf Stapleton is the well-known author of *Last and First Men* and *Star Maker*, science-fiction novels that map a two million year history of humanity. Stapleton went to Abbotsholme School, which I briefly attended along with both of my siblings, and which is considered one of the prototypes for "progressive" schooling in Britain. Stapleton's novels have influenced writers as diverse as H. G. Wells, Arthur C. Clarke, Jorge Luis Borges, J. B. Priestley, Bertrand Russell, Arnold Bennett, and Virginia Woolf (as well as Winston Churchill). They describe humanity's evolution via genetic engineering and space travel into a sort of galactic god-being. While generally regarded as *progressive fiction*, C. S. Lewis described the ending of *Star Maker* (in a letter to Arthur C. Clarke in 1943) as "sheer devil worship" (Edwards, 2007, p. 54).

CHAPTER V

Progressive schools: Abbotsholme, Theosophy, Wicca, Grith Fyrd

"Darwin made it possible to consider political affairs as a prime instrument of social evolution. Here was a pivotal moment in Western thought, a changing of the guard in which secular purpose replaced religious purpose, long before trashed by the Enlightenment. For the poor, the working classes, and middle classes in the American sense, this change in outlook, lauded by the most influential minds of the nineteenth century, was a catastrophe of titanic proportions, especially for government school children. Children could no longer simply be parents' darlings. Many were (biologically) a racial menace. The rest had to be thought of as soldiers in genetic combat, the moral equivalent of war. For all but a relative handful of favored families, aspiration was off the board as a scientific proposition. For governments, children could no longer be considered individuals but were regarded as categories, rungs on a biological ladder. Evolutionary science pronounced the majority useless mouths waiting for nature to dispense with entirely. Nature (as expressed through her human agents) was to be understood not as cruel or oppressive but beautifully, functionally purposeful—a neo-pagan perspective to be reflected in the organization and administration of schools."

—John Taylor Gatto, *Underground History of American Education*

One of the things I'd been looking to find was some indication that any of my family (either my generation or my father's) had been sent to any "dodgy" schools where they might have suffered some sort of sexual interference. I knew that my father (and his siblings) had been sent to various Quaker boarding schools from a very early age (Fairhaven Home School in Goathland, in the middle of the Yorkshire Moors, Keswick Grammar School, Bootham School, and The Mount School). I had found almost nothing online suggesting that any of these schools, or the Quakers, were connected to any sort of organized abuse.[1] And then there was Abbotsholme.

I went to Abbotsholme for two terms in 1978, when I was eleven. My brother and sister went there for several years. It is located in Derbyshire, thirty miles from Ripley, the town where Alec was born. There is a small town five miles from Ripley called Horsley, probably named after an aristocratic bloodline since there is a ruined castle there known as Horston Castle.[2] At least one Horsley (a soldier killed in World War I) is buried in Horsley cemetery, also suggesting a family lineage. Is it possible my grandfather belonged to or was named after such a lineage, and for some reason concealed it?

As far as I know, we weren't sent to Abbotsholme on Alec's recommendation, but that of our stepfather, Michael Vodden. Michael taught English in India after the Second World War and I remember him speaking of meeting Lord Mountbatten. Mountbatten is widely rumored to have been connected to the Kincora Boy's Home abuse scandal in Belfast, Ireland (*UK Data Base*, 2015), and of being the man who introduced Jimmy Savile to the royal family.[3] In light of everything else, this can hardly be dismissed as coincidental, but nor does it imply any actual secret agenda. My family considered itself "progressive," and there were only a few schools in the UK that fit that bill. In fact, Abbotsholme, founded by Cecil Reddie, was considered the *original* modern progressive school. No surprise then to learn that Reddie was influenced by the ideas of the Fellowship of the New Life, in other words, a Fabian. I visited the school around 2010 with my sister and niece (who was thinking about going there), and I was surprised to see that the school symbol was a pentagram.

A thesis essay called "The Vegetarian Movement in England, 1847–1981" (presented at the London School of Economics, again), describes how, in the early twentieth century, Quaker schools were introduced into this

progressive schooling stream. The long tradition of Quaker boarding schools, the separateness of Quaker society, and their repudiation of the classical syllabus and the teaching of science, "marked these schools apart from the public schools. In the early twentieth century the differences became more pronounced with the spread among them of co-education." For whatever reason, Quaker schools were drawn to the world of progressive education, as part of "the shift that occurs in Quakerism generally that takes it into the orbit of liberal progressive thought" (Twigg, 1981). The essay also mentions how, "In 1893, A. C. Badley, an ex-master at Abbotsholme, founded the co-educational Bedales." My sister went to Bedales briefly before attending Abbotsholme.

And then there was this:

> The second important influence was theosophy, which was in the early years of this century much involved in progressive social causes and had not yet adopted the social introversionism that came later. In 1915 a number of progressively minded theosophists led by Mrs. Ensor and George Arundale founded the Theosophical Fraternity in Education, and in the same year the Garden City Theosophical School was founded .... A number of these schools and other movements of the period aimed at bringing children into direct contact with nature, with particular stress put on the idea of the woodland, as a means of developing confidence and skills. The feeling is best expressed in Ernest Westlake's Order of Woodcraft Chivalry which was intended to be a more adventurous and libertarian version of the Boy Scouts, and with none of its militaristic

tone .... In 1929 he founded the Forest School—a mixture of Freud and Red Indians, according to one master—and here the aim was to restore children to their "lost birthright of freedom." In all these movements the paradise theme was strong, and Ernest Westlake speaks of the ultimate purpose as "to regain paradise." (ibid.)

Fabianism, Quakers, Wicca, Theosophy, children's education, "a return to nature," sexual freedom, all tied up together via the school which I and my siblings ended up at. Who knew? I left after two terms by mutual agreement. I was unhappy being away from home, at least that's how I remember it. I also got into a lot of trouble while I was there. I don't remember anything especially strange about the teachers or the education methods, but I do have a set of slightly anomalous memories from my short time there. I recall being woken up in the middle of the night by two or more boys pouring water into my ear. The explanation they gave was that it was a method for inducing trance, something they had heard or read about somewhere. I also remember how there was a practice going around of hyperventilating and then having another boy pick you up by the torso and squeeze you. It was meant to be a means to enter into an altered state of consciousness. (As far as I know, neither of these peculiar techniques worked on me.) Lastly, and most curiously of all, I have a vague, seemingly inexplicable memory of running around in a field with all the boys from my dorm room, in the middle of the night, holding sheets over our heads. I have never been able to make sense out of this strange quasi-memory. One other thing, perhaps unrelated: A few years ago, I was reading a small collection of letters I wrote home from that period: in one of them I mention seeing a UFO from the window in my dorm.

Moving on ...

Directly connected to this Fabian-Quaker-Theosophical-vegetarian-progressive-schooling-plan was a radical alternative educational movement started in England during the 1930s, called Grith Fyrd. Grith Fyrd ("Peace Army" in Old English) was founded (surprise surprise) by members of the Order of Woodcraft Chivalry, and began with two permanent work camps, one at Godshill, in Hampshire, the other at Shining Cliff in Derbyshire, five miles from Ripley. Grith Fyrd took in unemployed men and tried to use them as a basis for creating a land-based community. The movement's vision represented a mixture of socialism, co-operativism, eugenics, and anti-urbanism. It was strongly internationalist, but had particularly close contacts with the German youth movement. The Order's main practical aim was to create an outdoor movement that would allow boys, girls, men, and women to work and learn together (Field, 2000).

The Grith Fyrd campers—or Pioneers—were a mixture of young unemployed men (who were able to continue to draw benefit) and idealists who mostly came from middle-class backgrounds. The Pioneers built the camp buildings and furniture themselves, and produced their own food. Aldous Huxley wrote in the *Sunday Chronicle* that the Godshill camp was "almost a replica of an American backwoods settlement of a century ago" (Huxley, 2001, p. 150). For Huxley, the primitive conditions were an admirable counterblow against the standardization of modern urban, industrial society. (As well as Huxley, J. B. Priestley paid a visit to the camp.) Grith Fyrd was never a large movement (camps consisted of between thirty and fifty "inmates" apiece), and it had effectively died out as a living experiment by the late 1930s. A handful of veterans organized in the late 1940s to plan the Braziers Park community—bringing us full circle.

Before setting up the School of Integrative Social Research, Norman Glaister had been involved in the Grith Fyrd barter-for-work system. The School (which also functioned as a commune) aimed to explore the dynamics of people living in groups, to develop better methods of interpersonal communication and to find new ways of combining knowledge to make it more meaningful.

> After 1937 [the year Northern Dairies was founded], Grith Fyrd members went on to found the Q Camp movement (Q stood for "quest"), which ran outdoor camp communities for troubled young men, and in turn influenced later outdoor education approaches to young offenders. It also had an influence on adult education, mainly through the Braziers community, where Glynn Faithfull and others ran what was effectively an adult residential college (and brought up his daughter, Marianne). It had an influence on psychoanalytic approaches to the management of therapeutic communities. Finally, it was part of a wider network of people and institutions who have tried to develop sustainable communities and peaceful living between the wars, and therefore has a place in the history of British environmentalism. (Field, 2012)

Just like many of the Fabian ideas about progressive education, free sexuality, and consciousness expansion, Grith Fyrd was very much an early expression of what would (thirty years later) become known as "the counterculture." Its heyday was in the 1930s, before the idea of camping out became tainted by associations with fascism (and youth movements associated with Hitler Youth). During that period, its history was "littered with characters one might fairly describe as crackpots: sandal-wearing, fruit juice-drinking vegetarians with beards, curious medieval yearnings and unscientific theories on child rearing, sun worship and gymnosophy" (Clements, 2011).

And not just sun worship: In its first editorial, "Dion" Byngham's *Pinecone* made it explicit that the pinecone represented "not only the pine cones strewn about Sandy Balls but also the head of a penis" (ibid.).

CHAPTER VI

Sex, drugs, rock & roll, and Dandies: Marianne Faithfull, the Stones, Tom Driberg, and LSE

"From an evolutionary perspective, schools are the indoctrination phase of a gigantic breeding experiment. Working-class fantasies of 'self-improvement' were dismissed from the start as sentimentality that evolutionary theory had no place for."
—John Taylor Gatto, *Underground History of American Education*

This work began as an attempt to better understand my older brother's self-destructive path and uncover the poison-roots beneath it. Ironically—or perhaps not—Sebastian was as far from a hippy or a liberal as it's possible to get (though he did once call Jesus a dandy). He mocked granola-crunching hippies, political correctness, and New Age/neoliberal values, and was infinitely more likely to speak fondly of Hitler than to praise Gandhi or Mother Teresa. Does this imply that the Fabian indoctrination didn't take, or that he rebelled against paternal influences by adopting the very inverse values (as so many of us do)? Or does it imply something subtler and more obscure, namely, that the value-set *apparently* promoted by Fabians, Quakers, Grith Fyrdians, and progressive leftists concealed a very different set of values, and that there was a wolf lurking under the liberal fleece? In fact, dandyism is far more compatible with the "back to nature" aesthetics of the Order of Woodcraft and Grith Fyrd—and with fascism—than might at first be supposed.

The Men's Dress Reform Party was an outgrowth of the eugenics movement that, like the camping movement and progressive schools, began in the late 1920s and early 1930s. Its purported aim was to encourage men to dress in "more beautiful, flowing clothing reminiscent of what they wore during the Elizabethan era." By dressing up, it was reasoned, middle class men would become more desirable to women as mates, and "thus reverse the perceived evolutionary decline of the middle classes." Summer rallies of the MDRP were regular events during the 1930s, and an event of 1931, staged at the Suffolk Street Galleries, was attended by about 1,000 people, including H. G. Wells. The pine-cone-worshipping Dion Byngham even wrote about it for the *New Health Journal*, in 1932: "[A] renaissance of beauty for men—true masculine beauty of the body and mind, the bloom of a joyful spirit—might mean happier marriages, well-born and beautiful children, a healthier and more beautiful race" (*The Dish*, 2013).

One of the prime influences on this mini-movement was Edward Carpenter, an early Fabian whom George Bernard Shaw called "a noble savage," and whom *The Guardian* called one of "the founding fathers of socialism" (Hunt, 2009). Carpenter hung out at Millthorpe, a Derbyshire village not far from Sheffield and about forty miles from Abbotsholme School. There he was visited by Shaw, Bertrand Russell, D. H. Lawrence, and Cecil Reddie (founder of Abbotsholme). He corresponded with Walt Whitman, Annie Besant, Isadora Duncan, Havelock Ellis, Roger Fry, Mahatma Gandhi, J. K. Kinney, Jack London, George Merrill (his lover), William Morris, and John Ruskin, and he probably knew the pedophile-artist Eric Gill too (they were both of what was called "the Bloomsbury set"). As *The Guardian* recalled: "Millthorpe emerged as a countercultural hub in the face of Victorian materialism, becoming an essential stopping-off point for all sorts of confused humanists .... Millthorpe was also renowned for its air of sexual liberation" (ibid.).

A question occurred to me while discovering all of this, regarding those royal bloodlines that fell on hard times: Was part of the reason they lost their wealth and social standing that they became lazy and spoiled, as aristocrats tend to, and their kingdom slipped away? If so, perhaps one way to address this problem was to send the children to "natural schools" where they would have to learn to live in nature and develop a "wild" edge—turning them not so much into noble savages as savage noblemen?

My brother might well have enjoyed such a description. He could not have cared less about eugenics or creating a more beautiful race (he would have insisted that ugly and poorly-dressed people were necessary for him to stand out). Nor did he have any time for camping or nature movements. And while he was certainly hell-bent on his own sexual "liberation" and self-beautification, using fine clothes as a way of standing out had nothing to do with attracting a mate, because according to his credo, "Dandies do not breed." His interest in clothes was sourced in a particular blend of hedonism, narcissism, and materialism; yet it was not entirely uncoupled from a philosophy of living, far from it. Without wishing to oversimplify his choices, my brother's daily preoccupations were threefold: clothing, sex, and drugs. Art and self-expression (or self-worship) were equally essential, but it was as if the three "vices" were the means to this end, the paints on his easel. If we switch clothes for rock and roll (i.e., pop music, which my brother claimed to love more than all the other arts combined), then the chosen value set of the counterculture (and the imagined means of their social and spiritual liberation) is more or less intact.

Rock and roll (as well as dandyism) also overlapped with the "back to the roots" Fabian schooling movement ("a mixture of Freud and Red Indians"). An important member of the Braziers Park community, for example, was Glynn Faithfull, who met Glaister through the Order of Woodcraft Chivalry. Faithfull had been an academic at the University of Liverpool, studied the Italian Renaissance, and worked for MI6 during World War II. He was married to Baroness Eva Erisso, a former ballerina, and their daughter was the singer and actress Marianne Faithfull. According to Marianne's second memoir (*Memories, Dreams, Reflections,* curiously the same title as Jung's autobiography), Glynn Faithfull was the person called in to interrogate Heinrich Himmler after Himmler surrendered himself to the US government on realizing that the Nazis would soon be defeated. Faithfull *allegedly* failed to search Himmler well enough to find a cyanide capsule on his person, thereby allowing Himmler to *allegedly* take his own life, *allegedly* to be buried in an unmarked grave somewhere. This is a curious enough little tale even before noting that all this happened during the same period in which, via Operation Paperclip, leading Nazis were being incorporated into the OSS, soon to become the CIA.

Marianne was born the following year, and by her own account she moved to Braziers Park when it first began, in 1950 (at age four), and lived there until she was seven. In her first memoir (*Marianne:*

An Autobiography), she describes recurring nightmares of "frightening entities" who were "just like my father," strange men with moustaches who would tickle her and pour hot tea over her. "Every year," she writes, "we took deprived children on an annual camping holiday to the New Forest"—there to participate in "quasi-mystical" rituals (2000, pp. 6–7).

Faithfull reminisces in *Memories, Dreams, Reflections*:

> Things were madder, wilder, more eccentric, more randy, in the early years—some of the things that went on there were quite peculiar …. They appeared to be studying Dante and the Destiny of Man, but what they were also doing was fucking like rabbits—with what were technically the *wrong* people …. There was sex going on everywhere at Braziers. Not exactly an entirely happy and positive experience for a kid, I guess …. The mixture of high utopian thought and randy sex might seem incongruous but it was very much of its time—the 1950s—and an uncanny harbinger of the heady free-love, let's change the world vibe of the sixties. It was the fifties, the intellectual, Bertrand Russell-ish fifties, when Braziers began and there were all these ideas—grand, world-mending ideas, small groups of people isolating themselves from the big bad world to study Big Ideas, ideas about the Nature of Man, the foundations of civilization, the complexities of communicating ideas. Along with the metaphysical deliberations came experiments in group consciousness. This combo—shagging and Schopenhauer—was as rampant at Braziers as it is in the novels of Iris Murdoch. [My father] was a philosopher of the group mind, almost a technician of group dynamics—how to deal with ego within the group. (2007, pp. 135–136, 141–142)

Further along, in a chapter titled "The Girl Factory," Faithfull describes meeting the Italian writer and publisher Roberto Calasso, "an archeologist of myths." When Faithfull told Calasso about her childhood at Braziers, she recounts, Calasso compared it to a story by the playwright Frank Wedekind, called *Mine-Haha: the Bodily Education of Young Girls*. *Mine-Haha* is about a vast girls' school located inside a castle where unwanted females are raised from infancy to the age of sixteen, "a sort of geisha finishing school where they are brought up to please others." At the age of sixteen, these girls are either placed into *show business or prostitution*. Faithfull responds to Calasso by insisting,

"Nobody forced me to go to London and become a pop singer. *Tempted me*, definitely, *seduced* me into it, but I wasn't actually *compelled* to become a pop singer, whereas the girls in the castle are made to become performers with whips and torture." Calasso's response is to note how Faithfull "grew up in a similarly cloistered place … and at the age of seventeen … burst out into the world, trained, in a strange way, for all sorts of things—group politics, sex, books, dance, acting, singing—that were useful to you in your career." Faithfull agrees that the "group mind concept my father taught at Braziers must have helped me a lot in fitting in. Probably why I fitted in so easily with the Stones."

"Before the girls are sent out into the world," Faithfull writes, "they're examined head to toe, internally, externally, the whole thing. It's really perverse. Anyway, none of that happened to me, obviously." Why obviously, I wonder? Faithfull winds up the chapter by mentioning an Italian dance troupe (Gruppo Polline) who created a performance piece based on *Mine-Haha*, the themes of which were, "the persistence of memory, isolation, the hesitation about the future, alternating static and frenetic [resistive and sensory, again], and *the negation of the body as a result of an education based on theories and exploitation of the young*" (emphasis added). She then adds that she wrote the song "In the Factory" with Polly Harvey, inspired by one of Calasso's essays. She had wanted to call it "The Girl Factory," she says, but Harvey talked her out of it. Faithfull regretted the change, adding by way of explanation that Polly was "quite intimidating."[1]

Marianne Faithfull met Mick Jagger sometime at the start of her music career in 1964–65, and he wrote her first hit, "As Tears Goes By" (though they didn't become a couple until 1966). Jagger was fresh out of the London School of Economics, having got a grant to study there in late 1961 and staying on through to 1963. This two-year period was the same period in which the Stones were first formed and grew into a known act, soon after to become "the vanguard of British rock and roll." Before this, Jagger had been working in a psychiatric institution called Bexley Hospital, in the summer of 1961, where, by his own account, he learned invaluable lessons about human psychology, as well as losing his virginity to a nurse! (Norman, 2012, p. 44).

According to one story, Jagger ran into old schoolmate Keith Richards "coincidentally" on a train platform in 1961, on his way to LSE, and the rest is history. There's a well-known anecdote—I remember hearing it from my sister as a teenager—about how Jagger kept on studying to be an accountant even while the Stones were taking off, just in case it should turn out to be a flash in the pan. What's considerably less well known (in fact it's hard to corroborate, my only source so far is the singer Sally Stevens) is that, besides giving Jagger a grant, *LSE also bankrolled the Stones in 1963*. Stevens reports a conversation from that year with Derek Bell, Gertrude Stein's nephew:

> From what I recall of the ensuing conversation, during their first year, students at LSE were allowed to write a grant proposal for project funding from LSE. According to Derek, Mick had written a good grant proposal, using the Rolling Stones as his business model, and asking for financial aid to buy equipment so they could improve their stage sound. Of course, not one member of the Board, including Derek, had much of an idea about the financial soundness of rock music, though obviously it was becoming an economic powerhouse, and they'd sort of heard of the Beatles, but when it came to the niceities[sic] of the business, LSE needed an expert opinion, in this case, me. The Board wanted to know if the Stones had any future, and I was able to say I thought so, based on what I was seeing. Would they be a good risk? "Er—yes," quoth the expert. So, Mick got some grant money from LSE which he bought gear with, after which he gave LSE the salute, and took off for the sky. (Stevens, 2011)

Apocrypha or not, the Stones became the biggest band in the world, after the Beatles, and Mick Jagger and Marianne Faithfull became one of the most famous couples in rock and roll. Jagger also came to stay with Faithfull at Braziers Park, after his release from prison in 1967.

If more evidence is required of the implicate order of popular culture, intelligence operations, and politics, Mick Jagger was associated for a period with the Labour MP and alleged MI5 (and possibly KGB, and even Church of Scientology[2]) informant, Tom Driberg. Driberg was impressed with Jagger, having been introduced to him in 1965, and tried unsuccessfully over a number of years to persuade him to take up active Labour politics. Driberg belonged to one or more of the same groups my grandfather belonged to, fraternized with Richard Acland, and was even briefly earmarked by Aleister Crowley as his natural successor for world teacher! Nothing came of the proposal, though the two continued to meet.

Even more ominously, Driberg (who fully embraced the social and cultural freedoms of the '60s) enjoyed a lengthy friendship with the Kray twins, and in July 1964, both he and Lord Boothby (a well-known Conservative peer) were alleged to have been sexually propositioning males at a dog track and to be involved with a criminal underworld scene. Driberg and Boothby attended parties at the Krays' flat where "rough but compliant East End lads were served like so many canapés," according to Driberg's biographer Francis Wheen (1992, p. 350). While Driberg avoided publicity, Boothby was hounded by the press and forced to issue a series of denials. After the twins had been convicted of murder in 1969, Driberg frequently lobbied the Home Office about their prison conditions, requesting that they be given more visits and allowed regular reunions. In passing, I note that the author and psychotherapist Anthony Storr described Driberg "as the only person he ever met who could truly be called 'evil'" (Baker, 2009). Even more tantalizingly, author Robin Bryans noted that "Many of Driberg's Oxford friends enjoyed the black mass" (1992, p. 482; we will hear more from Bryans in Part II; Driberg started at Oxford in 1924, around the time Alec graduated).

When he wasn't participating in satanic rituals—or perhaps simultaneously—Driberg belonged to the aforementioned 1941 Committee, which besides Acland and Astor also recruited Julian Huxley (Aldous's older brother, a eugenicist and social engineer), and probable MI5-asset Christopher Mayhew (who became the under-secretary of state of the Foreign Office in 1945 and formed The Information Research Department to counter Soviet propaganda and infiltration). This was the same period that the CIA was embarking on its MKULTRA mind control program (with the help of those paper-clipped Nazis), which included the early use of psychedelics, and in 1955, Mayhew took part in his own experiment with psychotropics. Ostensibly intended as part of a *Panorama* special for the BBC but never broadcast, under the guidance of his friend Dr. Humphry Osmond, Mayhew ingested 400 mg of mescaline hydrochloride and allowed himself to be filmed for the duration of the trip (Drokhole, 2013). Part of the footage was included in the BBC documentary "LSD—The Beyond Within," released in 1986. Dr. Humphry Osmond gave Aldous Huxley mescaline the following year (1952), which led to Huxley's countercultural bible, *The Doors of Perception*.

Since my grandfather was also on the 1941 Committee (according to LSE Marxist historian, John Saville), was he also ingesting mescaline on the frontline of the psychedelic revolution? If so, I had no clue about any of this while growing up. Yet hallucinogen-ingestion apparently *was* a central element in the Fabian experience: over fifty years before Huxley made mescaline famous, Havelock Ellis wrote an article called "Mescal: A New Artificial Paradise," for *The Contemporary Review*, January 1898, making him one of the very first Western experimenters with "entheogens."

Once again, my brother continued this tradition in both exact and inverse ways: he wrote an article for *The Observer* (formerly edited by MI6-asset David Astor) about his Ibogaine experience, called "Trip of a Lifetime" (Horsley, 2004; I am even mentioned in it, though not by name). More famously, he wrote lovingly of his heroin addiction in various places, and on his self-designed death-coat of arms he included syringes, as well as skulls. He wore with pride the weapons of his self-destruction.

The creation of cultural figures through applied extremity inevitably gives rise to some kamikaze models.

CHAPTER VII

Food control, world control: Suez Crisis, Northern Dairies, Marks & Spencer

> "You needn't carry a card or even have heard the name Fabian to follow the wolf-in-sheep's-clothing flag. Fabianism is mainly a value-system with progressive objectives. Its social club aspect isn't for coalminers, farmers, or steam-fitters. We've all been exposed to many details of the Fabian program without realizing it. In the United States, some organizations heavily influenced by Fabianism are the Ford Foundation, the Russell Sage Foundation, the Stanford Research Institute, the Carnegie Endowments, the Aspen Institute, the Wharton School, and RAND. And this short list is illustrative, not complete."
> —John Taylor Gatto, *Underground History of American Education*

In the early 1950s, Northern Dairies was approached about going public and the firm was approved by the aforementioned Lord Piercy, who then approached Labour MP and Fabian Society member Ian Mikardo. Mackintosh was also represented in the Northern Dairies board, and Alec was "reasonably certain of a successful issue in 1956" (Ounsworth, 1987, p. 10). It was at this point that Alec was approached by the Orthodox Church of Russia to take a team of churchmen to the Soviet Union. "Then came the Northern Dairies share issues in 1956,"

Alec writes in his short memoir, "and happily, providence decided that General Nasser would nationalize the Suez Canal on that very day, so demand was not high" (ibid.). I am not well-versed in stock-talk (despite being myself a major shareholder in Northern Foods from the age of eighteen to twenty-four), but what I deduce from this is that, because of the timing of the company going public with an international crisis, there was a flurry of insider trading while the price of shares remained low. "Although all shares were taken up the price hovered around ...' the same price that our friends and customers the Mackintosh Group had acquired theirs." Alec adds that "several members of the Mackintosh family actually bought significant quantities of our shares, and a happy relationship has continued to this day" (ibid.).

When I first began this exploration of my family history, I had not even heard of the Suez Crisis, but I soon discovered that it was a major turning point in global politics. For one thing, it spelled the end of the then British Prime Minister Anthony Eden's career, due to a combination of failing health and a seriously compromised reputation. For another, it is on record as heralding the end of British predominance in the Middle East (once the US refused to back Eden's government in trying to kill Nasser and retake the canal)—which is not far from saying the end of the British Empire. (The canal was of major importance to European industry due to the fact that two-thirds of oil supplies to Europe passed through it.) So in 1956, on the very same day that Northern Dairies was going public, General Nasser, the president of Egypt, seized the canal in response to the withdrawal of Anglo-American funding for the Aswan Dam.[1] As a result of this act of "providence," Alec and his buddies were able to make a big business score. Considering Alec's close relationship to power, it begs the question as to just how "providential" this timing was.

Also of note here is that David Astor's media empire was instrumental in bringing down Eden's government after the crisis: *The Observer* accused Eden of lying to Parliament, and of working in collusion with France and Israel to seize the canal. (Of passing interest, Astor was psychoanalyzed by Freud's daughter, Anna, around the time the Tavistock Institute was founded.) The Suez Crisis also comes up in relation to my father, in his *Guardian* obit: "[His] politics were always radical. In his youth, he had been a prominent protester against the Suez fiasco and an Aldermaston marcher" (Haskins, 2004). If my father was protesting against Eden's siding with France and Israel in 1956, this would have been a year or so before he left the UK and began traveling around the US and Canada, trying, or at least hoping, to be a writer (he met my mother in New Orleans in 1958). Did something happen to drive him from the UK, and from intense pressure to join the family business (which he ended up doing anyway, after he married my mother)? And if so, did it relate to Northern Dairies' "happy" transition from a private to a public corporation? Was this a time when my father got a whiff of the sort of insider interests Alec was really serving? (It's probably also worth noting here that, after going public, Northern Dairies' first major expansion was into Northern Ireland.)

To give a little background to this story, the transformation of Alec's local dairy into an international corporation began during World War II. As the website *Reference for Business* (2010) relates it:

> Recognizing that the time of the small dairyman was over, Horsley embarked upon an energetic and ambitious campaign of expansion, acquiring other dairies one by one. The larger the business grew, the more attractive it became to small firms beset by the bombing (Hull was very hard hit during the war), the chronic shortages, and the difficulties of adapting to rationalization [rationing]. As the firm expanded it actually became more efficient with each new addition, as Horsley chose the best dairies and plants when consolidating operations. By 1942 Horsley controlled a considerable network of retail and wholesale businesses scattered throughout Humberside and Yorkshire, and the retail end of the company was renamed Northern Dairies to reflect this (although the wholesale operations continued to be known by their individual names).

For a company to become public as Northern Dairies did in 1956 means it can begin selling shares to "the general populace"—that is, to rich people—and so become part of the stock exchange. This allows the company to raise funds and capital through the sale of its securities, in other words, to make money off money. Shareholders don't *do* anything to make money, they just own shares and receive dividends. It's pure capitalism, and about as far from a socialist philosophy as it's possible to get. I should know: as one of these shareholders, from about the age of fifteen or so, I knew that (if I played my cards right) I would never have to work a day in my life (I didn't, and I do). Once I turned eighteen and took ownership of my stock, I embraced a life of social freedom and irresponsibility (i.e., I did whatever the hell I pleased). Here's a description of my lifestyle from the one piece I ever managed to get into *The Guardian* (the "Experience" section, open to everyone):

> On an average day, I woke around 1pm, ate, drove my black Opel Manta to the West End and spent £200 on records, videos, comics and books. On less adventurous days, I rented three or four movies from the local video store, ate an M&S dinner, rolled five or six joints, and spent half the night getting high. If I already had movies, I often didn't get out of bed, just rolled a joint and turned on the TV. On my 20th birthday, I moved to New York. Beyond the locale, nothing much changed. When I wasn't enjoying pot and movies in my Bowery bedsit, I was drinking tequila and snorting cocaine in an East Village bar. If anyone asked what I did for a living, I took great pleasure in telling them: "You're looking at it." (Horsley, 2006)

This was the legacy of my "socialist" father and grandfather, and it was one that, within six or seven years, I found so burdensome that I effectively threw all my shares away. Today I run a thrift shop in a small town. Our clientele includes the poorest, most damaged, and disenfranchised people in town.

*

Returning to the Northern Dairies going public/Alec's Russian journey/Suez Crisis/end of British Empire nexus of 1954–56: it may seem a bit of a stretch to imply that Northern Dairies (soon to be Foods) was a significant player in this realm of geopolitics—were it not for the fact that food distribution is one of the most essential components in social engineering. Every bit as much as oil, food is fundamental to the smooth functioning of society—making it also a powerful means to control and direct it.

Northern Dairies became Northern Foods ten years after my father took over, and three years after Alec retired. (According to some sources, it was only then that my father came into his own as chairman, suggesting he'd been operating under the shadow, if not the thumb, of Alec.) My uncle, Christopher Haskins, joined the company in 1967. The "official" (Wikipedia) story is that he wanted to marry Alec's daughter, Gilda, and the condition given was that he join the business. The truth is the exact reverse: Alec agreed to let Haskins into the business only if he would marry his daughter. When given a choice between fact and legend, print the legend, yet whichever version of the story you read, it has an archaic, darkly mythological flavor to it. Either Alec used his youngest daughter as a bribe to recruit what he saw as a company asset (Haskins certainly turned out to be that), or, the reverse, he bribed his future son-in-law with a job in exchange for marrying off his daughter, thereby increasing the chances of expanding the family dynasty. In both narratives, Gilda is cast in the more or less "traditional" role—as chattel.

By Haskins's own account (always best questioned, in my view), he was instrumental in first forming an alliance between Northern Foods and Marks & Spencer, in 1970, via a "chance meeting" with a Marks & Spencer executive on a plane (*Reference for Business*, 2010). 1970 was also the year Northern Dairies passed the million-pound annual profit mark; once again, happy providence seems to have been at work. Northern Foods soon became Marks & Spencer's biggest supplier, employing its "typical enthusiastic blend of acquisition and innovation." It implemented a policy of "acquiring existing suppliers to Marks and Spencer wherever it could" (e.g., Park Cakes in 1972 and Fox's Biscuits in 1977) while also creating new products especially for its favored customer: "… by 1988 Northern Foods was producing a range of 250 products for Marks and Spencer" (ibid.).

In 2014, Lord Haskins (as he was by then known) stated: "My company was built up on the principles of Marks & Spencer—being fair and equal with those we worked with. It was very much above board and we treated our suppliers with respect" (Neville, 2014). Maybe so, but Marks & Spencer is more than just a clothing and food chain. It has been both directly and indirectly affiliated with Zionism and the state of Israel from its inception on, most overtly in that M&S chairman and founding member Israel Sieff was a Zionist, and chairman Joseph Sieff a British Zionist Federation member (Joseph Sieff survived an assassination attempt in 1973, allegedly by the Palestinian Liberation Army). Israel Sieff was also a member of the New Fabian Research Bureau, along with Julian Huxley and J. B. Priestley, and "regarded as one of the Fabian Society's more able permeaters" (Martin, 1966, pp. 302–303).

In 1987, under the chairmanship of Haskins, Northern Foods built a massive food factory in Europe:

> As a gesture of its goodwill and enthusiasm, Northern Foods built
> this Marks and Spencer dedicated plant—at a cost of £8 million—
> before it had yet been established what products were to be made

there. Echoing Alec Horsley's 1937 achievement with his first milk processing plant, Fenland Foods, which has been hailed as Europe's most advanced food factory, was built in 40 weeks—and was selling to Marks and Spencer three weeks later. (*Reference for Business*, 2010)

Apparently this gesture of goodwill was rewarded. "Ironically for a company whose own name is never seen on its products, Northern Foods is the largest fresh food manufacturer in the United Kingdom. The company's 1993 sales figures elevated it to the coveted status of membership in the 'two billion club'" (ibid.). After he left the company, Haskins remained a member of the club. He went on to become "rural tsar" (at the height of the foot and mouth disease epidemic) to prime minister and Fabian Society member Tony Blair. This would suggest that the business of running a food company and that of running a country are not so far apart as many might imagine. Who knew?

CHAPTER VIII

Mass observation and dance halls:
Jimmy Savile's beginnings

"[I]t would not be too far out of line to call the twentieth century the Fabian century. One thing is certain: the direction of
modern schooling for the bottom 90 percent of our society has
followed a largely Fabian design—and the puzzling security
and prestige enjoyed at the moment by those who speak of 'glo-
balism' and 'multiculturalism' are a direct result of heed paid
earlier to Fabian prophecies that a welfare state, followed by an
intense focus on internationalism, would be the mechanism ele-
vating corporate society over political society, and a necessary
precursor to utopia. Fabian theory is the *Das Kapital* of financial
capitalism."

—John Taylor Gatto, *Underground History of American Education*

On January 2, 1937 (Northern Dairies' birth year, again), a British surre-
alist poet named Charles Madge published a letter in the Fabian magazine *New Statesman and Nation*. With the title "Anthropology at Home,"
the letter announced the formation of a group of writers, painters, and
filmmakers committed to social documentation. Soon after, Madge (who
was married to poet Kathleen Raine) joined forces with Tom Harrisson,
whose poem was "coincidentally" published on the same page as

Madge's letter.[1] Harrisson was an ornithologist-cum-anthropologist who wrote for *The Observer* and did intelligence work during WWII.[2] They were then joined by the filmmaker, Humphrey Jennings. Jennings had founded the Cambridge literary periodical *Experiment* in 1928, with two of my grandfather's known cohorts, Jacob Bronowski and Yorkshireman William Empson (who later joined Mass Observation). Jennings worked for Crown Film Unit, a filmmaking propaganda arm of the Ministry of Information, during WWII. Together, these "artists and poets" created an organization dedicated to developing what they called "a science of ourselves."

> In its original guise, Mass Observation (M-O) was an organiza-
> tion dedicated to the documentation of everyday life amongst the
> British working classes .... M-O thus sought out facts and figures,
> through interviews and covert surveillance, which highlighted the
> nature of their fellow Britons' day-to-day existence. The range of
> the Mass-Observers' interests—from the "behaviour of people at
> war memorials, the aspidistra cult, [and] anthropology of football
> pools" to "bathroom behavior; beards, armpits and eyebrows; [and
> the] distribution, diffusion and significance of the dirty joke"—was
> intended to form a comprehensive topography of workers' lives,
> and in so doing, provide a new basis for social democracy. (*Visual
> Culture and Mass Observation*, 2015)

This all sounds deceptively agenda-free, but the context for this program of national research into the mores of the common man is considerably more fraught than the calm, rational, faintly caring tone of the proposal, with its suggestion of a benefactor doing impartial social research to "provide a new basis for social democracy" (ibid.). The fraught social context, one major factor of it anyway, was that M-O came into existence in the years following the massive General Strike of 1926, a strike that "shook the British ruling class out of their thrones and showed brilliantly how collective working class action can change society" (*Libcon*, 2012). During the height of the strike, London transport was crippled:

> On May 4, 15 out of 315 tubes ran, 300 out of 4,400 buses (by the end
> of the week this was down to 40), nine out of 2,000 trams operated.
> By the end of the first day builders, printers, dockers, iron, steel,
> metal, heavy chemical, transport and railway workers were out

on strike. All with the TUC [Trade Union Congress] stuck like rabbits in headlights. The working class was truly in the driving seat. Nothing moved unless the workers said it could move …. The ruling class had spent hundreds of millions of pounds but they would have lost had it not been for the concerted campaign of sabotage carried out by the TUC. Had the workers organized themselves into independent rank and file organizations and had the same revolutionary vision as their Spanish counter-parts did ten years later, then the results may have been very different. (ibid.)

The workers' struggle—an example of a genuine socialist movement?—was one that presented a genuine threat to capitalist interests, for obvious reasons. The ruling class needs "workers" (slaves) to maintain its rule and keep industry going. The idea of "educating" the mass populace—M-O's ostensible goal—was, in John Taylor Gatto's view at least, Orwellian newspeak for making sure they didn't educate and empower themselves. As Gatto writes in *The Underground History of American Education*:

Forced schooling was the medicine to bring the whole continental population into conformity with these plans so that it might be regarded as a "human resource" and managed as a "workforce." No more Ben Franklins or Tom Edisons could be allowed; they set a bad example. One way to manage this was to see to it that individuals were prevented from taking up their working lives until an advanced age when the ardor of youth and its insufferable self-confidence had cooled. (2006, p. 38)

This indicates a deliberate policy of "hobbling" the working class to neutralize them as a threat to the entrepreneurial class. And not only were working class people rising up against working conditions, they were also protesting forced schooling—first implemented in Prussia in the 1700s *expressly as a means to control human behavior and curb independent thinking*, and steadily introduced in the UK and the US in the late 1800s and early 1900s. Nonetheless, the avowed aim of M-O (and no doubt many of its implementers believed it) was:

to empower Britons with information about themselves and their country such that they could make informed political choices, take political action when necessary, or pick adequate political representation; properly interpret current events; and consequently, not become victims of baseless rumor or suggestion (particularly related to the situation in Europe) spread by mass media and the government. Yet these publications were not merely intended to pass information laterally, but also upward, such that the Prime Minister, Cabinet, and Members of Parliament could be informed of the "real" concerns of the nation …. Surveillance was an effective way of collecting information, if only because the individuals surveyed were unaware of that fact and thus presented themselves in a relatively natural state. Yet, once this method of research had been publicized, it likewise bred a form of popular paranoia. (*Visual Culture and Mass Observation*, 2015)

M-O was supported by the aforementioned Fabian economist, John Maynard Keynes, in its early stages:

> Madge had renewed contact with Maynard Keynes, who responded enthusiastically to his offer to test out the public acceptability proposals for financing the war through compulsory saving. Giving Madge an immediate subsidy of £50 from his own pocket, Keynes urged the National Institute of Economic and Social Research (NIESR) to fund the project. Harrisson and Madge, he wrote, "are live wires, amongst the most original investigators of the younger generation and well worth encouraging," and this was "an enquiry of first class importance, which I have long wished to see undertaken … more purely economic-scientific [in] character than some of their previous enquiries," and "vastly more deserving" than many of the dreary and fruitless academic projects customarily financed by the NIESR. (Hinton, 2013, p. 160)

Other cultural movers and shakers who joined the M-O movement were the painter Julian Trevelyan, Tom Driberg, and, as ever lurking behind the scenes, Sir Richard Acland. Tom Harrisson briefed Acland on the aims of M-O and Acland spoke in favor of M-O, while drawing "a sharp line—over-generous in the circumstances—between the WSS [Wartime Social Survey], whose findings provided the state with a secret weapon for the manipulation of public opinion, and the MO, who published its results for all to see" (ibid., p. 183. After Acland published his book, *Unser Kampf (Our Struggle)*, he commissioned M-O to pretest his "Manifesto of the Common Man.")

One of the aims of M-O was to popularize science and so introduce increased rationality into the public debate. Harrisson came up with a plan to provide the major newspapers with written reports of the latest scientific research. In 1940 he presented "Memorandum on Propaganda for Science" to Solly Zuckerman's scientific dining club, Tots and Quots, whose members included Julian Huxley. Popularizing scientific research was meant to combat

> "the sway of superstition in the midst of science." Another was to tackle the problem from the other end, by working directly with these "large new groups of semi-intellectuals and semi cre-ative persons" employed in *commercial entertainment, whose work played a role in encouraging superstitions and escapist modes of think-ing among the masses.* [Emphasis added. This included pop music and dance clubs.] Richard Acland had responded enthusiastically to Harrisson's suggestion of a meeting with "some people in the dance music world … I wonder if it would be worth trying to con-vert any of these to our ideas and try to get them to express them in dance tunes. I can imagine for example an immense popularity for something with the refrain of "When are they going to let us build a better world?" (Hinton, 2013, pp. 256–258)

M-O's interest in dance clubs was so extensive that a 375-page study of dance culture "On with the Dance: Nation, Culture, and Popular Danc-ing in Britain, 1918–1945," cites M-O's findings 85 times. A brief perusal of this document makes clear that, not only were dance clubs of great interest to M-O as venues for observing British citizens and learning about their behaviors and interests, but dance music, and by extension dance halls, were *an intrinsic part of an ongoing effort to shape public behav-ior and interests.* Specifically, the study cites the plethora of dances that were contrived as a means to instill people with patriotic feelings dur-ing wartime! Like M-O itself, this is an aspect of history that seems to have gone mostly unremarked upon, but which very clearly shows how popular culture can be directed—and even *created*—to serve sociopoliti-cal ends. Mick Jagger and LSE come to mind once again.

The British public also embraced this notion that the Lambeth Walk, and dancing in general, were symbolic of democracy and the national spirit. Mass Observation's Tom Harrisson and Charles Madge justified their inclusion of an entire chapter about the dance in a book about the national reaction to the Munich Crisis by noting, "we may learn something about the future of democracy if we take a closer look at the Lambeth Walk." ... This was a crucial time period, in which Britain moved closer to war, and ideas about national identity transitioned accordingly .... Some people seemed to have seen through the commercialization of the nation represented in the dance, and to have viewed the content as exploitative. Alec Hughes speculated in his report for Mass Observation that the timing of the dance was designed to coincide with the institution of conscription in the summer of 1939. (Abra, 2009)

Entertaining the masses to keep them distracted has worked at least since Roman times (bread and circuses); add to that a loosening of sexual mores means more women getting pregnant sooner, which is one way to ensure men are sufficiently motivated to keep their jobs and not to want to strike.

Allegedly Jimmy Savile started playing records in dance halls also in the early 1940s (when he was supposedly working down a coal mine). This is difficult to corroborate, but according to his autobiography at least, he was the first to use two turntables and a microphone at the Grand Records Ball, in the Guardbridge Hotel, in 1947. If so, it's perhaps not unthinkable that he was cutting his teeth as a teenager in local dance clubs at *exactly the time* Acland, Harrisson, et al. were working out how best to incorporate the dance club scene into social research and "progressive" movements.

The evidence provided by the Mass Observation material indicates that the world of pop music and dance halls was of crucial interest to the ruling class and, in fact, that it was being used to implement long-term social goals. Before attaining prominence as the dean of pop music in the 1960s, Savile (as well as the Kray twins) ran his own clubs in the 1950s, a period when wartime dance halls steadily morphed into gangster-run venues for drugs and prostitution. And not only did the budding new dance culture overlap with the crime underworld populated by the Kray twins and Jimmy Boyle (and possibly Ian Brady, Myra

Hindley, and Savile's pal Peter Sutcliffe), it also intersected with the interests of Members of Parliament, from social reformers like Acland to occult-dabblers like Driberg and known child molesters like Lord Boothby. Is it a leap to suppose that Savile's involvement with the world of dance music was part and parcel with his connection to, or employment by, governmental agencies?

CHAPTER IX

Evolutionary theory and social engineering: Richard Acland's Common Wealth

"I've neglected to tell you so far about the role stress plays in Fabian evolutionary theory. Just as Hegel taught that history moves faster toward its conclusion by way of warfare, so evolutionary socialists were taught by Hegel to see struggle as the precipitant of evolutionary improvement for the species, a necessary purifier eliminating the weak from the breeding sweepstakes. Society evolves slowly toward 'social efficiency' all by itself; society under stress, however, evolves much faster! Thus the deliberate creation of crisis is an important tool of evolutionary socialists. Does that help you understand the government school drama a little better, or the well-publicized doomsday scenarios of environmentalists?"

—John Taylor Gatto, *Underground History of American Education*

At the beginning of World War II, Norman Glaister and his friends joined Common Wealth, the new political party formed by Sir Richard Acland. Acland began as a "junior whip" for the Liberals. His politics apparently changed course and, in 1942, he broke from the Liberals to found Common Wealth with J. B. Priestley, thereby opposing the coalition between the major parties (see Acland, 1981). He helped form the

Campaign for Nuclear Disarmament in 1957, of which my grandfather was a cofounder and, according to family history, helped design the famous Peace symbol that would be adopted by the counterculture. Common Wealth's interest in optimizing social organization consistent with its principles also led it to develop close links with the School of Integrative Social Research at Braziers Park.[1] But we know all this.

Of Common Wealth, etc., George Orwell wrote: "I think this movement should be watched with attention. It might develop into the new Socialist party we have all been hoping for, or into something very sinister." Orwell, like Kitty Bowler, believed that Richard Acland had the potential to become a fascist leader (Simkin, 2014). Richard Acland also wrote a bunch of books, including his homage to *Mein Kampf* and *What it Will Be Like in the New Britain*, in which he talks about the need to break down the family unit. It was published by Victor Gollancz in 1942 (Gollancz was another member of the 1941 Committee, and Alec sent him regular donations). Sixty years later, Gollancz, the publishing house, would be part of Orion House Publishing, which is owned by Hachette, one of "The Big Five" publishing houses. In 1992, Hachette merged with Matra, the French automobile and missile building company. Gollancz, a.k.a. Orion, a.k.a. Hachette, a.k.a. Matra, would publish my book *Matrix Warrior: Being the One*, in 2003, about the need to break down, not just the family but the entire social "unit." When I was offered the contract with Gollancz in 2002, I had a brief period of conscience-wrestling over the thought of making money for a company that would use it to build weapons of mass destruction. I had no idea how ironic Gollancz's affiliation was, in light of its original *alleged* ideological goals—or how closely that irony touched upon my own family background.

Yet here we are again. It is all of a piece, even though many of the parts have been lost or concealed to history—and not only my own. Growing up, I never had the slightest idea that socialism not only overlapped with, but was in some sense either a parallel project to or a cover *for*, social experimentation involving sex, drugs, and strange rituals. I was always under the impression that these areas were worlds apart (at least until the 1960s). A natural assumption, on discovering this strange overlap, is simply that the leftist reformers of my family and beyond were freethinkers and sexual libertines, and that, back in the day, they had to be discreet about it. But how well does this perhaps-too-easy assumption hold up when the sexual experimentation overlaps, not only with social and psychological research, but with the criminal underworld and the sexual exploitation of children for profit?

When it comes to attempting to map the shape of the past, there is always the tendency to try to create a narrative out of the available data and so force it to fit into that context. Ideally, the data *reveals* the context, and as it does so, the emerging context recontextualizes the data, allowing the two to feed into and support each other until a more or less complete picture emerges. Yet, when what is being explored is by definition incomplete, hidden, and inherently unfamiliar, even controversial, the chances of ever reaching a full picture are slim at best. Knowing and acknowledging the difference between fact and theory is never more crucial than when exploring the realms of hidden history (family or otherwise), since it inevitably overlaps with the phenomenon of conspiracy—that is, of individuals working together in secret, to bring about desired, usually criminal, ends.

I really don't want to theorize about conspiracy, only to lay out the evidence *of* conspiracy and let it speak for itself. At the same time, without *some* speculation, there's the danger that the material being presented will be confusing and overwhelming to the reader, raising too many questions for them to process. What *does* it all mean? What *am* I suggesting by presenting all of this apparent evidence—and evidence of *what*? Clearly, even by choosing to write this down, I must have *some* idea of what it means. So then why be evasive about that, especially when so much of the material seems quite contradictory?

The main hypothesis, or even deduction, which I think this data demands, is that seemingly unconnected, even disparate, groups and individuals *appear* to have been collaborating in ways that throw into question their *public* aims and characters. At which point, everything truly begins to look like a massive conspiracy. This may be a premature deduction. The easiest example that came to my mind while working on this piece was that of a body, human or otherwise, experienced from the inside, for example by a single blood cell. There may be an experience of the heart, the liver, the intestines, and the digestive tract. It may be possible to observe these different organs performing their various tasks, and to notice that certain processes are occurring, for example, that food coming into the stomach via one channel is being processed by a separate system and then conveyed down another channel. From the inside, there is no awareness of being *on* the inside of anything, because the body is its own internal environment. It's only through noticing the ways in which the various organs seem to be cooperating with each other and assisting with various processes that the idea of a larger body, containing everything, can be inferred.

It may be the same with the various groups and individuals which this work is exploring. The fact they take part in shared processes and *seem* to collaborate, while serving ostensibly separate, even opposed ends, suggests they are part of a larger system *directing them externally*. There is no need to assume that the majority of these individuals or groups are aware of being used by a larger governing intelligence, any more than a heart or a liver necessarily knows that it's working for the body. The way to recognize such a controlling intelligence is twofold: to trace the connections between apparently unconnected agencies; and to attempt to deduce from this the processes being implemented *through* these agencies. This then allows for the hypothesis of a containing body, whatever that might be, without really saying anything about it *outside* of its methods, means, and apparent aims.

In "The Childhood Origins of the Holocaust," the psycho-historian Lloyd deMause talks about Weimar culture, the flourishing of the arts and sciences in Germany during the Weimar Republic. This period between Germany's defeat in World War I and Hitler's rise to power, deMause writes,

> may have produced "exuberant creativity and experimentation" but also created "anxiety, fear and a rising sense of doom." By the end of the 1920s, so many reactionary anti-democratic backlash parties had spontaneously sprung up that Weimar was called "a Republic without republicans." People began to call for "emancipation from emancipation" and "a restoration of authoritarian rule." (deMause, 2005)

What deMause is describing, in bald terms, is how a period of social and sexual freedom allows for a release of collective unconscious or "id" material in a people, and how this then leads to a corresponding reaction from the controlling ego, that is, to even more "Draconian" social restrictions. It's possible to extrapolate from such observable trends in history—both individual and collective—how such a principle could be *consciously applied* at the level of social engineering. If the aim, say, is totalitarianism, first promote the *opposite* ideas pertaining to individual freedom, sexual liberation, artistic expression, human rights, and drug experimentation. Such a form of deep psychosocial engineering could, hypothetically, proceed over generations, propagating a set of values to one generation so as to create an opposing reaction from the next. It could also proceed at a more localized, short-term level, over periods of months, days, and hours, even down to a micro-level, such as when a TV show promotes "radical" or anti-capitalist values while at the same time serving as product placement for corporations.

A very broad example of this might be how the promotion of individualistic, capitalist, consumer values over the second half of the twentieth century led to a supposed dead-end and "environmental crisis" in which individualism is frowned upon and seen as something to be curbed (often via draconian laws) in order to save "the planet" (collective). It also goes the other way, as when the collective "countercultural" values of the '60s, promoting peace and harmony, led to the capitalist feeding frenzy of the '80s—many of the feeders being former hippies who "wised up."

It's possible to trace a direct correlation between this kind of social engineering and the psychological and biological model (and possibly agendas) of the Fabians, regarding evolutionary management through stress. Adversity breeds character, necessity is the mother of invention, and so on. The many bohemian artistic communities-cum-survival camps that arose in the 1930s (in tandem with National Socialism), and that combined sexual freedom, self-expression, and back-to-nature primitivism (paganism), may have started with the thinnest end of the wedge being gently inserted into the child-psyche (naked children encouraged to explore their sexuality rather than being shamed about it); but pretty soon, the id monsters were running the show.

From the LSE Vegetarianism thesis quoted previously:

> During the twenties the influence of Freud on the progressive school movement—and indeed on progressivism generally—was marked, and Freudian theory was used to underpin the liberation of the child from adult repression and to justify the belief that the natural impulses should have free expression. In certain of the schools this produced a move towards a libertarian and anarchic ideal. The progressivism of the period, however, largely used Freud as *a dissolvent of conservative social values*, taking up the attack on traditional religion and upon patriarchal authority. It was, however, *an essentially selective reading of Freud, one that passed over the darker*

Hobbesian aspects of his thought, focusing instead on its *libertarian potential*, which was then grafted on to an essentially non-Freudian model of man and his destiny—one that derived from *the older romantic tradition*. (Twigg, 1981, emphasis added)

What happens when you attempt to mix half-baked Freudianism with an older, incompatible philosophy is that you wind up with a potentially explosive chemical reaction. The demiurge of superego gets its "liberation," but the devil of the id is denied its due. And when the id starts to rumble and grumble, there's a corresponding clampdown from the superego. As the darker impulses take over, over time, sexual abuse becomes part of the unofficial curriculum. And since sexual abuse leads to trauma, is it any real surprise if trauma is reframed—whether by early Fabian "evolutionary socialists" or by today's spiritual spokespeople (such as Esalen-biographer Jeffrey Kripal or LSE-student Whitley Strieber[2])—as *a means to access the divine and accelerate evolution*?

CHAPTER X

The Gates of Hell: MKULTRA, Robert Graves, William Sargant, and Wasson's Magic Mushroom

"Fabianism was a principal force and inspiration behind all major school legislation of the first half of the twentieth century. And it will doubtless continue to be in the twenty-first. [T]he 'purpose of education' was to supply the teacher with 'fundamentals of an everlasting faith as broad as human nature and as deep as the life of the race.'"

—John Taylor Gatto, *Underground History of American Education*

All of this inevitably conjures associations with the CIA's notorious mind control program of the 1950s and beyond, MKULTRA. In case anyone is unfamiliar with this subject (or only aware of it via Hollywood product such as *Conspiracy Theory, The Bourne Identity*, or *American Ultra*), MKULTRA is the codename given to a program of experiments on human subjects, at times illegal, designed and undertaken by the CIA for a number of reasons, including developing drugs and procedures to force confessions through mind control. Organized through the Scientific Intelligence Division of the CIA, the project coordinated with the Special Operations Division of the US Army's Chemical Corps. It began in the early 1950s, was officially sanctioned in 1953, reduced in scope in 1964, further curtailed in 1967, and officially halted in 1973.

The program engaged in many illegal activities, including the use of unwitting US and Canadian citizens as its test subjects. MKULTRA research included at least 80 institutions, 44 colleges and universities, as well as hospitals, prisons, and pharmaceutical companies. The CIA operated through these institutions using front organizations, although sometimes top officials at these institutions were aware of the CIA's involvement. The program consisted of some 149 subprojects which the Agency contracted out to various universities, research foundations, and similar institutions. At least 80 institutions and 185 private researchers participated. Most of the official records were destroyed in 1973 by order of then CIA director Richard Helms.[1]

As it happens, there *is* an overlap with the cultural movements, programs, and agendas I have already been mapping, and it takes the form of William Sargant, a contemporary of my grandfather and a British psychiatrist best remembered for promoting treatments such as psychosurgery, deep sleep treatment, electroconvulsive therapy and insulin shock therapy. Sargant worked in some capacity for MI5 (Streathfield, 2008, p. 243), and corresponded with the infamous psychiatrist Ewen Cameron (who was performing MKULTRA research in Canada). While he reputedly wanted the British government to distance itself from the CIA project (he called it "blacker than black"), he remained committed to the principle of mind control, and allegedly became the link between British Intelligence and MKULTRA (Thomas, 1989).

Besides his affiliations with the Tavistock Institute,[2] the first reason Sargant is relevant to my own family history is that, once again, there is a curious overlap with the world of Fabianism, leftist movements, and progressive creative circles. In 1954, a convalescing Sargant was completing his book *Battle for the Mind* in Majorca, and had Robert Graves on hand to help him edit it. Robert Graves is of course the famous poet, novelist, and critic who is as responsible as Joseph Campbell for reintroducing ancient myths into popular culture (*The White Goddess*), and a primary influence in popularizing ancient history (*I Claudius*). In passing, he was teaching at Oxford during my grandfather's tenure there, but if they met, I never heard about it.

So what's the connection between a poet-mythologist and the world of mind control? The answer I found was surprising because also familiar: the world of hallucinogens. In 1952, Robert Gordon Wasson (the man who brought the magic mushroom to the West) wrote to Graves asking him about the kind of mushroom which had allegedly been responsible for Claudius's death. Graves sent Wasson an account of ancient Mexican religious ceremonies that included the ingestion of mushrooms—mushrooms that had "eluded botanists and explorers for nearly five hundred years and, as a result, were generally considered to be mythical" (Streathfield, 2008, p. 60). Graves claimed there was new evidence for their actual existence, but that currently the only thing known about them was that they were referred to as "the flesh of God." It was allegedly Graves's tip that sent the Wassons down to Mexico in 1955, where they made the discovery that would help kick-start the counterculture and spark off the "psychedelic revolution."

Among the first people to hear of Wasson's discovery were Graves and his "friend," William Sargant. "In a bizarre turn, the war poet and the psychiatrist had struck up a friendship and agreed to collaborate on a book about brainwashing; two years later *Battle for the Mind* was a bestseller and had cemented Sargant's fame. Sargant provided the opinions, Graves the structure and layout to 'make the saliva flow,' as he put it" (Streathfield, 2008, p. 79).

A few months after Wasson's discovery, the CIA was reporting on the work of "an amateur mycologist" and the potential to incorporate his findings into what was then Project Artichoke, soon to be MKULTRA. Small world. (Wasson's team was then allegedly "infiltrated" by CIA agent James Moore, before the next trip to Mexico.) As for Wasson being "an amateur mycologist": maybe so, but he was also vice president for public relations at J. P. Morgan at the time, one of the biggest banks in the world, so not exactly an "independent researcher." Researcher Jan Irvin (2015) ran a series of well-documented articles presenting evidence of just how deep Wasson's background was. For example, that Wasson headed the CIA's MKULTRA Subproject 58 program. That he served as a chairman to the Council on Foreign Relations (the CFR). That he had close ties to Allen Dulles, head of the CIA and MKULTRA initiator. That he earned a directorship at a pharmaceutical company for his mushroom discovery. That he was an account manager to the Pope and Vatican for J. P. Morgan. That he was in charge of promoting the Russian Orthodox Church for Russian immigrants. (This an odd overlap with my grandfather's invitation from the Russian Orthodox Church to visit the Soviet Union in 1954, "without any strings." Though I have read his 35-page report, I am still unclear about the exact purpose of this visit. There is an appendix in the booklet titled: "Decree of the Central Committee of the C.P.SU [Communist Party Soviet Union]:

About mistakes in conducting scientific-atheistic propaganda among the population.")

Wasson also had a Russian wife, Valentina, who was religious and was from the Russian intelligentsia. Primary documents reveal that Wasson was involved in helping to cover up J. P. Morgan's involvement in the Civil War's Hall Carbine Affair, and that Wasson directed the disinformation campaign, earning him his position as vice president for public relations for J. P. Morgan. Wasson was close friends with Edward Bernays, the father of propaganda and spin and nephew to Sigmund Freud. Wasson was also friends with George Kennan, one of the engineers of Operation Paperclip (the program to secretly bring top Nazi officials and scientists into the USA). Wasson's superior at J. P. Morgan, Henry Davison, was a member of the infamous Skull and Bones secret student society at Yale University, as was Henry Luce at *Time-Life*. Davison created *Time-Life* for his boss, J. P. Morgan. C. D. Jackson, head of US psychological warfare (and purchaser of the JFK Zapruder film), was VP at *Time-Life* and later became its president. And so on (all this via Irvin, 2015).

To cement Wasson's finding of the mushroom, *Life* magazine ran a piece in 1957 called "Seeking the Magic Mushroom." *Life* magazine was published by Henry Luce, close friend of Allen Dulles. Wasson claimed the article came about due to "a chance meeting with Luce, yet according to Irvin (2015), Luce and Wasson were long-time members of the Century Club, an elite/CIA/OSS intelligence front posing as an exclusive "art club," where Wasson gave lectures on his mushroom research. According to Carl Bernstein (1977), Luce "readily allowed certain members of his staff to work for the Agency [CIA] and agreed to provide jobs and credentials for other CIA operatives who lacked journalistic experience." An organization called the British Security Coordination (which included children's author Roald Dahl among its members) played an important role in the Council for Democracy, a group established by Luce and his wife Clare Boothe Luce. This and other groups came under the control of William Donovan, the head of the OSS, before it turned into the CIA in 1947. The origins of Operation Mockingbird, a secret campaign by the CIA to influence media initiated in the 1950s by Cord Meyer and Allen Dulles, date back to the OSS and the Second World War. Luce's *Time-Life* was a central weapon in this cultural war, and (we have no reason not to suppose) remains so to this day.

In his memoir, author Tom Robbins talks about the impact the *Life* article had in "turning on" countless young Americans—himself and Timothy Leary included—all thanks to an English war poet who became famous writing historical novels about ancient Rome! Henry and Clare Boothe Luce were introduced to LSD in the early '60s by Gerald Heard, who also "turned on" Bill Wilson (cofounder of AA) and edited a short-lived British magazine called *The Realist* that published authors such as H. G. Wells and the Huxley brothers. Heard also introduced Huston Smith to Huxley, who went on to introduce Huxley to Timothy Leary. Huxley and Leary immediately became "close." According to Irvin, Wasson worked as a director of Sandoz pharmaceuticals and may have worked with Dr. Timothy Leary to distribute LSD. Maybe the CIA also coined the phrase "truth is stranger than fiction"?

Following Graves's own mushroom eating ceremony (with Wasson in New York in 1957, soon after the *Life* article came out), Graves decided that "the sacred mushroom should be distributed across Europe and America" (Streathfield, 2008, p. 89). The CIA may well have agreed. Four months after that, Graves took LSD and reported his experience, negatively, to his brainwashing buddy William Sargant. (Graves felt LSD was a deceptive imitation of the mushroom that led "to Coney Island and not to Eden.")

In 1961, Graves waxed paradisaically to members of the Oxford Humanist Society about his mushroom experiences, and during that same period, the British military took a keen interest in the substance. All of this was occurring congruent with the CIA's use of LSD and countless other drugs in their MKULTRA program. Two histories running side by side—one selling Eden, the other storming Hell.

CHAPTER XI

A Scientific Outlook: Congress for Cultural Freedom, Bertrand Russell, William Empson, and the New Criticism

"The state not only had a vested interest in becoming an active agent of evolution, it could not help but become one, willy-nilly. Fabians set out to write a sensible evolutionary agenda when they entered the political arena. Once this biopolitical connection is recognized, the past, present, and future of this seemingly bumbling movement takes on a formidable coherence. Under the dottiness, lovability, intelligence, high social position, and genuine goodness of some of their works, the system held out as humanitarian by Fabians is grotesquely deceptive; in reality, Fabian compassion masks a real aloofness to humanity. It is purely an intellectual project in scientific management."
—John Taylor Gatto, *Underground History of American Education*

According to a citation-free source which is possibly apocryphal, another of Graves's affiliations was with a late-night drinking circle at Oxford consisting of poets and occultists, some but not all of whom were contributing writers for Alfred Orage's magazine *The New Age*. This latter is worth a brief mention. It began as a journal of Christian liberalism and socialism before being reoriented to promote the ideas of Nietzsche and Fabian socialism. It famously published a debate on the role of private property, with H. G. Wells and G. B. Shaw on one side, and G. K. Chesterton and Hilaire Belloc on the other. It also discussed the need for a socialist party as distinct from the newly formed Labour Party. The editorial line moved from initial support to bitter opposition over the issue of women's rights in 1912. As *The New Age* moved away from Fabian politics, the leading Fabians founded *The New Statesman and Nation* to counter its effects, in 1913. *The New Age* also concerned itself with the definition and development of modernism in the visual arts, literature, and music, and consistently observed, reviewed and contributed to the activities of this movement. It also became one of the first places in England in which Sigmund Freud's ideas were publicly discussed.

Orage's collaborators and cohorts included Aleister Crowley, W. B. Yeats, Ezra Pound, and (allegedly) Robert Graves. There's certainly a significant area of overlap, and once again, the intelligence community seems to have colonized, if not created, the *vesica piscis* in the Venn diagram. In this case, the fish takes the form of the Congress for Cultural Freedom, an anti-communist advocacy group created by the CIA in 1950, via the Ford Foundation. The CCF:

> was headquartered in Paris and later discovered to be a CIA front organization during the cultural Cold War, was among the most important patrons in world history, supporting an incredible range of artistic and intellectual activities. It had offices in 35 countries, published dozens of prestige magazines, was involved in the book industry, organized high-profile international conferences and art exhibits, coordinated performances and concerts, and contributed ample funding to various cultural awards and fellowships, as well as to front organizations like the Farfield Foundation. (Rockhill, 2017)

This first came to public awareness in 1962, via the *World Marxist Review*. Four years later, the *New York Times* ran an article about how the CIA secretly funded the CCF's British magazine *Encounter*; soon after (also in 1966), it revealed that the CIA had been instrumental in creating the group. *Encounter* attracted some of the leading intellectuals of the period and beyond (despite having its intelligence roots revealed, *Encounter* continued until 1990). Contributors included Graves, Stephen Spender (founder), Melvin J. Lasky (cofounder), John Strachey, Evelyn Waugh,

Virginia Woolf, W. H. Auden, Arthur Koestler, Anthony Burgess (who had his own MI5 affiliations), Ted Hughes (whom I met as a child), Jorge Luis Borges, Dwight Macdonald, Arthur Schlesinger, Jr., Kingsley Amis, Malcolm Bradbury, Tavistock employee R. D. Laing, Aleksandr Solzhenitsyn, Marshall McLuhan, Philip Larkin (who according to my brother's memoir visited our childhood home), Paul Theroux, Elias Canetti, D. M. Thomas, David Lodge, Martin Amis, and Clive James. It's been only half-jokingly called "some of the best money the CIA ever spent."

My grandfather's friend J. B. Priestley attended a CCF meeting hosted by Arthur Koestler in 1956, and Bertrand Russell was one of its chairmen during the early years. Since Russell was viewed as a great philosopher and humanitarian, it's easy to see how the CIA could use his caliber to lend credibility to their cultural battleship. On the other hand, a chairman has power to steer the ship, so it seems unlikely the CIA would take a chance on someone who was not already in their employ—or perhaps that of a higher governance body? While trying to ascertain Russell's possible intelligence connections, I ended up reading online passages from Russell's 1931 work, *The Scientific Outlook*. I was surprised to see that it reads like a manual for totalitarian control. Ostensibly, Russell intended this text (just as Huxley ostensibly intended his novel *Brave New World*) as a *warning* about the possible dystopian future in store for us if we continued to pursue the mechanistic approach to solving social problems. *And yet*: This was not at all clear to me while I was reading passages online, because Russell's method is simply to describe the means and methods of such a scientifically organized future state, not in the style of cautionary prophecy but very much in the nature of *a blueprint to follow*.

> [T]the scientific rulers will provide one kind of education for ordinary men and women, and another for those who are to become holders of scientific power. Ordinary men and women will be expected to be docile, industrious, punctual, thoughtless, and contented. Of these qualities, probably contentment will be considered the most important. In order to produce it, all the researches of psycho-analysis, behaviourism, and biochemistry will be brought into play …. All the boys and girls will learn from an early age to be what is called "co-operative", i.e., to do exactly what everybody is doing. Initiative will be discouraged in these children, and

insubordination, without being punished, will be scientifically trained out of them .... Except for the one matter of loyalty to the world State and to their own order, members of the governing class will be encouraged to be adventurous and full of initiative. It will be recognized that it is their business to improve scientific technique, and to keep the manual workers contented by means of continual new amusements .... In normal cases, children of sufficient heredity will be admitted to the governing class *from the moment of conception*. I start with this moment rather than birth since *it is from this moment and not merely the moment of birth that the treatment of the two classes will be different*. If, however, by the time the child reaches the age of three it is fairly clear that he does not attain the required standard, he will be degraded at that point. [T]here would be a very strong tendency for the governing classes to become hereditary, and that after a few generations not many children would be moved from either class into the other. This is especially likely to be the case if embryological methods of improving the breed are applied to the governing class, but not to the others. *In this way the gulf between the two classes as regards native intelligence will become continually wider and wider* .... Assuming that both kinds of breeding are scientifically carried out, there will come to be an increasing divergence between the two types, making them in the end *almost different species*. (pp. 181–188, emphasis added)

The next chapter of Russell's book begins: "The scientific society which has been sketched in the chapters of this Part, is, of course, not to be taken as serious prophecy. It is an attempt to depict the world which would result if scientific technique were to rule unchecked." He acknowledges that it has "features that are repulsive," "likely to be disastrous," and that it describes a world "devoid of beauty and joy." For this and other reasons, the general consensus is that Russell was a humanitarian who regarded his scientifically engineered future society with abhorrence. This may be true and it may be not true. It's also possible (I think probably most likely) that he had mixed feelings about it and that he regarded his own abhorrence as an unfortunate lapse into nonscientific thinking, and as something that could be overcome in the fullness of time (by future humanity).

If someone can be quoted in large, pages-long passages that give *no indication* of irony or abhorrence but which read like calculated prescriptions for social engineering, isn't it reasonable to suppose that they were intended to be read this way? At the very least, it would be irresponsible of Russell to write in this fashion if he wished to avoid that risk, and there's nothing to indicate that Russell was irresponsible as a writer or public speaker. (That he chaired a CIA front, fraternized with Fabians, was given the nickname "Mephisto," and described himself as a vampire, however, is a matter of public record.[1]) It is also wise to take into account the audience for which Russell was writing. Any given passage (such as the above quoted) means something very different to one class of people than it does to another.

To the ruling class—those subscribed to the kind of thinking Russell is apparently warning against—the text starkly illustrates ways to exploit human beings via the appliance of science and technology with a clear end in mind. If "common" people were to read it, or the more "sentimental" among upper classes and intelligentsia—it appears as a warning against such exploitation. Fine and dandy. But who generally studies philosophy in college? For the most part, it is those who are being groomed to rule. (Poor kids generally don't study Bertrand Russell.) With all this in mind, it's possible to suppose that Russell's expression of abhorrence was partially sincere, but also partially strategic. The bulk of the text, after all, is dedicated to describing the means by which a scientific outlook can create a more smoothly functioning society, albeit at the price of certain humanitarian values. In 1932, the year after he published *The Scientific Outlook*, Russell published *Education and the Social Order*, with the following introductory passage:

> [I]nternational cohesion, and a sense of the whole human race as one co-operative unit, is becoming increasingly necessary if our scientific civilisation is to survive. I think this survival will demand, as a minimum condition, the establishment of a world State and the subsequent institution of a world-wide system of education designed to produce loyalty to the world State. No doubt such a system of education will entail, at any rate for a century or two, certain crudities which will militate against the development of the individual. But if the alternative is chaos and the death of civilisation, the price will be worth paying .... Loyalty to the world State ... might entail considerable curtailment of the intellectual and aesthetic impulses. I think, nevertheless, that the most vital need of the near future will be the cultivation of a vivid sense of

> citizenship of the world. When the world as a single economic and
> political unit has become secure, it will be possible for individual
> culture to revive. (pp. 19–20)

As one biographer put it, "For the public good, as it were, [Russell] was
prepared to abandon what was finest in himself" (Monk, 1996, p. 476).
The biographer doesn't pause to ask what good ever came from aban-
doning what is finest, however.

If this was my grandfather's colleague, correspondent, and fellow
Fabian, to whom he made an unknown number of monetary donations,
does that mean he *approved* of Russell's plan for a world state? Even if it
required (temporarily, for a century or two) a scientifically engineered
society in which the division between classes—like in H. G. Wells's
The Time Machine—would eventually become a species divide? Where
exactly does socialism or the avowed concern for the rights of "the common man" fit into this vision? Roughly as a sheep's clothing fits into the
strategy of wolves?

Russell is also attributed with introducing the possibility of peaceful protest in the 1950s and 1960s, for example with CND's sit-downs
against nuclear weapons, thereby setting the template (one he learned
from Oxford alumnus Mahatma Gandhi) for *nonviolent* resistance ever
since. (Gandhi even had a Russell "endorsement blurb" hanging on his
house wall.[2]) While it might be argued that violent resistance is easier
for the ruling classes to deal with because they can meet it with greater
force, there is a degree of social chaos that results from such open conflict that may interfere with business. It also forces the iron fist of government to remove its velvet glove, thereby alerting the public to the
exact nature of the oppression they are under, and potentially sowing
the seeds of future revolt. It's possible that Russell (and by extension
my grandfather), by rechanneling social unrest into peaceful forms of
expression, were, in the long run, serving the interests of the state and
not the people.

*

> "The anti-traditional action necessarily had to aim both at a
> change in the general mentality and at the destruction of all tra-
> ditional institutions in the West, since the West is where it began
> to work first and most directly, while awaiting the proper time

for an attempt to extend its operations over the whole world,
using the Westerners duly prepared to become its instruments."
—René Guénon, *The Reign of Quantity*

Returning briefly to Robert Graves: According to *The Birth of New
Criticism: Conflict and Conciliation in the Early Work of William Empson,
I. A. Richards, Robert Graves, and Laura Riding*, by Donald J. Childs,
Graves was the unacknowledged father of what's known as "New
Criticism": a formalist movement in literary theory that dominated
American literary criticism in the middle decades of the twentieth
century. New Criticism emphasized close reading, particularly of
poetry, to discover how a work of literature functioned as a self-
contained, self-referential aesthetic object. This is the equivalent to
removing a literary work from its context. Teaching people to think in
boxes (separate compartments that have no need of any deeper context to be understood) is a way to get them to *live* in boxes, and eventually to become *like* boxes: separate, isolated individuals. "Every
man is an island" becomes the truth of the modern mindset, and
plays into the notions of the "self-made man" and the "meritocracy."
Compartmentalization or boxing was also key to the Prussian education system, the breaking up of learning into arbitrary "classes"
separated by the ringing of a bell. It's also central to the shaping
of information in TV (and even newspaper) media, each show or
article boxed off from the others via commercial breaks or margins
on the page. All of this might well lead to an internal state, that of
the "objective"—that is, decontextualized—experience of self and
world: a *self-objectification*.

The New Criticism movement derived its name from John Crowe
Ransom's 1941 book *The New Criticism*, and its early practitioners
formed a loose-knit community sometimes referred to (because of a
literary magazine that featured much of their work) as the Fugitives,
and also as the Agrarian poets (linking them up loosely with the camping movement of Glaister, Byngham, and co.). Primary influences were
the critical essays of T. S. Eliot and the work of English scholar I. A.
Richards, especially his *Practical Criticism* and *The Meaning of Meaning*,
which offered what was claimed to be *an empirical scientific approach* to
poetry and literature. In a similar way, Eliot had argued that "the study
of literature ought to strive towards scientific objectivity" (Makaryk,
1993, p. 120). A scientific outlook.

Perhaps the key player in this movement was my grandfather's friend and fellow Yorkshireman, William Empson. Empson is one major cultural influence known by Alec but not named by him. (This would suggest that, despite his proclivity for name-dropping, there may be others.) In fact, the only reason I found out about their friendship was via a book called *Hetta and William: A Memoir of a Bohemian Marriage* (2012), by Jacob Empson (William's son). In it, Jacob writes how his father was living in London in 1953, having enjoyed some success as a critic, and due to travel to the US, looking for a permanent job, specifically a chair in English literature. "He had applied to Hull University, giving his old friend Alec Horsley as a reference (Alec was a hugely successful Hull businessman with a dairy and a brewery to his name, who was to found the multinational Northern Foods)". Apparently Alec's influence was insufficient to land Empson the job, however, and he ended up taking the chair at Sheffield.

Childs describes Robert Graves as being "… the first to practice what is known as close reading …. Even New Critics who did not know Graves' early work directly nonetheless, by mid-century, knew it indirectly through the work of two major influences on New Criticism most influenced by him: [I. A.] Richards and [William] Empson" (2013, p. 3). The New Criticism movement, like the other cultural movements I have stumbled upon while looking into my family history, seems not to have come about purely through the natural evolution of ideas, but also with a degree of social, shall we say, *facilitation*. In the late 1940s and early 1950s (i.e., just before he showed up on my grandfather's doorstep), Empson taught a summer course for the intensive study of literature at the Kenyon School of English, at Kenyon College in Ohio. According to *Newsweek*, "The roster of instructors was enough to pop the eyes of any major in English" (Haffenden, 2006). In addition to Empson, the faculty included the members of the Vanderbilt Fugitive set, such as Robert Penn Warren, John Crowe Ransom, and Allen Tate.

In *American Literary Criticism Since the 1930s*, Vincent B. Leitch writes that the major development in the history of academic criticism, post-Great Depression, was the overwhelming success of the "New Critics" in pioneering and institutionalizing formalist concepts and methods. He describes four stages of this development. The first occurred during the 1920s, with T. S. Eliot, I. A. Richards, and William Empson in England, and the Fugitives and Agrarians (especially John Crowe Ransom and Allen Tate) in America. The second stage occurred during the 1930s and

1940s when "[T]he number of critics sympathetic to this emerging for-
malism increased, and the New Critics *spread their beliefs effectively into
literary quarterlies, university literature departments, and college textbooks
and curricula*" (2009, p. 21, emphasis added). The third stage of development occurred from the late 1940s to the late 1950s, when the movement
lost its "'revolutionary' aura and occupied the mainstream, its followers
produced intricate canonical statements of its theories" (ibid.).

> That the New Criticism was over by the late 1950s as an innovative
> and original School was clear to both adherents and opponents.
> Nevertheless, after that time the New Criticism served for grow-
> ing numbers of academic critics and scholars as "normal criticism"
> or simply as "criticism." This transformation of a particular school
> into a cultural status quo distinguished New Criticism from all
> other competing schools, marking a special—a fourth—stage of
> development. Often critics practicing New Criticism during this
> phase were unaware that they were doing so: the ideas and meth-
> ods of the School had become so deeply embedded and broadly
> generalized among critics as to form the very essence of "criticism."
> (ibid., p. 22)

Leitch quotes William Cain, writing in 1984:

> The New Criticism appears powerless, lacking in supporters,
> declining, or on the verge of being so. No one speaks on behalf of
> the New Criticism as such today .... But the truth is that the New
> Criticism survives and is prospering, and it seems to be powerless
> only because its power is so pervasive that we are ordinarily not
> even aware of it. So deeply ingrained in English studies are New
> Critical attitudes, values, and emphases that we do not even per-
> ceive them as the legacy of a particular movement. On the contrary
> we feel them to be the natural and definitive conditions for criti-
> cism in general. (ibid., pp. 22–23)

According to this view, the "'death' of New Criticism in the 1950s signaled a kind of normalized 'immortality'—a strange feat which no other
critical school in this era was able to accomplish" (ibid., p. 23).

It is also curious that I myself, whose first published work was a
work of film criticism, had never heard of the New Criticism until I was

working on this piece. I have included so much about it, partly out of personal interest, but also because I think it serves as an example of how the Fabian eel proceeds to worm its way through culture and transform it. Russell's "scientific outlook" was extending itself into modern culture and thought in more ways than one, via the work of individuals and groups who were both openly and discreetly affiliated. The ways in which these memeplexes embed themselves into the culture and transform it may not be as apparent as we think—or even apparent *at all*.

Ellis's and Shaw's and Wells's and Russell's and Glaister's and Huxley's vision for a brave new world may *seem* to be one that never quite took hold. But, like the school of New Criticism, it may be that the reverse is in fact true: that it so effectively insinuated itself into modern society that, like fish in water, we are entirely unaware of its having done so. We have been engineered.

CHAPTER XII

Tentacles across the ocean:
Edward House, Woodrow Wilson,
the Council on Foreign Relations

"As trusty Fabian Socialists, frequently wearing the 'liberal' or 'progressive' label, established themselves gradually, firmly and increasingly in the professions, literature and popular journalism; in higher education and research; in reform movements, labor union leadership, politics and government service, they trained and carried their successors along with them. Thus the movement for 'peaceful' social revolution in the United States expanded, becoming ever more diffuse and more difficult to pinpoint, until it assumed the aspect of a nationwide fraternity with a largely secret membership held together by invisible ties of ideology."

—Rose L. Martin, *Fabian Freeway*

One obvious question at this juncture is, how influential can Fabianism have been in the shaping of world history when most people have never heard of it—or if they have, would be hard-pressed to say what it is? Ironically, Fabian influence seems dependent on a degree of historical invisibility or apparent marginality. I am aware that this is rather like the skeptics' trope about how conspiracy theorists claim that a *lack* of evidence is itself proof of conspiracy. Of course this is absurd, and in my experience it's generally a straw man argument, meant to discredit a claim without really addressing it. While lack of evidence of a conspiracy obviously does not suggest a conspiracy, evidence that certain key individuals, ideas, and events have been highly influential in world history, and have been downplayed almost out of existence by the history books, does indicate a conspiratorial element at work. This appears to be very much the case with Fabianism—the very meaning of which is *incremental* (hence largely invisible) change.

According to history books, the little-known but hugely influential historical figure, Edward M. House, was not even a Fabian, *per se*. Yet evidence indicates that he was a channel for Fabianism and, through his relationship with Woodrow Wilson, a means for it to shape world events at a crucial time in history while leaving only the faintest of traces.

House was born in 1858 in Texas of a prominent Houston businessman, the last of seven children (in folklore, that makes him a witch). He was schooled for a period in Bath, England, and studied at Cornell University, New York (where "The Sexual Child" course would one day be taught), and there joined Alpha Delta Phi, a North American Greek-letter secret college fraternity. Later, House helped to make four men governors of Texas, and after their election acted as unofficial advisor to each of them. One of them, James Hogg, gave House the title "Colonel" by appointing House to his staff. In the period between 1902 and 1911, House "made a point of cultivating key persons in the academic world" (Martin, 1966, p. 156). He met Woodrow Wilson in 1911, through publisher and later ambassador to England Walter Hines, whereupon "… an immediate bond of sympathy was established. It was the beginning of what Woodrow Wilson called 'the perfect friendship,' one of the strangest friendships in American history" (ibid., 156–157).

As Rose L. Martin writes in *Fabian Freeway*:

> House believed the United States Constitution, creation of eighteenth century minds, was "not only outmoded, but grotesque" and ought to be scrapped or rewritten. As a practical politician, he realized this could not be done all at once, given the existing state of popular education; he favored gradual changes which, in the long run, would produce the same results. A similar point of view was expressed in Woodrow Wilson's campaign speeches, afterwards printed as The New Freedom. (p. 157)

In 1912, House anonymously published a novel entitled *Philip Dru, Administrator: A Story of Tomorrow*. It was released by B. W. Huebsch, "a favorite publisher of the Left and for many years a valued collaborator of American Fabian Socialist groups" (ibid., pp. 157–158). There were many similarities between the fictional Dru's program and the legislation requested over the years by Woodrow Wilson, to the degree that Wilson's secretary of the interior (Franklin K. Lane) wrote: "All that the book has said should be, has come about." The use of fiction as a means to shoehorn new social, cultural, and political values and goals into society is a tried and true method, and it underscores the reason men like House—who wished to implement major change via hidden leverage—"preferred the company of authors, playwrights and professors, of which the British Fabian Society boasted a noteworthy assortment" (ibid., p. 161).

> In those pre-World War I years British Fabian lecturers were already roaming the campuses and cities of America. Fiction by British Fabian authors, whom few Americans recognized as Socialists, headed the best seller lists. The novels of H. G. Wells, Arnold Bennett and John Galsworthy, the published plays of George Bernard Shaw, became standard reading matter for literate Americans and were favored as high school graduating gifts to boys and girls preparing for college. (ibid., p. 193)

Regarding *Philip Dru, Administrator*, Martin writes that "Few works of fiction have so deeply affected, for better or worse, the trends of contemporary life in the United States. In effect [the book] became a kind of handbook or Cooke's guide for Democratic presidents" (p. 159). Among those who read the novel and took it to heart was Franklin Delano Roosevelt, whose mother was a friend of House. Martin continues:

> It is hard to say just when House conceived the bold plan of penetrating America's Democratic Party ... in the interests of a Socialist program to change the face of America. Whether the idea was his own or inspired by Fabian friends in Britain, every step he took over the years appeared to be directed towards its fulfillment .... His career was a living example of Socialist gradualism at work. With the election of Woodrow Wilson, House became a power at home and abroad. From then until their final break at Paris in

1918, the President relied on House, trusted him completely and never made a move without consulting him .... The understanding between them was based on ideology as well as affection. It was as if they shared a mutual secret not to be divulged to the American people. (p. 162)

One of the primary aids to House's crypto-Fabian agenda was the *New Republic*, a magazine financed in 1914 by heiress Dorothy Whitney Straight (also known as Dorothy Payne Whitney), whose brothers both belonged to the Skull and Bones secret society (according to Martin, p. 166, one of them was also a J. P. Morgan partner). Straight also cofounded the (Fabian) New School for Social Research, in 1919. Among the *New Republic* staff was Walter Lippmann, a member of the London Fabian Society since 1909 (when he was only twenty), also initiated into the Phi Beta Kappa secret society at Harvard. Lippmann was the man who brought John Maynard Keynes to America, having arranged for the publication of Keynes's early work, *The Economic Consequences of the Peace*, in 1919 (oddly enough, Keynes was apparently opposed to Wilson and to the peace treaty at the time). Decades later, Lippmann would become an informal advisor to John F. Kennedy, and, following Kennedy's death, to Lyndon Johnson.[1]

"The British Marxist and Fabian, Professor Harold J. Laski [also of the New School], teaching at Harvard from 1905 to 1919, was a frequent wartime contributor" to the *New Republic*, and the magazine supported Woodrow Wilson up to and during the war. (Laski also "had the rare distinction of helping indirectly to select and educate two Democratic Presidents of the United States: Franklin D. Roosevelt and John F. Kennedy," see Martin, p. 316.) "By what Lippmann prudently calls 'a certain parallelism of reasoning,' the *New Republic* often suggested policies that President Wilson followed" (Martin, 1966, p. 167). The senior editor of *New Republic* (Herbert Croly) and Walter Lippmann met twice monthly with House to discuss problems "relating to the management of neutrality" leading up to the reelection of Wilson in 1916 (ibid., p. 167).

Following the example of top-level British Fabians, *New Republic* editors moved in good society and were considered eminently respectable. Penetration and permeation were their tasks. Like the Webbs and other worldly-wise leaders of the London Fabian Society, they accepted the war as inevitable and concentrated on planning for the New Order, which all good Socialists felt sure must emerge from the social unrest anticipated after the war. (ibid., pp. 167–168)

Considering that *Fabian Freeway* was published in 1966, its references to a "New World Order" were somewhat ahead of their time. What the author lays out is a long-term plan—spanning two world wars—to bring about a united governmental front based on socialist or pseudo-socialist (Fabian) principles. The first step to this international government was the creation of a League of Nations, which was also the last of the famous Fourteen Points put forward by Woodrow Wilson in January 1918 as the basis for peace negotiations to end World War I. According to Martin, "The demands outlined in the Fourteen Points ... were conceived by Sidney Webb and the London Fabian Society" (p. 169). Fabian Leonard Woolf "was the author of *International Government*, which supplied the first blueprint for the League of Nations" (ibid., p. 327). Picking up where point 14 left off:

> The first American version of a "convention" for a League [of Nations] was drafted by the President's friend, Colonel House, on July 13 and 14, 1918 .... Fully three years earlier the Fabian Research Department in London, then shepherded by Beatrice Webb, had prepared two reports of its own on the subject .... The draft so speedily produced by Colonel House on two summer days in Massachusetts bore a striking resemblance to the Fabian proposals, whose Socialist authors were not otherwise in a position to impose their ideas on the British Foreign Office. House's twenty-three articles formed the basis for the President's tentative draft, which adopted all but five of those articles and became the first official American plan for the League of Nations. (ibid., pp. 172–173)

Mere months after this, the friendship between Woodrow Wilson and Edward M. House ended. Though the details are unclear, Wilson was apparently disillusioned with House and felt deceived by his advice and direction around the Paris peace treaty.

> In those days it was a generally accepted fact that the treaty making power of the United States resided not merely in the President, but in the President *with* two thirds of the Senate present and voting.

> [N]obody in America except a handful of Socialist intellectuals and foreign-born radicals wanted any part of International Government. So Wilson, the bitter-ender, went home to failure and collapse; while House, the gradualist who never stopped trying, remained in Paris, attempting to salvage by negotiation whatever fragments of his program could still be saved. As it had been from the beginning, the real quarrel was still with the Constitution, and on that rock they foundered separately. (ibid., p. 174.)

While the Fabians' first attempt to infiltrate the US government failed, House "had set the pattern and outlined goals for the future, and he still had a scheme or two in mind." House foresaw the necessity of "a top-level Anglo-American planning group in the field of foreign relations." The purpose would be "to secretly influence policy on the one hand and gradually 'educate' public opinion on the other." House's "experience in Paris had shown him that it must be a bipartisan group" (ibid., p. 174). Many of the younger men House had been counting on to pave the way for the "New World Order" (including Lippmann and Franklin D. Roosevelt) had already left. Fortunately for House, there were still a few American intellectuals in Paris, men of "undefined political affiliations and excellent social standing—such as John Foster and Allen Dulles" (ibid.). House arranged a dinner meeting in Paris on May 19, 1919, for a small group of British and American diplomats and scholars, including the Dulles brothers and a select group of Fabian-certified Englishmen, among them John Maynard Keynes. All of them, according to Martin's account, "were equally disillusioned, for various reasons, by the consequences of the peace."

> They made a gentleman's agreement to set up an organization, with branches in England and America, "to facilitate the *scientific* study of international questions." As a result two potent and closely related opinion-making bodies were founded, which only began to reach their full growth in the nineteen-forties, coincident with the formation of the Fabian International Bureau. The English branch was called the Royal Institute of International Affairs. The American branch, first known as the Institute of International Affairs, was reorganized in 1921 as the Council on Foreign Relations. (ibid., pp. 174–175.)

As every self-respecting conspirologist knows, no secret history wall chart is complete without the CFR. By 1939—and through the course of World War II—the CFR achieved prominence within the US government and the State Department and established a strictly confidential War and Peace Studies, funded entirely by the Rockefeller Foundation. The secrecy surrounding this latter group was such that the CFR members who were not involved in its deliberations were completely unaware of its existence. It was divided into four functional topic groups: economic and financial, security and armaments, territorial, and political. The security and armaments group was headed by Allen Dulles, who later helped form the OSS, and then the CIA.

CHAPTER XIII

Jimmy's Kingdom: LSE, NHS, and the beginnings of psychiatric social work and child care

"These 'educational missionaries' spoke of schools as if they were monasteries. By limiting the idea of education to formal school instruction, the public gradually lost sight of what the real thing was. The questions these specialists disputed were as irrelevant to real people as the disputes of medieval divines; there was about their writing a condescension for public concerns, for them 'the whole range of education had become an *instrument of deliberate social purpose*' [emphasis added]."
—John Taylor Gatto, *Underground History of American Education*

As a possibly last series of connections to map, I am returning to Robert Graves's buddy William Sargant, who worked at St Thomas' Hospital from 1948 to the end of his career as head of the department of psychological medicine. In 1962, Sargant found himself a new assistant in one David Owen, a neurology and psychiatric registrar who had only just qualified as a doctor. Two years prior to becoming Sargant's assistant, Owen had joined the Vauxhall branch of the Labour Party and the Fabian Society. Before that, Owen studied at Mount House School, Tavistock, an English town written about by Arthur Conan Doyle and Neal Stephenson. Tavistock is tied from late medieval times with the

Russells, the family name of the Earls of Bedford and, since 1694, the Dukes of Bedford (the same family Bertrand belonged to). The second title of the Duke of Bedford is the Marquess of Tavistock. The importance of this Devon town to the Russell family fortunes is attributed in part to its hinterland and the minerals beneath it, and the Russell family is said to retain considerable interests in the locality. According to writer David Livingstone, the Tavistock Institute took its name from Bertrand Russell's cousin Herbrand, the 11th Duke of Bedford/Marquess of Tavistock. It is this Russell family connection through the Bedford Estates which gives the name (by ownership) to Russell Square and Tavistock Square in London, home to the Tavistock Clinic. Tavistock Square was also the location of the exploding bus of 7/7/2005, the last bomb to go off in an alleged series of coordinated "terrorist" attacks in central London using the public transport system during rush hour.

Returning to Tavistock-born David Owen: the only reason his name showed up on my radar at all is that it was thanks to him that Jimmy Savile "came to be in charge of Broadmoor for a period in the 1980s when he was put in charge of a task force to run the secure hospital." In fact, Savile's "involvement at Broadmoor was rubber-stamped in 1974 by Dr. David Owen, now Lord Owen, who was health minister" (Lewis & Duffin, 2012). Savile had a personal set of keys to the hospital and it allowed him to abuse countless patients over three and a half decades, between 1968 and 2004.

It's generally been assumed that the reason Savile wanted (and was given) access to Broadmoor (besides visiting his pals Reggie Kray and Peter Sutcliffe) was to indulge his sadistic sexual proclivities by taking advantage of defenseless young women (many of whom were adolescent runaways or simply troublemakers at school). No doubt this is partly true, but it may not be the whole truth. It's also possible, in the light of all the other evidence of similar "schooling" programs going on through the UK and the US and elsewhere for decades, that Savile had a specific *role* at Broadmoor, and that the institution was being used as a locale for the sorts of sexual and social research and experimentation which has fascinated the Fabians and others since at least the turn of the twentieth century. Maybe Broadmoor was, like Wedekind's Sadian castle, a prison-school for "the bodily education of young girls"?

Nor are we talking only about Broadmoor. In 2014, Kate Lampard carried out an independent review of Savile's predations within the British National Health Service (NHS), including more than forty hospitals. Her report was quoted in *The Guardian* in 2015: "Savile's status and influence ... *was enhanced by the endorsement and encouragement he received from politicians, senior civil servants and NHS managers. His access within NHS hospitals gave Savile the opportunity to commit sexual abuses on a grand scale for nearly 50 years*" (Laville & Halliday, 2015, emphasis added).

The article goes on to quote Liz Dux, a lawyer who represents 44 of Savile's victims, calling the report a "crushing disappointment" because it held no one accountable.

> "It beggars belief that a report which has revealed Savile was widely known as a sex pest at Stoke Mandeville can find no evidence of management responsibility," Dux said. "Ten victims had reported their assaults to nursing staff on the ward, including one complaint being made to management, yet still his deviant and sickening behaviour continued." She said the revelation in the report that three other doctors had committed serious sexual offences at the hospital in the past four decades suggested "something seriously amiss." (ibid.)[1]

I have said that I wish to avoid unnecessary speculation in this work; but on this occasion I'm willing to go out on a limb, because without the horrifying context provided by Savile's activities, the following information may seem random and bizarre. And maybe it is, but the only way to find out if the pieces fit is by placing them side by side.

The following facts are taken from a Mental Health History Timeline assembled by Middlesex University:

"In 1926 [the year Jimmy Savile was born] An appeal to The Commonwealth Fund (New York) by Cyril Burt and Amy Strachey (born Amy Simpson 1866), 'Mrs. St Loe Strachey' for funds to start training psychiatric social workers at the London School of Economics (see below) and support for Child Guidance." (What exactly do economics have to do with psychiatry or child guidance, I wonder? No explanation is offered.) Three years later, in 1929 (the year Ernest Westlake founded his Forest School): "With money from The Commonwealth Fund, a Diploma in Mental Health started at the London School of Economics to train Psychiatric Social Workers." The fund's Director, Barry Smith, had written in 1928 that "[T]he training of psychiatric social workers is an essential and fundamental part of [a] child guidance program" (Roberts, 2017).

Some corroboration comes from the US National Library of Medicine:

> When the Commonwealth Fund agreed to finance the establish-
> ment of child guidance clinics in Britain, it stressed the need to train
> social workers in a university setting. Thus in 1929, the London
> School of Economics established the first course to train social
> science graduates with some experience of social work as PSWs. In
> the same year, the Association of Psychiatric Social Work (hereaf-
> ter APSW) was inaugurated with the dual objectives of promoting
> mental hygiene, and raising the professional status of psychiatric
> social work. (Long, 2011)

The Commonwealth Fund is a private foundation that is still around
today. It was founded in 1918 by the widow of Stephen Vanderburgh
Harkness. Harkness was the American entrepreneur and silent partner
of John D. Rockefeller, Sr., in the founding of Standard Oil (and a director of Standard Oil until his death). Today, the Rockefeller Foundation
houses all the archives for the Commonwealth Fund. From its website:
"As an independent, nonpartisan organization, the foundation has
aimed to help develop *common ground from which policymakers across
the political spectrum can lead the nation* toward a health care system
that assures its residents have long, healthy, and *productive* lives" (*The
Commonwealth Fund*, 2014, emphasis added).

Cyril Burt, mentioned above, was a member of the London School
of Differential Psychology, and of the British Eugenics Society, hence
most likely a Fabian. Amy Strachey, a.k.a. "Mrs. St Loe," was the
wife of John Strachey, a British journalist and father of the *other*
John Strachey already mentioned in this work, the Fabian and
Labour politician who was at Oxford in 1922, around the time my
grandfather arrived. Strachey joined the Labour Party the following year in 1923. From 1946 to 1950, he was the minister of food,
which would have given him plenty of reason to have had dealings
with Alec. While I have found no definite links to MI5 or MI6, his
name crops up a lot in related literature, and he was certainly *one of
the circle*. Strachey also has traceable links to Lord Boothby—whom
he probably met at Oxford—Tom Wintringham and Victor Gollancz
of the 1941 Committee, John Maynard Keynes, Harold Laski (who
joined the Fabian Society while he was at Oxford), Richard Acland,
Tom Driberg, and so on.

The Mental Health Timeline continues (for 1929) by mentioning a work called *Our Baby—For Mothers and Nurses*, eventually published in 1936 by John Wright/Simpkin Marshall, which "on page 126 lists Idiocy under Congenital Defects":

> This is a term for mental weakness which dates from birth. It varies in degree from a mere feebleness of intellect, to a state in which the mind seems wholly absent. Should a child fail to answer to most of the tests of normal progress given on page 88, it must be considered backward, and the child should be taken to a doctor, as systematic training should be begun very early, considerable improvement being then almost always possible.

This description clearly evokes what would become standard operating procedure with autistics in the coming decades. And do I need to remind the reader of Russell's plan for close surveillance, categorization, and the use of "behaviourism" with children, from the moment of conception onward?

The Timeline then quotes a "Wood Report on Mental Deficiency published by the Board of Control"[2] from the same year:

> The majority of the feeble-minded are to be found within a relatively small social group, a group which may be described as the subnormal or social problem group, representing approximately 10 per cent of the whole population. Most of the parents in this subnormal group are themselves of poor mental endowment, and would no doubt have been classed, when children, among the dull or retarded. Similarly the dull children of the present generation, who form a large majority amongst children in this subnormal group, are the potential parents of many feeble-minded in the next generation. Therefore, from the standpoint of the prevention of many social evils it is of the utmost importance that the problems of the education and social care of the borderline retarded child should be effectively tackled .... Let us assume that we could segregate as a separate community all the families in this country containing mental defectives of the primary amentia type. We should find that we had collected among them a most interesting social group. It would include, as everyone who has extensive practical experience of social service would readily admit, a much larger proportion of

insane persons, epileptics, paupers, criminals (especially recidi-
vists), unemployables, habitual slum dwellers, prostitutes, inebri-
ates and other social inefficients than would a group of families not
containing mental defectives. The overwhelming majority of the
families thus collected will belong to that section of the community
which we propose to term the "social problem" or "subnormal"
group. This group comprises approximately the lowest 10 per cent
in the social scale of most communities. (Gillard, 2013)

The Mental Health Timeline then refers to the April 1929 *Journal of the American Medical Association* about the establishment of the London Child Guidance Clinic (citing "Bowlby 1936" and "Tavistock 1967") and cites (in 1929) a "Conference on Mental Health convened by the Joint Committee of the National Council for Mental Hygiene and the Tavistock Square Clinic. Held in Westminster."

The Bowlby referred to is Edward John Mostyn Bowlby, a British psychologist, psychiatrist, and psychoanalyst, notable for his interest in child development and for his pioneering work in attachment theory. (*A Review of General Psychology* survey published in 2002 ranked Bowlby as the forty-ninth most cited psychologist of the twentieth century.) Bowlby worked during World War II in Canonbury in the child psychiatry unit with maladapted and delinquent children, which led to an interest in the development of children, and to his work at the Child Guidance Clinic in Islington, London. By his own account, he had help getting established from some "academic economist" friends.[3]

As for the Child Guidance Clinic, it was founded by the Jewish Health Organization in 1927 and was *the first children's psychiatric facility* in the UK, and allegedly also Europe. From *The Use of Psychoanalytic Concepts in Therapy with Families*, by Hilary A. Davies:

> It was set up to meet the needs of the immigrant population who had settled in that part of London since the beginning of the century and whose children were perceived to have emotional, psychological, behavioral, and educational difficulties. A foreword to an early report by the Clinic is quoted as saying that "in its efforts to adjust the groping child mind to life, to make useful citizens of difficult and abnormal boys and girls [it] is doing the work of civilization." ... The Clinic was able to offer a service to almost 1900

children and families from all over the UK in the first 4½ years of its existence. The Clinic later moved and became the Tavistock. (Davies, 2010, p. 15)

(The citation about doing the work of civilization is attributed, via a website, to "Lady Lawrence" who was chairman of the Clinic in 1934 and had written a foreword to a report. The website states its source as *The Times* and makes a guess as to the identity of the Lady Lawrence in question being Lady Rosamond Lawrence, a British novelist who wrote several popular books before marrying and relocating to India. However, it's also possible the Lady Lawrence referred to was the British Labour MP Susan Lawrence, who was appointed parliamentary secretary to the Ministry of Health in 1929. Susan Lawrence the Fabian Society a few years previously, and was close friends with Sydney and Beatrice Webb.)

Returning to the Mental Health Timeline, John Bowlby joined the Tavistock Clinic in 1946 as deputy director and set up the Children's Department to develop clinical services, training and research. In 1948, he obtained a small grant from the Sir Halley Stewart Trust to *"empirically study the effects of early separation and deprivation"* (emphasis added). For his research, he hired a psychiatric social worker (James Robertson, presumably LSE-trained). The London Child Guidance Clinic eventually became the Child Guidance Training Centre and was housed in the Tavistock Centre from 1967. In 1985, it merged with the Tavistock Clinic's Department for Children and Parents and became the Child and Family Department.

I noticed in the Timeline at this point (1986) the mention of "MBE [first appointment to the Order of the British Empire, the one before OBE] in New Year Honours: Miss Eve Saville, General Secretary, Institute for the Study and Treatment of Delinquency." A quick search revealed that Miss Eve Saville was a Fabian.[4] Whether she was related to Jimmy, OBE, I do not know and I doubt anyone else does (not counting those who do). The names Savile and Saville seem to be more or less interchangeable, and one easy way for Sir Jimmy (who called his mum "the Duchess") to cover any possible aristocratic ancestral tracks might have been to remove one of the l's. Eve is a somewhat mysterious character, considering there is almost nothing about her online and yet there is a memorial lecture named after her. She was the author of an obscure tract called "A History of the I.S.T.D. [Institute for the Study and

Treatment of Delinquency]: A Study of Crime and Delinquency from 1931 to 1992." After a period searching through Google Books, I found a most unexpected affiliation between Eve Saville and Victor Neuburg, Crowley's ill-fated homosexual partner and disciple, and with fellow phallus-worshipper Dion Byngham. In *The Magical Dilemma of Victor Neuburg*, the author Jean Overton Fuller reveals, through her correspondence with Eve Saville, that Neuburg was one of the founding members of the ISTD. In a letter to Fuller, Saville writes that Neuburg "was present at the very first meeting [at Primrose Hill, near Hampstead, and] appeared as one of the original members of the Executive Committee and as Honorary Secretary at the beginning of 1931." A list of thirty-nine vice-presidents for 1934 included Freud, Jung, Adler, Havelock Ellis, and H. G. Wells.

CHAPTER XIV

Strategy of wolves: UK child care system as sex abuse network

"Tavistock underwrites or has intimate relations with thirty research institutions in the United States, all of which at one time or another have taken a player's hand in the shaping of American schooling."

—John Taylor Gatto, *Underground History of American Education*

Is it really possible that Savile's predations of various care homes and psychiatric institutions were facilitated by Lord David Owen, Labour MP, not merely out of some sleazy tit-for-tat, but as part of a decades-long, multinational agenda (related to Owen's former boss William Sargant, and thence to MKULTRA) involving the deliberate sexual abuse of children as both a form of dark research/experimentation and a fully operational social engineering program, dating at least as far back as Havelock Ellis and the formation of the Fabian Society? If the answer is no, is it really possible that all of this is just "coincidence"? If the answer is again no, what does that leave? Is there a middle ground between "all a plot" and "just coincidence"?

The middle ground seems to be that dark research and social engineering have a knack for making use of groups and individuals who are genuinely attempting to bring about social reform through more humanistic methods, and who either remain oblivious (while useful) to these hidden goals, or eventually "wise up" and adapt their methods, values, and goals to fit with the deeper program—in other words, who "follow the money" and align with the power. It's easy to imagine how this might be especially the case if they were to discover that all their efforts were being blocked by the same power structures, and that the only way to at least *try* to beat them, would be to join them.

So here's another coincidence for the rapidly mounting pile: 1752, the Quakers in Philadelphia, USA, were the first group in America to make an organized effort to care for the mentally ill. Pennsylvania Hospital provided rooms in the basement with shackles attached to the walls, designed to house a small number of mentally ill patients. Within a couple of years, the demand was so high that another ward was opened beside the hospital. A new Pennsylvania Hospital for the Insane was opened in a suburb in 1856, and continued to do business under differ-ent names until 1998 (*U.S. National Library of Medicine*, 2006). In the UK meanwhile, in 1796, the (Quaker) Society of Friends set up The Retreat in Yorkshire, commonly known as the York Retreat, for the treatment of people with mental health needs. It operates to this day as a charitable organization, and is known for having pioneered the humane treatment that became a model for asylums around the world.[1] Which of course it is supposed can only be a good thing.

Another coincidence: the London Child Guidance Clinic was first established in Islington, North London, in 1929. Some seventy years later, an alleged ring of child molesters, working in and through a net-work of care homes across the country, was discovered operating in Islington. At the time (1993), it was Britain's biggest police inquiry into the organized sexual abuse of children.

> For the past five months officers from the squad have secretly liaised with directors of social services in more than half a dozen London boroughs amid fears that organized gangs have targeted vulnerable children in their areas. Several of the most prominent offenders under surveillance are wealthy businessmen. They have been linked to a sex ring abusing young people living in children's homes in the London borough of Islington. Due to the missing files, nobody can check which local authorities Islington sent children to, but some evidence remains in the form of statements from children who were in Islington's care. (Palmer, 1993)

No convictions were made and the investigation was apparently shut down. The investigation into child protection expert, social care worker, and founding member of PIE, Peter Righton, was shut down in 1994. Twenty years later, in 2013, the Metropolitan Police began an investigation into claims (including ones made by Labour MP Tom Watson) that Righton was part of a child molestation network with connections to the British Government (*Spotlight on Abuse*, 2013).

At least one boy from the Islington care home system was taken to New Barns School, an independent boarding school in Gloucestershire where Peter Righton was a governor, and where music teacher Alan Stewart was convicted of sexually abusing girls in 1994. Despite allegations of widespread sexual abuse at the school, the Crown Prosecution Service dropped the case. After Righton's 1992 conviction, he and his partner Richard Alston (the headmaster of New Barns School) were invited to stay at Lord Henniker's estate in Eye, Suffolk. Lord Henniker's estate was run as a "children's activity centre," and Islington council had been sending children there for years (ibid.).

In August 2014, the BBC described Righton's role in the UK child care system as one of "considerable assistance" to the Home Office, specifically to a government report in 1970, when "Righton travelled extensively carrying out research work [and went] to children's homes 'all over the country' where he interviewed individual boys in 'approved schools' and spoke to 'the heads of homes.'" While working to establish PIE, Righton "became increasingly influential in the field of residential child care. According to Ian Pace, Righton was "'deeply involved with the cult of the classical world that was very important to ... the paedophile movement,' focusing on stories of 'Greek love' between men and young boys" (Bateman, 2014).

As leader of Islington Council, Margaret Hodge was responsible for allowing this alleged, nationwide network to continue its predations of children in the care system. Indifferent to the implications, Prime Minister Tony Blair made Hodge children's minister in 2003, ten years after the abuse first became public. According to *The Daily Telegraph*, reporting on April 6, 2014, one victim from an Islington care home alleged that "Jimmy Savile taxis" regularly came to the home, "suggesting that children were collected there and ferried to Savile, who used his position as a celebrity to procure children .... Michael Gove, the Education Secretary, has instigated investigations into 21 children's homes around the country where Savile is suspected of abusing vulnerable young people" (Mendick & Fairweather, 2014).

That same day, the *Telegraph* ran another article, citing the 1995 White Report which was a response to the *Evening Standard*'s 112-page dossier of evidence.

> Parents, children and staff reiterated to White the paper's allegations—including that violent pimps openly collected children from the home, and were even allowed by staff to stay overnight in children's rooms. White, then director of Oxfordshire social services, confirmed that Islington allowed at least 26 workers facing "extremely serious allegations" to leave its employ without investigation. Staff accused of everything from rape to child prostitution had been allowed to resign, often with good references. He described Islington as a "classic study" in how paedophiles target children, aided by the council's naïve interpretation of gay rights. Islington was deeply influenced by and had many connections to the Paedophile Information Exchange. In the fatally naïve 1970s to mid-80s, PIE openly campaigned for sex to be legalized with children from age four, and for incest and child pornography to be legalized. The National Council for Civil Liberties—now Liberty—allowed it to affiliate and its then legal officer Harriet Harman wrote a paper effectively backing some PIE demands. The assumption in those "progressive" days was that paedophiles simply loved children and wanted to "liberate" their sexuality. (Fairweather, 2014)

Harriet Harman has described Margaret Hodge as her best friend in Parliament. Hodge's late husband, Henry Hodge, was also an Islington Labour councilor, and a former chairman of the National Council for Civil Liberties. In 1985, Margaret Hodge "announced that Islington Council would positively discriminate in favour of gay staff. It exempted self-declared gay men from background checks, and paedophiles pretending to be decent gay men cynically exploited this." Righton meanwhile had founded a training course for residential workers. Pedophilia, he declared in one essay, was "no more bizarre than a penchant for redheads" (ibid.).

The article quotes a "whistleblower" called Dr. Davies: "I think there could be more than one home with Savile connections. Children from Islington's home at 114 Grosvenor Avenue were taken to Jersey by Rabet, and Savile visited Jersey's Haut de la Garenne home. Survivors of abuse there have described being taken to an Islington children's home" (ibid.). Haut de la Garenne was visited by the Kray twins and Lord Boothby. The crimes that allegedly occurred there were considerably more severe than "mere" pedophilia, involving as they did the violent rape, torture, and murder of children. In February 2015, the independent journalism site *Exaro* alleged that Righton was involved in the sadistic murder of a boy at Lord Henniker's estate (Wood, 2015; unfortunately, *Exaro* no longer exists and the site has been taken down).

Although much of this seems almost unthinkable when written down in black and white, all of these crimes appear to be sourced in roughly—or exactly—the same social circles and value set as those of my own family.

*

"All that is necessary for totalitarianism to triumph is for people to mistake its practitioners for liberators."
—Theodore Dalrymple

There is another quite damning chain of associations to be found by looking at Sir Harold Haywood, a skilled social organizer who worked with certain celebrities during the 1960s and '70s. For almost twenty years, Sir Harold occupied one of the top positions at the National Association of Youth Clubs (NAYC), and under his directorship (from 1955–1974), Sir Angus Ogilvy, husband of Princess Alexandra, was appointed president. A slew of celebrity-attended fundraising events were organized, enlisting the support of Jimmy Savile, Cliff Richard, and Rolf Harris, among others, and membership swelled to 600,000. In 1973, Haywood was given an OBE for "services to youth," and in 1974, NAYC organized with Albany Trust to set up a two-day training conference on youth sexuality for people who train youth workers. Haywood's involvement with NAYC is listed as having ended in 1974, but even after his departure,

> [Jimmy] Savile stopping by was still a frequent occurrence and he maintained close links with both NAYC and PHAB [Physically Handicapped and Able Bodied] beyond Haywood's tenure. During 1974 and 1975 Savile was holding annual fundraising

events "Tea-rific" for NAYC and while writing his autobiography (published in 1974) referred to himself as Vice-President to Angus Ogilvy's President. In 1974 Savile had also become Honorary President of PHAB when it became an independent charity [Savile did charity runs for them]. During Haywood's time in 1970 PHAB had launched a TV fundraising appeal with Cliff Richard fronting the advert. Cliff along with Savile, Rolf Harris and Ed "Stewpot" Stewart were to become four major entertainers appearing publicly for PHAB fundraising. (*Bits of Books*, 2015)

In 1975, Sir Harold became chairman of Albany Trust; soon after he met with four or five PIE members at the MIND Sexual Minorities workshop. Having stated that there was a moral imperative for the Trust to assist pedophiles, he enlisted the aid of Trust director Anthony Grey (born Anthony Edgar Gartside Wright). Grey (then Wright) had been a journalist in Leeds, Yorkshire, in the 1940s (he may even have known Savile) before joining the Fabian-affiliated Homosexual Law Reform Society in 1958; he became secretary for Albany Trust in 1962 and director from 1971–77. In 1992's *Quest for Justice: Towards Homosexual Emancipation* (a book which includes a photograph of Alec's wartime associate, J. B. Priestley, with his wife, Jacquetta Hawkes), Grey writes:

> I arranged for a few private discussions to be held at the Trust's offices between psychiatrists, psychologists and social workers whom I knew to be concerned with paedophiles in their professional work, to explore with them the nature and availability of support needed. I also invited some paedophiles to join in these talks, including the young man who had spoken at the MIND conference and other members of the newly-formed (and ill-fated) Paedophile Information Exchange (PIE) and another group, PAL (Paedophile Action for Liberation). (2011, p. 209)

Albany Trust teamed up with PIE to create a booklet called "Paedophilia: Some Questions and Answers." It proposed that child abusers were a social benefit and that without them voluntary services and youth welfare work would be practically impossible! (According to researcher Simon Ricketts, it was "essentially [proposing] pedophiles as a 'free' source of labor for social services" (*Bits of Books*, 2015). "In the belief that knowledge dispels prejudice, this booklet sets out to answer the commonest questions and suppositions about paedophilia, and to argue that those involved represent no special threat to society, but *on the contrary are often a force for social good*" (emphasis added).[2]

In 1977, Sir Harold Haywood was appointed director of the Queen's Silver Jubilee Trust at the queen's behest, which went on to raise over £15 million for "disadvantaged youth." He also became a director of The Prince's Trust, and in 1985 "took the Prince on a 'plain clothes' visit to London's Centrepoint Hostel and charity centers in Soho's red light district, to see the plight of young homeless people for himself" (*Philanthropy Impact*, 2010).

CHAPTER XV

Child abuse as sex magick and sexual research: Aleister Crowley, Margaret Mead, Alfred Kinsey

"For that group, the book of books was Davidson's *History of Education*. William James called its author a "knight-errant of the intellectual life," an "exuberant polymath." ... Its purpose was to dignify a newly self-conscious profession called Education. Its argument, a heady distillation of conclusions from Social Darwinism, claimed that modern education was a cosmic force leading mankind to full realization of itself."

—John Taylor Gatto, *Underground History of American Education*

An *Evening Standard* report from 1994 regarding the Islington care home child abuse wrote that, "For years a group of gay social work academics were able to abuse young boys with terrifying ease shielded—unwittingly—by colleagues who didn't dare challenge their views on child-sexuality for fear of appearing anti-liberal." They described Scotland Yard's Obscene Publications Squad as "investigating a network of gay intellectuals who are believed to have run child sex rings for decades through schools and children's homes" (Payne & Fairweather, 1994).

When I was growing up, I was not exactly surrounded by gay intellectuals, but they were certainly around, and I was suffused in the sort of liberalism that *would* have been afraid to challenge pro-pedophilia views—at least if they were coming from respected peers within our community. Would this have extended to the point of shielding abuse? Certainly, it is not at all hard for me to believe this.

One of the things I concluded about my brother's carefully crafted public persona as a dandy, drug user, and sexual libertine, was that it was an elaborately disguised cry for help—that he had been engineered through trauma to become the clothes-Horsley that he was, and that his every insistence on being his own man was an unconscious cry from the soul of the very opposite, that he had been colonized internally by a malign force. This book is neither disguised nor unconscious as a cry for help; and yet it's perhaps equally irrational, since I neither expect help to come nor believe that I need it. That time has long passed. Even so, some of the individuals who *could* have intervened on my behalf as a child *are* still alive, and they may be implicated, some directly, in this investigation. But the main participants—those who were either most responsible or who could most effectively have intervened, or both—my grandfather, my father, my brother (and my mother and my stepfather), are all dead. They were also the principal carriers of the Fabian legacy which I have inherited, being the firstborns of the firstborn; and since they are gone, I am now the only surviving son of the firstborn son of Alec. The buck stops here.

If this written exploration is for anyone besides myself, and those very few surviving family members willing to look at the hidden aspect of their heritage, it's for those that have passed on. Perhaps there are family members being wrongly implicated by this piece. There is always the possibility that even my grandfather was duped, that he was a useful liberal idiot, oblivious to the geopolitical social engineering agendas that were moving, like vast cosmic tides, around and finally over his castles in the sand. Yet, if one of those sand castles is Northern Foods—possibly the largest Food conglomerate in Europe, whose legacy in geopolitics continues to this day—it seems rather naïve, not to mention a disservice both to Alec and to history, to reduce it to a sand castle.

Before I get to the geopolitical picture and how Northern Foods' influence—via my uncle Lord (or is it Baron? I can't keep track of peerages) Haskins—continued into the 2000s, I want to return to the intersection of progressive leftist movements and homosexuality, within the already described larger context of social reform, economics, psychiatry and the medical establishment, hallucinogens, literary movements and liberal intellectualism, pedophilia and, most distressing of all, intelligence operations in mind control. That means going back to the beginning once more.

A decade after the founding of the Fabian Society, in 1897, The Order of Chaeronea was founded by George Cecil Ives (friend of Oscar Wilde). It was a secret society for the cultivation of a homosexual, ethical, cultural, and spiritual ethos. It was secret because homosexuality was illegal at that time and homosexuals needed a means of underground communication. The organization was inspired by and closely tied to the "Uranian" movement, Uranian being a nineteenth-century term that referred to a "third sex," originally someone with "a female psyche in a male body" who was sexually attracted to men (making it a *very* early precursor of the transgender movement).

Although there's no mention of Aleister Crowley in the records of The Order of Chaeronea, they could hardly have been unaware of one another, since Crowley was both a pioneer of "sexual liberation" and a practitioner of homosexual sex magick. The subject of sexual magick, while it's really of central importance to this investigation, is one I've avoided until now, because it becomes all-too-easy to lose the ground of factual reportage once we stray into more esoteric and philosophic waters. However, it's worth mentioning in brief (having just come across this material myself) that the Theosophical Society (tied to the Fabians via Annie Besant) was implicated in child sexual abuse in the early 1900s because of Charles Leadbeater. Canadian sociologist Stephen Kent writes:

> Leadbeater's practice of sex magick involved homosexual abuses, but this tradition is by no means limited to homoerotic activities …. Leadbeater was a pederast, and he used the Theosophical Society to gain access to boys so that he could engage them in various forms of sex magick (see Washington, 1995, p. 121). Remarkable, perhaps, about Leadbeater's pederasty was that he was able to sanctify it under the guise of spiritual training. Apparently, Leadbeater taught a sexual technique to an inner circle of initiates who claimed that "the energy aroused in masturbation can be used as a form of occult power, a great release of energy which can, first, elevate the consciousness of the individual to a state of ecstasy, and second, direct a great rush of psychic force towards the Logos for His use in occult work." (2012)

According to occultist Phil Hine, this

> gave rise to the rumors that there existed groups of "Black Magi-
> cians" who obtained occult power by psychically vampirizing
> young boys. [Author] Dion Fortune … alleged that there was a con-
> spiracy of male occultists who used "homosexual techniques" to
> build up what she called "dark astral power." She also blamed the
> decline of the Greek and Roman empires on those cultures' relaxed
> attitude to homosexuality. Although she never named any of these
> "black adepts," it is clear that she was probably referring to C. W.
> Leadbeater, and perhaps, also Aleister Crowley. (1991)

Hine refers to Crowley's male lover, the poet Victor Neuburg, "his partner in a series of homosexual sex-magick operations known as The Paris
Working, where Neuburg & Crowley performed a series of invocations
using anal intercourse as the means of achieving gnosis." The six-week
ritual included strong drug use, as well as the occasional attendance
of a Liverpudlian journalist named Walter Duranty. Inspired by the
results of the Working, Crowley authored his treatise on sex magick,
Liber Agapé. Following the Working, Neuburg distanced himself from
Crowley, Crowley "cursed" Neuburg, and Neuburg (allegedly) suffered a nervous breakdown.

That was in 1914; a year before, in 1913, George Cecil Ives, along with
Edward Carpenter and others, founded The British Society for the Study
of Sex Psychology (BSSSP), to advance a radical agenda in the field of
sexual reform. It was particularly concerned with homosexuality, aim-
ing to combat legal discrimination against homosexuality with scientific understanding. Members included Havelock Ellis, George Bernard
Shaw, and fellow Chaeroneans Laurence Housman and Montague Sum-
mers (a clergyman with a leaning towards the occult who translated
Malleus Maleficarum into English). Ernest Jones was also a member, and
he is worth lingering on.

In the early 1900s, Jones had worked with and mentored under
Wilfred Trotter, of Tavistock. He experimented with hypnotic techniques
in his clinical work and applied Freudian psychology as an inspector of
schools for "mentally defective" children. In 1906, he was arrested and
charged with two counts of indecent assault on two adolescent girls
he was interviewing. In court, Jones insisted the girls were fantasizing
and was acquitted. He founded the British Psychoanalytical Society in

1919 and was president until 1944. In 1931, the BSSSP was renamed the British Sexological Society, and it seems to have continued until some point in the 1940s. It was largely through Jones's advocacy that the British Medical Association officially recognized psychoanalysis, in 1929. There's that year again—the same year that "Idiocy" became a diagnostic term for a congenital defect, and the London School of Economics began its training courses for psychiatric social workers.

No study of how the seeds of the sexual revolution were sown is complete without mentioning Margaret Mead, whom Theodore Dalrymple called "the patron saint of these ideas" (2005, pp. 240–241). In 1928, at the tender age of twenty-seven, Mead published *Coming of Age in Samoa*, the book that made her famous. Mead was a student of anthropologist Franz Boas, "an extreme cultural determinist who wanted to prove that the angst of adolescence was, like most important human realities, the product of culture, not of biology" (ibid.). *Coming of Age in Samoa* provided the "proof" her mentor had been seeking. It described

> a South Sea paradise in which adolescents spent the years between puberty and marriage in uninhibited sexual activity, as much as possible with as many as possible. There was no jealousy, no rivalry, no anxiety, no guilt, just fun ... here was a culture that dealt with sex better than we, as the absence of Samoan adolescent unhappiness proved. Of course her depiction of Samoa was in error: she was taken in by her ironical informants. Sexual morality in Samoa was puritanical rather than liberal, and owed much to the efforts of the London Missionary Society, no advocate of free love during adolescence or at any other time. [And yet] Few university students during that half-century did not read [the book] or at least know its message [and] generations of educated people accepted Mead's ideas about adolescent sexuality as substantially correct and reasonable. (ibid., pp. 240–241)

Mead was married to fellow anthropologist Gregory Bateson, whom she met in New Guinea in 1933, and who served in the OSS in the Second World War (along with over two dozen other anthropologists, see Price, 1998)—the OSS being "the direct institutional predecessor to the CIA" (ibid.). Bateson's specialty was "black propaganda," for which he "applied the principles of his theory of schismogenesis to help foster disorder among the enemy" (ibid.). CIA documents show how Bateson recommended that US intelligence agencies gather as much data as possible about native cultures in India, and that they use it "to control the direction of native social and political movements." This sort of "culture-cracking," or psychological warfare, "would become one of the CIA's standard techniques of subversion and conquest" (ibid.). Perhaps unsurprisingly at this point, Bateson has been named as one of the leading players in the seeding of the '60s counterculture (Atwill, 2015). He was an early teacher at Esalen and a member of the Lindisfarne Association, whose goal was the creation of a planetary culture. He was also one of the pioneers of cybernetics, and his studies in schismogenesis and "the double-bind" may have been formative to MKULTRA's mind control program (Winter, 2018). Mead appears to have shared some or all of Bateson's affiliations, and certainly was sympathetic to them. In 1971 she led a committee whose purpose was to argue that "[T]here was nothing inherently sinister about [anthropologists] working with the military, even on counterinsurgency projects." Such collaborations, the committee's report pointed out, "were the historical norm, not the exception" (Baker, 2016). All of this may give us pause to wonder if Mead's "error" about the sexual mores of the Samoans—being as widely influential as it was—was entirely *innocent*?

*

Returning to the timeline: While in 1930s Germany, homosexual groups and individuals were being targeted as subversives (and eugenics was becoming national policy), in the 1940s, many countries in Europe (starting with Iceland) decriminalized homosexuality. In 1948, Alfred Kinsey—the natural heir of Mead, published *Sexual Behavior in the Human Male*, which made the claim that homosexuality was far more widespread than was commonly believed. The book also reported Kinsey's findings about child sexuality. Tables 31–34 were the tables or lists in the book which purported to display the number of times infants and young children were aroused when the researcher attempted to masturbate them. Kinsey noted "groaning, sobbing, or more violent cries, sometimes with an abundance of tears (especially among younger children)" (Reisman, 2010, p. 31).

Even though this sexual abuse of children was displayed in the text of the work itself (a study often said to have kick-started the sexual revolution), it was not until 1981 that Dr. Judith Reisman drew attention to the implications. Her charges were eventually confirmed, in the August 25, 1997 issue of the *New Yorker*, by James H. Jones, former member of the Kinsey Institute's Scientific Board of Advisors; they were then validated by the Institute for Media Education. According to Reisman, however, Jones avoided any mention of the hundreds of infants and children under Kinsey's control.

> This table lists 188 children who were stimulated by pederast employees who observed children's reactions, timed them, and followed this abuse by keeping copious pederastic interpretive notes. The abusers *could definitely have been Kinsey, Pomeroy, Martin, Gebhard, and/or others hired for their team*. In an audio-taped interview, Paul Gebhard later acknowledged that they asked child rapists to get data on child orgasm, use stopwatches "take notes … time it and report back to us." … Kinsey asserted that our culture restricted and inhibited child orgasms to children's detriment. If infants and children are not having orgasms, Kinsey said, they are being psychologically harmed by foolish adult puritanical inhibitions …. Kinsey admonished readers to have orgasms as often as possible, any way they could get them. For health, he urged early masturbation, all but mandating childhood masturbation as early as possible if a child was to be "normal." … Further, Kinsey claimed that promiscuity was harmless, without consequences of venereal disease, illegitimacy, or anything else. And, worst, his data and "orgasmic" narrative claimed that rape, incest, and pedophilia/pederasty were also harmless. (ibid., pp. 27, 34, 35)

In an audio-taped interview, Kinsey team member Paul Gebhard told Reisman that most of the "research" on children was done by "one individual, a man with scientific training, and not a known scientist. The other cases were done by parents [and] by nursery school personnel." The "man with scientific training" was known as "Mr. X," later discovered to be Rex King, a serial child rapist responsible for the rape of more than 800 children. "Some of these rapes were rendered to Kinsey in graphic detail, which he considered "scientific research." Kinsey never reported King to the authorities (Brinkmann, 2005).

In 1992, Gebhard confirmed that "some of the men on Kinsey's child sexuality team included child molesters who were easily obtained from prisons and pedophile organizations around the world …. He also admitted to having personally collaborated in the child abuse inherent in Kinsey's research." A 1998 Yorkshire-produced documentary, "Secret History: Kinsey's Paedophiles," uncovered more facts about the "trained persons" who participated in Kinsey's experiments, naming Dr. Fritz Von Balluseck, "a notorious Nazi child molester who contributed his child abuse data during the twenty year period of 1936 to 1956 to Kinsey's research data base" (ibid.).

Kinsey's "research" was funded by the Rockefeller Foundation (Jones, 2004, p. 555); Kinsey corresponded with MKULTRA-psychiatrist Ewen Cameron and was an admirer, and possible correspondent, of Aleister Crowley. Kinsey tried hard to obtain Crowley's sex-magickal diaries after Crowley's death, and even made a pilgrimage to Crowley's Thelema Abbey, where Crowley allegedly conducted sexual rituals that included children (Pomeroy, 1972, p. 413; see Part II for more on this).

James H. Jones described Kinsey as a militant propagandist, a sadomasochist, and homosexual, "campaigning with scientific cover and on tax-exempt funds for *his goal of undermining American morality to establish a sexual utopia*" (emphasis added). What's perhaps most remarkable about this hidden history is that it remains hidden to this day, despite being very much on public record. The 2004 Hollywood movie, *Kinsey*, with Liam Neeson, presented a glowing picture of the sexologist. Despite some protests, mostly from Christian activists, the film was well reviewed and won a bunch of major awards. Kinsey's reputation remains intact. *How is this even possible in a cultural climate that views pedophiles as the most depraved and irredeemable of monsters?* The answer would appear to be simple: *science*. Place blatant crimes in the context of science, and most people will not question them.

Ellis's, and Mead's, and Bateson's, and Kinsey's "research"—black propaganda or not—was effective in spreading the "gospel of free love" and kick-starting a revolution, one that continues to this day with no apparent end in sight. As Dalrymple writes:

> Having been issued the false prospectus of happiness through unlimited sex, modern man concludes, when he is not happy with his life, that his sex has not been unlimited enough .... Another rhetorical technique the sexual revolutionaries favor (apart from the appeal to a fantasy of limitless eroticism) has been to try to

dissolve sexual boundaries. They preached that all sexual behavior is, by nature, a continuum. And they thought that if they could show that sex had no natural boundaries, all legal prohibition or social restraint of it would at once be seen as arbitrary and artificial and therefore morally untenable: for only differences in nature could be legitimately recognized by legal and social taboos. (2005, pp. 244–246)

And not even differences in nature. As the current transgender movement makes clear—a clear descendant of the Uranian movement and a "natural" extension of gay rights—even biological distinctions are now becoming illegitimate.

CHAPTER XVI

World process: *Kinderladen*, Paedophile Information Exchange, and Labour

"My endeavor has been to present education as the last and highest form of evolution .... By placing education in relation to the whole process of evolution, as its highest form, I have hoped to impart to it a dignity which it could hardly otherwise receive or claim ... when it is recognized to be the highest phase of the world-process. "World process" here is an echo of Kant and Hegel, and for the teacher to be the chief agent in that process, both it and he assumes a very different aspect."

—Thomas Davidson, *History of Education*

Returning to the twentieth-century history of homosexuality, the Homosexual Law Reform Society was founded in Britain in 1958, publicly supported by Clement Attlee, Isaiah Berlin, Julian Huxley, J. B. Priestley, and Bertrand Russell, among others, with members including Victor Gollancz, Stephen Spender, MP Kenneth Younger, and the aforementioned Antony Grey. Most of the founders were not homosexual, at least openly. That same year, a related charity, the Albany Trust, was set up, using J. B. Priestley's apartment for its first meetings (Grey joined in 1962). The following year, in 1959, the US Supreme Court ruled in favor of the First Amendment rights of a gay and lesbian magazine, marking the first ruling on a case involving homosexuality. UK's ITV, at the time the only national commercial broadcaster, broadcast the first gay drama, *South*, starring Peter Wyngarde.

And then came the Sixties, towards the end of which the Gay Liberation Front (GLF) was formed. Homosexuality became legal in the UK via the Sexual Offences Act 1967, the year I was born. In the UK, the GLF had its first meeting in the basement of the London School of Economics, on October 13, 1970. Why the LSE, of all places? Apparently it was simply the place to be.

Another chapter in the hidden history of the sexual revolution occurred in Germany during this period. A movement in Germany of the late 1960s involved schools across the country known as *Kinderladen*. In a collection of reports found for one of these schools, the Rote Freiheit ("Red Freedom") after-school center, dated from August 13, 1969 to January 14, 1970, fifteen children aged between eight and fourteen were mentioned as being "taken care of during the afternoon." "The goal of the center was to shape the students into 'socialist personalities,' and its educational mission went well beyond supervised play." There was "a very strong emphasis on sex education. Almost every day, the students played games that involved taking off their clothes, reading porno magazines together and pantomiming intercourse" (Fleischhauer & Hollersenup, 2010).

An entry made on November 26 reads: "In general, by lying there we repeatedly provoked, openly or in a hidden way, sexual innuendoes, which were then expressed in pantomimes, which Kurt and Rita performed together on the low table (as a stage) in front of us."

> In the basement [were] found two rooms that were separated by a large, one-way mirror. There was a mattress in one of the rooms, as well as a sink on the wall and a row of colorful washcloths hanging next to it. [T]he basement was used as an "observation station" to study sexual behavior in children .... It has since faded into obscurity, but the members of the 1968 movement and their successors were caught up in a strange obsession about childhood sexuality. It is a chapter of the movement's history which is never mentioned in the more glowing accounts of the era. (ibid.)

The aim of the movement was the "sexual liberation of children." As with the Kinsey Institute, some of the leading German academics of the time were involved. (Alexander Schuller, a sociologist, was one of the pioneers of the movement and a founder of a Kinderladen in Berlin's Wilmersdorf neighborhood. "Like Schuller, the other parents were academics, journalists or university employees—a decidedly upper middle-class lot.")

> [I]t was precisely in so-called progressive circles that an eroticization of childhood and a gradual lowering of taboos began. It was a shift that even allowed for the possibility of sex with children. Sexual liberation was at the top of the agenda of the young revolutionaries who, in 1967, began turning society upside down. *The control of sexual desire was seen as an instrument of domination, which bourgeois society used to uphold its power.* Everything that the innovators perceived as wrong and harmful has its origins in this concept: man's aggression, greed and desire to own things, as well as his willingness to submit to authority. The student radicals believed that only those who liberated themselves from sexual repression could be truly free. To them, it seemed obvious that liberation should begin at an early age. Once sexual inhibitions had taken root, they reasoned, everything that followed was merely the treatment of symptoms. They were convinced that it was much better to prevent those inhibitions from developing in the first place. *Hardly any leftist texts of the day did not address the subject of sexuality.* (ibid., emphasis added)

This radical philosophy blamed "The de-eroticization of family life, from the prohibition of sexual activity among children to the taboo of incest," for people's "voluntary subjugation to a dehumanizing labor system. [F]or the revolutionaries of 1968, [what is today seen as sexual abuse] was *an educational tool that helped "create a new person"* (ibid., emphasis added).

> In the wake of the emerging gay movement, so-called Pedo groups soon appeared. Taking their cue from homosexuals, they also claimed that, as a minority, they were entitled to certain rights .... The Greens were not long immune to the argument that the government should not limit the sexuality of children [and] argued that "nonviolent sexuality" between children and adults should generally be allowed, without any age restrictions. (ibid.)

As with the Kinsey affair, and as with PIE in the UK, this chapter in German history has been all-but stricken from the record. It is generally assumed that these movements "petered" out because they were aberrational, a symptom of the times. But what if, like the New Criticism, by gradually becoming the norm (gradualism being the primary Fabian principle), they became culturally invisible?

*

In 1973, the American Psychiatric Association removed homosexuality from its official list of mental disorders, and in 1974, Paedophile Action for Liberation (PAL) developed as a breakaway group from South London Gay Liberation Front. It was the subject of a front page and centerspread article in the *Sunday People*, leading to some of the people exposed losing their jobs. In 1975, PAL merged with the Paedophile Information Exchange, a special interest group within the Scottish Minorities Group, with founding member Michael Hanson (a non-pedophile), as the group's first chairman. As already mentioned, PIE grew out of the National Council for Civil Liberties (now simply Liberty), originally formed in 1932 as a response to the National Hunger March. The first secretary of NCCL was Ronald Kidd, and the first president was the author E. M. Forster. Vice-presidents were the politician and author A. P. Herbert and the journalist Kingsley Martin of the *New Statesman*. H. G. Wells, Vera Brittain, Clement Attlee, and Harold Laski were also founder members.

Since the majority of enquiries were from England, PIE relocated from Glasgow to London in 1975, where twenty-three-year-old Keith Hose became chairman. The group's stated aim was "to alleviate [the] suffering of many adults and children" by campaigning to abolish the age of consent and legalizing sex between adults and children. PIE spokesman Tom O'Carroll advocated the normalization of adult-child sexual relationships. Each stage of the sexual relationship between an adult and child, O'Carroll claimed, can be "negotiated," with "hints and signals, verbal and non-verbal, by which each indicates to the other what is acceptable and what is not. [T]he man might start by saying what pretty knickers the girl was wearing, and he would be far more likely to proceed to the next stage of negotiation if she seemed pleased by the remark" (O'Carroll, 1980, p. 35).

By his own account, O'Carroll was not a homosexual: "I didn't feel gay at all, and although Quentin Crisp is firmly in my pantheon of twentieth-century heroes, I felt as out of place in GLF company as I would sipping tea with Mary Whitehouse" (ibid., p. 155). (In passing, Quentin Crisp was also one of my brother's acknowledged role models.) O'Carroll describes attending the early meetings of PAL:

> It was at these meetings that I first met other pedophiles, and experienced the sheer exhilaration and joy of suddenly finding a whole new social world—a world in which the Great Unmentionable was all at once the thing to talk about, a source of instant, garrulous rapport, between the unlikeliest combinations of people: at my first meeting there were maybe a dozen, all male, mostly young not easily pigeon-holed—by either dress, accent or manner—into any obvious social class stereotypes. Among them were a naval petty officer, a motor mechanic, a former child welfare officer, a medical-research technician, a high-ranking administrator and a bus driver. At a later meeting a middle-aged man introduced himself as the headmaster of a boarding school for boys. (ibid., pp. 155–156)

O'Carroll quotes a letter published in PIE's magazine, *Magpie*, from someone reluctantly leaving the group, stating, "[S]ome of the finest people I have ever met in the gay world are PIE members" (ibid., p. 161). Even more tellingly, Tom O'Carroll writes about how he was angrily criticized for his involvement with PIE—not by offended parents but by fellow pedophiles—for not being subtle enough. A professor at the British Psychological Society's conference on Love and Attraction, in Swansea in 1977, accused O'Carroll of trying to be a messiah. "He had wanted to introduce to an academic audience some ideas about paedophilia and child sexuality," O'Carroll wrote, "that were quite as 'advanced' as any I had to offer; but his ideas were to be safely couched in academic language, with an air of tentative, disinterested objectivity. Thus, carefully sown, the seeds of his radicalism would be nurtured in good soil, and would in their own good time propagate themselves more widely" (ibid., p. 163).

At his blog, in a 2013 post, Tom O'Carroll mentions PIE treasurer David Grove (a.k.a. Robin Brabban), whom O'Carroll worked with in London in the 1970s. Grove was at Oxford during the same period as Alec Horsley, and according to O'Carroll (who refers to Grove as a "colonial boy-lover"), Grove "... served as an assistant district commissioner in Nigeria from the 1920s. Alec was assistant district officer in

Nigeria in the 1920s, so it seems likely he met Grove there. He definitely knew him, because my aunt reported encountering Grove when
he visited my grandfather sometime in the past, probably the 1970s.
As my aunt remembers it, Grove was talking to Alec about the benefits
of sexual love between adults and children. I have no idea what Alec's
response was. My aunt's only comment on the encounter now was to
add how "naïve" they were back then. (None of this was told to me,
but only to my cousin, while my aunt was insisting that I had got it all
wrong about Alec's past.)

Like O'Carroll, Grove "was indicted on a charge of conspiracy to corrupt public morals and would have been tried alongside [O'Carroll]
and others at the Old Bailey but for the fact that he was gravely ill by
then and died before the trial began." O'Carroll writes that "Old David
used to talk with great affection about the boys in Africa—hordes of
little kids who were not banned from his verandah, nor from his heart
or his life. He loved them dearly and they, I am sure, would have loved
him. He was that sort of guy" (O'Carroll, 2013).

O'Carroll also describes attending MIND, the national mental health
organization, where it was suggested that PIE should submit evidence
to the Home Office Criminal Law Revision Committee on the age of
consent. O'Carroll writes that the report "caught the imagination of no
less a figure than the Home Secretary of the time, Roy Jenkins. He is said
to have been impressed ... but added words to the effect: 'Of course, it
hasn't a hope in hell'" (1980, p. 157).

Roy Jenkins is an important figure in this narrative. In Jenkins's
obituary, Labour MP David Marquand claimed that "Jenkins did more
than any other person to make Britain a more civilized country to live
in," that he played an "indispensable part" in taking Britain into the
European Union, an "equally indispensable part" in paving the way
for the single currency, and, by forming the Social Democrat Party
(with the aforementioned David Owen) and "breaking the mold" of
British politics, Jenkins created New Labour (Marquand, 2003). In the
late 1950s, Jenkins wrote a tract entitled "Is Britain Civilized?" in which
he attacked Britain's "archaic" laws on censorship, homosexuality,
divorce, and abortion, and argued for changes to the country's "Victorian" criminal justice system. Jenkins's progressive views on social
reform were still in the minority in the Labour Party at that time, but by
1964, when Labour regained power, a "group of middle-class, mainly
Oxbridge-educated 'intellectuals' had risen to prominence in the party

and, for these 'modernizers,' led by Jenkins and his Oxford friend Tony Crosland, the main aim was the social, rather than the economic, transformation of Britain" (Clark, 2003). Jenkins, who became home secretary in 1965, was "convinced that the 'permissive society' was the 'civilized society.'" In 1967, Jenkins embarked on what *The Daily Telegraph* called "the most radical program of penal reform since the Second World War. His Criminal Justice Act of 1967 said very little about the victims of crime, but plenty about the perpetrators" (ibid.).[1] Jenkins was a lifelong Fabian and chaired the Fabian Society from 1957–58.

Other leading Fabian and Labour figures more directly connected to PIE are the aforementioned Harriet Harman and Patricia Hewitt, who first encountered the group when they were working in the National Council for Civil Liberties. According to a *Daily Mail* piece from 1976, "the NCCL filed a submission to a parliamentary committee claiming that a proposed Bill to protect children from sex abusers would lead to 'damaging and absurd prosecutions' …. 'Childhood sexual experiences, willingly engaged in, with an adult *result in no identifiable damage*,' it read. 'The real need is *a change in the attitude which assumes that all cases of paedophilia result in lasting damage*'" (emphasis added). In 1978, Harriet Harman became the NCCL's legal officer and promptly wrote its official response to Parliament's Protection of Children Bill, which sought to ban child pornography. Harman argued that "a pornographic picture of a naked child should not be considered indecent unless it could be proven that the subject had suffered" (Adams, 2013).

Patricia Hewitt was part of the NCCL before PIE was formed and continued there throughout its existence. She stuck up for Tom O'Carroll after he was convicted in 1981 for "conspiracy to corrupt public morals" over the contact ads section of *Magpie*. "Conspiring to corrupt public morals," Hewitt wrote, "is an offence incapable of definition or precise proof." She argued that O'Carroll's involvement in distributing child pornography had "overshadowed the deplorable nature of the conspiracy charge used by the prosecution" (ibid.).

I only spend so much time on these characters because many of them show up again in the 2000s, as part of Tony Blair's "Brain Trust," a New Labour incentive that included Rupert Murdoch, two of Jenkins's devotees David Marquand and Peter Mandelson, Patricia Hewitt, famous film producer David Puttnam, my mother's old neighbor Melvyn Bragg and—my uncle, Lord Haskins (*Independent*, 1995). Also implicated throughout are British intelligence services MI5 and

MI6: On July 19, 2015, Australia's "60 Minutes" broadcast an investigation of an alleged pedophile ring which was supplied with children by PIE founder, Peter Righton, former director of education at the National Institute for Social Work and legal aide to the British government. The ring allegedly included senior politicians from all three main parties, including Leon Brittan, Greville Janner, and Cyril Smith, alongside British diplomat and long-time deputy director of MI6, Sir Peter Telford Hayman. Hayman also went to Worcester College, Oxford, where my grandfather majored.

As recently as 2015, the *Telegraph* reported that "… the statement that paedophilia is 'natural and normal' was made not three decades ago but last July. It was made not in private but as one of the central claims of an academic presentation delivered, at the invitation of the organisers, to many of the key experts in the field at a conference held by the University of Cambridge" (Gilligan, 2015). Among the speakers was Graham Powell "one of the country's most distinguished psychologists" and past president of the British Psychological Society, as well as "current provider of psychology support services to the Serious Organised Crime Agency, the National Crime Squad, the Metropolitan Police, Kent Police, Essex Police and the Internet Watch Foundation. In *Perspectives on Paedophilia*, Powell coauthored a chapter which included the statement: "In the public mind, paedophile attention is generally assumed to be traumatic and to have lasting and wholly deleterious consequences for the victim. The evidence that we have considered here does not support this view … we need to ask not why are the effects of paedophile action so large, but why so small" (ibid.).

Is all of this in keeping with the notion of weaponized academics described in *Fabian Freeway*?

> There was another secret weapon valued more highly than the atom bomb by Anglo-American Fabians of the New Deal era. Namely, the university professor, who … was to be the future secret weapon of national strategy …. a trend that had been gaining momentum in America since the turn of the century. With the Roosevelt Administration, the liberal-to-Left professor moved into his prescribed orbit as the planner and guide of national policies based on Fabian research, which officials and politicians would trigger. (Martin, p. 297)

Currently (2018), pedophilia is classified by the Diagnostic and Statistical Manual of Mental Disorders as both a "paraphilia" and a "sexual orientation":

> DSM-5 makes reference to the term Pedophilic Sexual Orientation. Sexual Orientation is ordinarily used to designate the category, or categories, of persons whom a given individual finds to be sexually appealing. Those who are heterosexually oriented are sexually attracted to adults of the opposite sex; those who are homosexual, to adults of the same sex; men with a heterosexual pedophilic orientation, to prepubescent females; and men with a homosexual pedophilic orientation, to prepubescent boys .... Experiencing ongoing sexual attractions to prepubescent children is, in essence, a form of sexual orientation, and acknowledging that reality can help to distinguish the mental makeup that is inherent to Pedophilia, from acts of child sexual abuse. (Berlin, 2014)

There are currently dozens of legal pro-pedophilia groups active throughout the world.[2] The unnamed professor who admonished Tom O'Carroll for his zealotry and incaution was advocating gradual, incremental change via the methods of subtlety, stealth, and subterfuge: the quintessential Fabian method of cultural engineering.

CHAPTER XVII

A master key: Northern Foods, MI5, Groucho Club, Lord Haskins

"Here is the intellectual and emotional antecedent of 'creation spirituality,' Pierre Teilhard de Chardin's assertion that evolution has become a spiritual inevitability in our time. Suddenly mere schooling found itself elevated from its petty, despised position on the periphery of the known universe into an intimate involvement in the cosmic destiny of man, a master key too important to be left to parents."
—John Taylor Gatto, *Underground History of American Education*

So where does all this leave me? Do I think my grandparents, my uncles and aunts, my father, were involved in/victims of the sexual abuse of children disguised as sociological research and/or radical leftist reform? Or simply that they were that way inclined? Or was my grandfather only trying to brush shoulders with those people and groups he recognized as having the power and influence that he so desperately coveted for himself? And at what point does the line, once reached, get crossed?

While I was researching all this, I got hold of copies of letters between Alec and Bertrand Russell, as well as a couple sent to Victor Gollancz and the rather cursory replies from his secretary. The impression I got overall was of a man trying a little too hard to gain the ear and the support of "great men," to enlist them to his cause (ostensibly that of world peace). Alec mentions several donations he has made, or is willing to make, to these men, in tandem with invitations for them to attend various meetings or lunches which he is setting up in the name of the cause. (It's never specifically stated, besides that word "peace.") He is fobbed off by Gollancz (who suffered a broken limb around that time, and at one point uses it as an excuse), and even by Russell, who does at least agree to meet with my grandfather, while declining to be a public spokesperson at one of his events.

It is easy for me to relate—to imagine my grandfather's plight, trying to gain the attention and approval of powerful men and being kept out of the "club." Of course, this is very much at odds with the picture which has been emerging, via all of the material gathered here. But then, it may not be either/or. I once asked a conspiracy publisher (Kris Millegan, whose father was in the OSS and the CIA) about the possibility my grandfather was an intelligence operative. His response:

> You have spooks and then you have the folks that spooks influence. Basically intel ops operate with deceit and subterfuge. Even if you're a spook they lie and compartmentalize. You are only told what is needed. If you want someone to go from A to B, if you can get him to go there without even knowing you exist is great. If you have to tell them to go from A to B, you never tell them the right reasons. So many that are involved are simply played, and are not under orders. Most that get involved do it for all the right reasons, god and country, but are used by higher-ups. I find the final agendas come from the secret societal system, beyond the nation states that they have captured.

This may be true in a larger sense also. I can imagine my grandfather— and in a very different way my father—pursuing his lofty social goals, making connections to people higher up than himself, and slowly, over time, learning that those in power operated in very different ways to how he had imagined, that the line between criminal activities and political ones was not only invisible but nonexistent. I can imagine him realizing, in slow, steady increments, that, in order to be able to move in those circles of power, circles in which he could be most effective, he would first have to cross that nonexistent line, and participate in activities which might have initially been abhorrent to him. And then discovering, over time, that these seemingly heinous activities were not merely the perks and peccadillos of the powerful, but also, in some strange and alien sense, the means to a "higher" goal that was, to whatever degree, in accord with my grandfather's. Why else would a socialist who claimed to be interested in the plight of the common man associate with social engineers like Russell and Acland (who claimed to have the same goals, and perhaps actually did); or with criminals like Jimmy Boyle? Why else would he give large amounts of money to semi-clandestine organizations and create a corporate empire that served the interests of the most powerful groups on the planet?

In *Dandy in the Underworld*, my brother writes how Alec's house "set the scene for the first business meeting between Gordon White and James Hanson" (Horsley, 2007, p. 23), both of whom became Lords, and later were known as "Lords of the Raiders" (*The Economist*, 2004). Hanson and White were controversial figures, notoriously devoted to making a fast buck by any means necessary. White was written into the script of Oliver Stone's *Wall Street* as Sir Larry Wildman (played by Terence Stamp), and Hanson went Hollywood in his own way, having affairs with Audrey Hepburn, Jean Simmons, and Joan Collins. If these were the sorts of people my grandfather considered bedfellows, clearly his political and ethical principles were a lot more "flexible" than we grew up believing. And, by all accounts, Alec's personality was anything but a "liberal" or compassionate one: He was unanimously described by his children (and by my mother) as a bully.

One of the things his bullying was in service to was achievement. He pushed all his children (but especially the males) ruthlessly to excel, whether at tennis, at school, or in business. Perhaps he practiced the Fabian evolutionary theory of stress? Henry Stewart remembers meeting Alec when he was working on *News on Sunday*, the radical newspaper he helped my father found in 1987:

> One of the investors was Alec Horsley, founder of Northern Foods. (His son, Nick Horsley, was Chair of the company.) I remember we were taking a group of investors round the company a month before launch. One of my colleagues was explaining the finances and said "The break even is sales of 800,000 copies a week." This outraged Alec. Though he was all of 85 at the time, he grabbed my colleague by the lapels and forcefully stated "Break even is not the

point. Don't you dare talk about break even. The aim of a business
is to make a profit." (Stewart, 2012, pp. 93–94)

Alec's core values can also be gleaned by the legacy he left behind, that
of Northern Foods, which under the steerage of my father and then
Lord Haskins, became one of the largest food corporations in Europe
and was, indirectly at least, via its partnership with Marks & Spencer, a
major supporter of Zionism, as well as an early adopter of GMO food.
This is very far from Alec's supposedly humble origins as a Quaker and
a man of the common people.

The "official" record (Wikipedia) states that my father "took early
retirement due to a rare genetic wasting disease." The truth, as always,
is more complex. In 1986, he tried to change horses and pursue his first
ambition of writing/journalism by helping to fund the radical tabloid
News on Sunday, originally proposed by journalist John Pilger (to be
editor-in-chief) and Alan Hayling (an acclaimed documentary filmmaker who worked for two decades at the BBC; he went on to produce
Michael Moore's *Bowling for Columbine*). Pilger dropped out before the
paper launched, however, and the project only survived seven months.
It was my father's only business failure, and when he tried to return to
chairing Northern Foods, Haskins, who had taken over in the interim,
refused to let him back in. This at least was the version we all heard in
my family. Now, in light of everything else, I can't help but wonder if the
doomed paper was a carrot to lure my father out of his Northern Foods
chair. It was after the *News on Sunday* fiasco that he retired to Barbados.
He seemed to have given up. His prime of power and influence was in
the 1970s and early 1980s, when Northern Foods was at its peak and I
was venturing into the troubled waters of adolescence. My memories
of my father from this time are of a man sitting in his armchair with a
whiskey and ice, hiding behind the Sunday paper, seemingly terrified
of any kind of meaningful contact. Naturally, his awkwardness trans-
ferred to me and I found it excruciating to be around him. The trouble
he had walking due to the "genetic wasting disease" which eventually
put him in a wheelchair, the time he took just to get out of his chair and
across the room, only added to the pain I felt in his company.

It was also during this period (1980-83) that my father served as
chairman for a consultative group on industrial and business relations
at the BBC—a fact I only recently found out by reading his Wikipedia
page (recently created by unknown persons), which cites *The Guardian*

obit. This is the same BBC that "turned a blind eye to the rape and sexual assault of up to 1,000 girls and boys by Jimmy Savile in the corporation's changing rooms and studios" (Boffey, 2014). By which I don't mean to suggest that my father was one of those blind eyes, only that, once again, the proximity of my family to power abuse is striking.

*

And of course there's more. In November 2010, the award winning filmmaker and writer Tyrone D. Murphy discovered that an online members' group operating under the name of "the Groucho Club forum" was providing child pornography and children for sexual purposes, among other illegal activities. Hundreds of web pages and links to pornographic videos and images of young children and infants available for sex were quickly deleted from the website forum, and within a week of the report to the police, Murphy discovered that even the cache pages were being discreetly deleted.

> Despite Murphy sending 24 emails, 4 letters and numerous telephone calls to the Police and [Child Exploitation and Online Protection Centre], he was neither consulted nor interviewed by the Police about the forum. Murphy said "This forum attracted the lowest form of individuals in society; the sheer scale of the illegal activity on the Groucho Club forum is overwhelming .... The forum has posts made by child pornographers as late as September 2010. The forum has 42,348 members, 663,709 topics and 900,987 posts. Hundreds of the web pages and links are dedicated to gross and indecent material of young children .... Whoever owns and operated the Groucho Club forum seems to be somewhat of a mystery. (Lattice, 2011)

My father was a founding member of the Groucho Club when it opened in 1985. Although his name is not mentioned in the official website history, literary agent Michael Sissons is listed as one of four founding members, and my father had been friends with Sissons since Oxford. He even put me in touch with him as a writer. My brother was a member of the club (I went there once with my sister), and he reportedly began the drug binge that ended his life (a day or two later) at the club. According to its website, by the 1990s the club had become "the preferred watering hole for the famous and infamous and of course like any bar with bed-rooms came tales of naughtiness and excess—and as many of the clien-tele were celebrities it was inevitable the notoriety of the Club would spread" (*Groucho Club*, 2014).

Another founding member was Stephen Fry (Burrell, 2010). Fry gave the "key note" speech at my brother's funeral, and I presume attended the after-funeral VIP party at the Groucho (since he wasn't at the one I attended). It was also Fry who optioned my brother's book for a film adaptation. Fry was born in Hampstead in 1957. In 1979 (aged twenty-two), he wrote a play called *Latin! or Tobacco and Boys* about a homosex-ual relationship between a teacher and a thirteen-year-old student at an all-boys prep school. The play ends up in Morocco, and the title derives from Christopher Marlowe's reported comment that "All they that love not Tobacco and Boys are fools." On a TV program called *Shrink Rap* in 2007, Fry described being sexually assaulted by a sixth-former dur-ing his first year of boarding school. "According to sources close to the programme, Fry denies that the event had lasting consequences for his mental health" (Dunt, 2007). (Though Fry is a lifelong sufferer of bipo-lar disorder and quite open about it.)

After Jimmy Savile's death Fry tweeted (2011): "Oh, Sir Jimmy Savile is no more. Spent a train journey from Leeds to London with him once. He was not as other men. Fascinating & rare: RIP." By 2014, however, he was describing Savile as "an absolutely monstrous, depraved and repulsive piece of work" (*BBC News*, 2014a). Yet since Fry has worked at the BBC from the mid-1980s to the present day, he could hardly not have heard the rumors about Savile's monstrous predations, long, *long* before they became public knowledge. (For example, John Lydon of The Sex Pistols knew about Savile in 1978 and was "banned from the BBC" for making on-air remarks about him; see *The Guardian*, 2015.)

In 2014, Fry was announced as president of the Hay Literary Festival at a dinner in London, where he "treated guests to a graphic story about Gore Vidal's stay at a top London hotel where he rang a gay escort agency to arrange a boy for an energetic afternoon session. Despite being attended by usually liberal-minded literary types, Fry's lurid details of the sex act with the young man and what he would or would not perform was too much for some guests" (Hardcastle, 2014). That same year, Fry publicly criticized Operation Yewtree, the sexual abuse inquiry instigated after Savile's death, claiming that "fewer than half" of the people arrested had been found guilty, and stating that "the law should be toughened up to deter people from inventing claims about sex abuse" (Gordon, 2014). He made a joke at the 2016 BAFTA awards ceremony about pedophilia, referring to the child abuse movie *Spotlight*: "Love abounds this year in film," he quipped. "The love between two women, love between a young Irish girl and an Italian American, love between Catholic priests …" (*Irish Examiner*, 2016). Later the same year, he was chastised in the media again, this time for telling victims of sexual abuse to grow up:

> It's a great shame and we're all very sorry that your uncle touched you in that nasty place, you get some of my sympathy, but your self-pity gets none of my sympathy because self-pity is the ugliest emotion in humanity. Get rid of it, because no one's going to like you if you feel sorry for yourself. The irony is we'll feel sorry for you, if you stop feeling sorry for yourself. Just grow up. (Elgot, 2016)

So much for Stephen Fry. Murphy's investigations into the club were initially sparked by a combination of factors. For one thing, two rapes had allegedly occurred in the club within a short time period but had not been reported. For another, a seemingly gratuitous number of surveillance cameras had been installed inside the club. Murphy was working on a book about the subject when the Groucho Club took out an injunction against its publication and sued Murphy for libel. At the last minute, however, the club managers withdrew their case. A combination of a statement from one of the club's own managers with "copious exhibits that included internal emails and CCTV footage from the club" … supported Murphy's contention that further cameras had been secretly installed at the Groucho [that] lacked any proper registration with the authorities as required under the Data Protection Act" (Ward, 2012). This naturally raised the question of why the Groucho Club needed all these additional (concealed?) cameras, constantly tracking the movements of its members. Speculation has arisen that they were installed not for security but for blackmail purposes. This would be perfectly in line with what's known about MI5/6 standard operating procedures (see Chapter XXVIII).

The Groucho Club has been called the largest celebrity hangout in the world and, though its member list is secret, it has included among its attendants Bill Clinton and Princess Diana (Rankin, 2015). The secret forum which Murphy discovered is evidence of probably the largest child pornography network to come to light in the UK to date. And yet there has been an almost complete media blackout around the subject.[1]

My strong sense, regarding my father and his proximity to (if not complicity with) all of these intrigues, is that it relates directly to why he always hated his father and never forgave him, even years after Alec had died. Of course, there was the bullying from an early age, which presumably had a lot to do with my father ending up taking over the mantle of Northern Dairies and turning it into Northern Foods (as well as his futile attempt to escape that fate by traveling around North America and marrying my mother). But I suspect there was a deeper reason for the recrimination, one that related to that wolf in sheep's clothing, and to my father's own slow, inexorable journey of discovery, regarding the true nature of power and the price of aligning with it. The power originally represented by the world which he had set out to reform, and the power that was slowly revealed as the legacy which he'd inherited. Simply put, if in some sense my father was deceived into picking up the family business and "the Horsley cause," under the impression that it was a means to bring about social reforms for the good of all, what must he have gone through on beginning to realize that the ends being served were those of the ruling class and always had been, and that the common man was—as made explicit in Bertrand Russell's scientific manifesto—no more than a basket of eggs for an elitist omelet?

*

The wolf would seem to be more nakedly apparent in the career trajectory of my father's successor as chairman, Lord Haskins. Haskins went from Northern Foods (where he strongly advocated the adoption of GMO products) to being a key player in Tony Blair's New Labour government. Haskins was placed in charge of something called the Better Regulation Task Force (BRTF), a program set up by New Labour "to free business from 'red tape' [and] save bosses from what they see as 'unnecessary' restrictions on their profits"(*PowerBase*, 2008). The BRTF was also involved in reviewing the standards in hospitals and care homes:

> —Fit Person Criteria: a review of the criteria used to judge people's suitability for certain occupations

—Early Education and *Day Care* ...

—Long-term Care: We said in May 1998, "It is essential that a clear distinction is made between mandatory requirements, *focused on the safety and protection of those in care*, and benchmark—or as we describe them, 'aspirational' standards." (The Better Regulation Task Force, 2003, pp. 24, 15, emphasis added)

After the Islington care home scandal of 1993, there can be no doubt that the Labour government was fully aware of sexual abuse that had been occurring in care homes, and while Jimmy Savile's predations within the NHS hospital system weren't exposed until 2015, they were ongoing in the 1990s. The question of whether the BRTF was involved in a genuine clean-up or merely a cover-up is one that clearly needs to be raised.

> *The state's regulatory role has also been greatly extended in care homes and private hospitals.* The Care Standards Act 2000 sets out all the areas in which Ministers may now make regulations—for private hospitals, care homes and boarding schools. It sets up the new Care Standards Commission, empowered to regulate all private and public care homes. While care homes have long been subject to some degree of regulation, *the new Commission enjoys unprecedented powers.* Persons wishing to become care workers will have to register with another new body, the General Social Care Council. (McElwee & Tyrine, 2002, emphasis added)

Haskins was chairman of BRTF from 1997 to 2002. He became Baron Haskins of Skidby when awarded a life peerage in 1998, and was recruited by Blair as "rural tsar" in 2001. The steps—or initiation rites—required of him to make the transition from a CEO to the House of Lords are unknown, to me at least. Nor do I have any plans on asking him.

Haskins also allegedly belonged to the Centre for European Reform (CER), a lobby group which, according to a well-referenced article at Wikispooks,[2] is closely associated with the American Enterprise Initiative and Atlantic Council, and appears to have "both UK and US intelligence connections as part of the UK's role as an agent for the US in the EU." As well as Haskins, its members include Jenkins protégé, Bilderberger, and high steward of Kingston upon Hull, Peter Mandelson. Haskins is also a patron of the Whitehall and Industry Group, "a body that aims to bridge the gap between business and government," and which seems to blur the line between corporations and intelligence work, specifically MI5:

> The practice of using the country's intelligence service to benefit companies is one performed in the United States for a number of years. There is evidence that it has used a communications eavesdropping system called Echelon to gather sensitive information on rivals in the European Union that has been passed on to US business. There is no suggestion that the British services intend to go that far, but this is thought to be the first time MI5 has brought in so many senior executives. (*Northern Voices*, 2012)

Haskins also belongs, or belonged, to think tanks The Adam Smith Institute and Demos, the latter being an independent organization recommended by the aforementioned Patricia Hewitt, in March 2010, "committed to radical thinking on the long-term problems facing the UK and other advanced industrial societies" (*Demos Report*).[3] The Demos Advisory Council includes CER board member and editor of the *New Statesman*, Ian Hargreaves, and Roy Jenkins's protégé David Marquand.

Whatever Haskins's affiliations with the ruling class and their abusive policies, he appears to have fallen from grace quite dramatically in 2005, when he was expelled from Labour for giving a donation to a young Liberal Democrat, Danny Alexander. Apparently there are rules against backing more than one horse in British politics; but considering the kinds of infractions that are simply business as usual within the higher echelons of power, it seems likely that somebody in those echelons was only waiting for a convenient reason to oust Haskins, and that he provided them with this opportunity. (Maybe it was even a set-up for this express purpose?) From my own point of view, in the light of what I have come to believe about power politics, his being scapegoated in this way can only speak in his favor. Or perhaps Haskins was planning for the future by backing a dark horse? Alexander is currently VP of the Asian Infrastructure Investment Bank. He was knighted in 2015.

I have almost no memories of Chris growing up, besides his Irish brogue and his love of whiskey and the fact that he liked to joke a lot. I spoke to my sister about him recently, and all she remembered was how afraid we were of having to stay with him and Gilda, because of how strict Gilda was with us. The last time I saw Chris was at my father's wake, in Hull. He was the main speaker, a fact I found darkly ironic. I had intended to speak but when I nodded to my uncle Jeffers to do so, for some reason he took the nod as my declining, and ended the ceremonies. I wasn't too regretful; the whole thing felt cursory to me. (My father had already been cremated in Barbados.)

I've avoided writing directly about Haskins until now because of his allegiance with power and the sensitivity of the material which I'm discussing. You do not stir up a hornets' nest without a good reason. At a certain point, for me at least, the consequences for not speaking out began to seem more severe than those for doing so. People are getting older and soon they will die. Peace remains unmade, truths remain concealed, traumas unhealed. Part of my fear of making this public is less reprisals than denials. Not that I expect anyone in my more distant family (besides the cousin I am in contact with) to do anything but ignore me. But even that feels fraught to me. Maybe the most hurtful response is none at all?

In fact, sometime after I wrote this, my cousin spoke to Haskins briefly on the phone and he mentioned that he'd heard about the writing I was doing. She asked him if he was bothered by it. He replied, "No. No one will read it anyway."

I wonder if that's as true as he thinks. Things are changing fast in terms of a growing public awareness of these realities, and it may be that the things I am uncovering here are a lot more relevant to common people than my uncle thinks. But even if he is right, it doesn't much matter.

There are deeper reasons to speak out than being heard.

CHAPTER XVIII

A Lamb among Wolves: Richard Dawkins, Gore Vidal, the Secret of Secrets

"The loss of the religious understanding of the human condition—that Man is a fallen creature for whom virtue is necessary but never fully attainable—is a loss, not a gain, in true sophistication. The secular substitute—the belief in the perfection of life on earth by the endless extension of a choice of pleasures—is not merely callow by comparison but much less realistic in its understanding of human nature."

— Theodore Dalrymple, *Our Culture, What's Left of It*

My grandfather sent all of his children to school at extremely young ages. My father was sent away at five, and his youngest sister, Gilda (the only other family member to suffer from the degenerative disease), was sent away at age three. I have looked into the schools but found no evidence of any direct affiliation with Fabian agendas, or with any kind of child abuse. But then, if John Taylor Gatto is right, education itself was a Fabian agenda; and in those days, people had a very different idea of abuse. Add to that the possibility that sexual interference with children may be an unacknowledged, intrinsic *part* of British schooling, particularly for the upper classes, then while the gun may not be smoking, there's definitely an echo of a shot.

In his best-selling book *The God Delusion*, Richard Dawkins describes his experience at three British boarding schools, all of which "employed teachers whose affections for small boys overstepped the bounds of propriety." Dawkins adds that, "if, fifty years later, they had been hounded by vigilantes or lawyers as no better than child murderers, I should have felt obliged to come to their defense, even as a victim of one of them (an embarrassing but otherwise harmless experience)" (2008, p. 355). He then warns against "false memories" concocted with the help of unscrupulous therapists and mercenary lawyers.

(Dawkins went on to study at Balliol College, Oxford, which a disproportionate number of Fabian Society members seem to have attended. He is also friendly with New School alumni and LSE professor Nick Humphrey, John Maynard Keynes's nephew and one-time friend of my grandfather. Humphrey dated my father's second wife, Sabitha, after she left him.)

The view that sexually interfering with children is harmless (combined with the seemingly contradictory one that a patient might invent traumatic memories of such an incident) is of course one that runs through the entirety of this investigation, and is very much the central argument for those who would exploit children for their own ends—and/or for imagined "social liberation" purposes. Except that, the social engineering programs underway, at least since Havelock Ellis, appear to be based on an even more radical belief, that sexual interference with children can actually be *beneficial* to them, at least some of the time. What's implicit in Dawkins's account is that he himself is the *proof* that these sorts of experience do no harm, being that he is now a successful, award-winning author (and social reformer), and a man of great intellectual prowess.

Dawkins follows up his personal anecdote by stating that the damage done by sexual abuse is "arguably less than the long-term psychological damage inflicted by bringing the child up Catholic in the first place" (ibid., p. 356). As evidence, he offers an anecdote about a young girl who was sexually abused in a car by her parish priest; around about the same time, a Protestant friend died and consequently the girl believed her friend had gone to hell. She wrote to Dawkins to say that the sexual fondling was just a "yucky" impression, while the memory of her friend going to hell "left a cold, immeasurable fear" that gave her nightmares (ibid., p. 357). What's interesting is how Dawkins uses the example, both to bolster his case against religion, and to downplay the psychological impact of sexual abuse. Putting the two examples of abuse side by side as an either/or—when it was clearly a case of both/ and—serves to further his *own* ideological ends. It also leaves completely unaddressed the question of whether sexual interference can harm a child's psyche in ways not immediately apparent, then or later. For example, the "cold immeasurable fear" the girl felt *consciously* when thinking of her friend's damnation might have been part of the unconscious *affect* of being molested. This would be especially so when the person who sexually molested her was also the person whom she had entrusted with *the care of her soul*: Might she not feel damned herself by such molestation, and hence all the more identified with her doomed and "sinful" friend?

My brother seemed to share Dawkins's views about both religion and sexual abuse. On one occasion in a teahouse in Soho, he passionately insisted to me that orally raping a baby would not do it any harm. When I argued with him fiercely, he would have nothing of it. Where did he come up with this idea? Based on everything I have uncovered in this investigation, this is a not-uncommon philosophy, albeit one that is generally kept private. Leaving out the very delicate question as to whether my brother was involved in such activities—as victim, perpetrator, or both—it seems likely he didn't come up with the idea at random.

Another example. After his death, it came out that (Stephen Fry's party pal) Gore Vidal had been "terrified" that William F. Buckley would release a file accusing Vidal of having sex with underage boys. According to family members, Vidal ran up a million-dollar legal bill trying to prevent this from happening. Vidal's half-sister told a Vidal biographer that she believed the records alleged that the author committed "Jerry Sandusky acts"—Sandusky being the Penn State University football coach convicted of sexually abusing young boys. Vidal also "had a 'very weird take' on the disclosures of sexual abuse of boys by priests in the Roman Catholic Church, dismissing the victims as 'hustlers who were sending signals'" (Swaine, 2013).

Vidal was also a cohort in sexual predation with the aforementioned Tom Driberg, as recounted by Christopher Hitchens in his memoir *Hitch-22*: "Rugged young men recruited from the Via Veneto would be taken from the rear by Gore and then thrust, with any luck semi-erect, into the next-door room where Tom [Driberg] would suck them dry. It shows what few people understand even now, which is the variety of homosexual conduct" (2011, p. 153).

In rather less glowing terms, the abuse researcher Ian Pace wrote about Vidal's sexual predilections, referring to his "most notorious novel, *Myra Breckinridge* (1968), specifically the passage which relates with relish the brutal rape of a teenage boy, Rusty, presented in terms of female/gay empowerment so as to titillate liberal left readers" (2014c). Pace argued that the chapter "indicates what type of a predator, rapist and child abuser Vidal was"; he then reproduces the chapter in its entirety. It is just under 9,000 words of grisly, salacious, and deliberately eroticized descriptions of Myra Breckinridge's medical rape (ending with the use of a dildo) of a young boy. Early on in the chapter, Myra persuades the boy, Rusty, to stay:

> "I'm sorry. But this is more important than your social life. After all, you want to be a star, don't you?" That was always the clincher in dealing with any of the students. They have been conditioned from childhood in the knowledge that to achieve stardom they might be called upon to do anything, and of course they would do anything because stardom is everything and worth any humiliation or anguish. So the saints must have felt in the days of Christendom, as they burned to death with their eyes on heaven where the true stars shine.

Later on, Vidal/Myra writes, "Now I sit at the surgical table, making the greatest effort to calm myself, to put it all down not only for its own sake but also for you … who never dreamed that anyone could ever act out totally his fantasies and survive."

*

> "Silence is the fourth of the so-called powers of the Sphinx, to know, to will, to dare, and to keep silent."
> —Aleister Crowley, *Magickal Diaries*

"Where once I was a universe had I become a mere star—maybe a black hole?" (Horsley, 2007, p. 316). My brother's all-consuming desire to stand out from the "mob"—to become a star—was apparently inseparable from his hedonistic quest for self-abasement, for "humiliation and anguish," and his inverted spiritual goal to "make the soul monstrous." Maybe all stars that don't go supernova implode and cave in on themselves. Are those unable to eradicate their moral sense—to fully turn decadence into a virtue, evil into good—inevitably the ones who are destroyed in the attempt—who turn their own destruction into a "dark art"?

I have cited the Vidal example because I think it provides a clue to the whole awful mess of my brother's and my childhood, and to the culture that enveloped it, and us, like an octopus's inky cloud. I think there is a view among the ruling class that sexual abuse—which they do not admit *is* abuse—is just an inescapable part of the world of the power elite. Everyone is fair game for such research/methods, and only those with the genetic mettle to turn abuse into power ever really understand the nature of the beast they are riding. The rest get thrown and trampled into the dirt.

In this view, sexual interference is, as my brother and Dawkins and Vidal saw it, a silly thing to get worked up about. Those who are selected to be part of the ruling class, who have gone through the "hazing" rituals of the private school system, Balliol, etc., have transitioned from being objects of abuse to perpetrators, acting at a consciously empowered level. The poison containers have become the poison deliverers. The sociopathic virus necessary to become one of the social engineers has taken root. We never really see the hideous truth of this, because the sociopaths present themselves to us, as social leaders and cultural heroes, as the proof of their own pudding.

To bring it down to very simple terms, and to what I know for sure: The conspiratorial legacy I have inherited is that my father hated his father and was never able, or willing, to tell us why. He died still hating him, perhaps partially because he could never talk about the reasons why. My brother also hated *his* father, and likewise died with (into?) that hatred. I am the last man standing, left staring at a powerful ancestral bond of hatred that, like Shakespeare, goes back countless generations. To begin to understand how and why this bond was created is to start to dissolve the hatred with understanding, which is the first stirring of love. But it also means looking more closely at the *reasons* for that hatred, and so finding the source of it. And the closest, most immediate source is right here and now, within myself.

At a deep level, the trauma I suffered, which perhaps we all suffer, was *betrayal trauma*. Betrayal trauma happens when someone we believe and *need* to be good turns out not to be so. When I asked for bread, I received a stone, hatred (or indifference) in place of love. After that formative experience, it doesn't feel safe for me to believe that goodness can exist *anywhere*. And in an ironic, tragicomic way, it's true, there is no "goodness" that isn't mixed up with "evil" in this world (no love without hatred), because this world is a divided sphere—"knowledge of good and evil" is the psyche split against itself. Yet I do not believe the soul can hate (only the ego can), and my challenge is to look past the ancestral stain and find the source of eternal goodness within us and *become* it. That means total, unconditional non-resistance to evil.

It is time to put down the stone I was given and look unflinchingly at the wolf within.

*

> "The work of cultural destruction, while often swifter, easier, and more self-conscious than that of construction, is not the work of a moment. Rome wasn't destroyed in a day."
> —Theodore Dalrymple, *Our Culture, What's Left of It*

Significantly, Dalrymple follows the above quote by citing an example of incremental (i.e., Fabian) cultural destruction, George Bernard Shaw's *Pygmalion!*, which caused a public sensation with the phrase "Not bloody likely!" In terms of verbal profanity, "A logic and a convention of convention-breaking was established, so that within a few decades it was difficult to produce any sensation at all except by the most extreme means" (ibid.). In the same essay, Dalrymple makes this sobering observation:

> [T]he boundless prurience of the British press concerning the private lives of public figures, especially politicians, has an ideological aim: to subvert the very concept and deny the possibility of virtue, and therefore of the necessity for restraint. If every person who tries to defend virtue is revealed to have feet of clay (as which of us does not?) or to have indulged at some time in his life in the vice that is the opposite of the virtue he calls for, then virtue itself is exposed as nothing but hypocrisy: and we may therefore all behave exactly as we choose. (2005, pp. 52–53)

In a somewhat different way, it's possible to see the galloping virus of "conspiratainment" of internet culture as having a similarly numbing effect, and hence an "ideological aim" behind it. This is known in con-spiracy research circles as "the revelation of the method": Expose the public to more and more information about the methods of our social engineers, and most people will either become gradually unhinged or paralyzed with despair. We may also—like my brother—find ourselves imitating our oppressors, even (or especially) as we discover what a morally bankrupt bunch of thugs our "betters" truly are.

The real question that drives this written investigation, of course, is: To what extent am I also carrying the power-abuse virus? *Was* I a victim of sexual interference as a child? If so, was it directly related to the groups and individuals, philosophies, methods, and goals being described here, or only indirectly? Part of me wants to write that I have no *reason* to believe I was sexually abused, while knowing that so far this book is practically a checklist of such reasons. Combine all of this with the fact that, like my brother, I exhibit countless symp-toms of being abused, from compulsive nose-picking to nighttime butt cramps and a bleeding anus, from low-level anxiety about physi-cal contact and ongoing discomfort with my sexuality to all manner of abuse-saturated dreams, nightmares, and waking fantasies—and it no longer really seems like a question of *if*, but only of when, who, how severe, how often, and under what circumstances? Yet while there is every reason to believe, I have as yet no mental memory to substantiate the belief. Yet the record of trauma is written into the cells of the body, and it is through *somatic* memory, not through the mind, that the truth eventually wills out. At least, so it has been for me (as I will get to in Part II).

For me at least, at the end of this epic uncovering of facts that may or may not make up a coherent narrative, the passage in my brother's book referring to my "marvelous beauty [as a child] which stopped strangers in the streets," and to "a pedophile invited into the family circle [who] could hardly have been expected to be indifferent," begins to look like the ferocious tip of an approaching iceberg of *affect*. If the evidence speaks as clearly as I hope it does, this affective iceberg prob-ably includes anyone who grew up in the UK or the US, in Europe or the world, during the '50s, '60s, '70s, '80s, or anytime at all. At the very least I hope this testimony makes clear that a person can be in the very thick of wolves—and even have one's psyche torn to shreds by them—and somehow maintain the illusion of living quietly among sheep, unharmed and whole.

That's the last thing this part of the book testifies to: the lasting damage done by such unwanted, undefended proximity to sexual predations and to destructive, deceptive, sociopathic ideologies. This is an ironic point, because the sheer fact of my compulsive need to map all of this out (which has gone on overtly for about five years, but which I see now has been underway my entire adult life, being what drove me to write in the first place) is the proof of how profoundly impacted I have been by those early, suppressed experiences, *whatever* they were. I have been cut off from my life force, my sense of reality; and there is nothing more tormenting than this.

If I write this, it's not because I want to but because I *have* to. Going into the past has been a way to identify all the ways in which I have been unable to *be* myself, and why: the false beliefs, values, complexes, neuroses, fears, drives, compulsions, obsessions, all sourced in a network of trauma that makes up both my own false identity and the Fabian-fueled, Savile-saturated culture that shaped it. All the ways in which I have been unable to live inside my own body, to have access to my total psyche, and to be my own man. All the ways in which my life has not been mine to live.

But compared to my brother or my father, I have been lucky. My father lived mostly for the sensual gratifications of food and sex, and for the mental and emotional relief which alcohol gave him. He was confined to a wheelchair for the last years of his life—not even a shadow of his former self (though that too), more the shadow of a self he never got to be. He was the shadow of a father I never had, living a ghost of a life, an emotional shell hiding behind the Sunday papers. Even from the first, he forbade his children to refer to him as "dad" or "father," and always as "Nick." As he denied the existence of a heavenly father, so he denied his own fatherhood.

The last time I saw him was in Barbados, where I spent a couple of weeks staying at his house. He spent the days in his wheelchair, near the pool, reading the papers and trashy novels. I sat with him some of the time but we hardly said a word. It wasn't until evening came and he had his first drink in his hand that he—and I—were able to relax enough to talk; even then, I don't think we ever had a conversation that lasted for more than ten minutes without requiring some form of artificial resuscitation. My father was like the man on the stair who was not there. To say I missed him even while he was there with me wouldn't be quite accurate though—because how can you miss what you've never had?

The legacy he left me (besides the money, which I threw away at twenty-four) was tragedy: the unlived life of the parent. My father's most treasured and frustrated goal was to write, and he was never able to do it. He was unable even to *speak* the truth of his life, about how he never got to live it. All of this that you've read has been a way for me to understand the depth of the ancestral wound I've been walking around with, the wound that crippled and then crushed both my God-denying father and my God-defying brother. It is the wound of being unable either to love or feel loved by one's own father. Understanding this, in the weirdest of possible ways via mapping this ocean of intrigue, has helped me to understand what made him the man he was, the father he was. As a result, I have come to know him, in absentia; and little by little, since to know someone is to love them, to establish him in my heart.

PART II

THE CROWLEY JOKE

"[T]he representatives of the 'counter-initiation' are in fact as completely ignorant as ordinary profane people, and more irremediably ignorant, of the essential, in other words, of all truth of a spiritual and metaphysical order, for this truth has become completely strange to them, even in its most elementary principles, ever since 'heaven was closed' to them."

—Rene Guénon, *The Reign of Quantity & the Signs of the Times*

"Magic is something primeval, heroic, unsentimental, something violent, aristocratic, bodily-concrete, which resists every abstraction, universalism, and moralisation. Magic is the plunder of the demonically imbued man."

—Ernst Schertel, *Magic: History, Theory, Practice*

"For it must needs be that offences come; but woe to that man by whom the offence cometh!"

—Matthew, 18:7

CHAPTER XIX

Pedophilia and organized ritual abuse

"While we look not at the things which are seen, but at the things which are not seen; for the things which are seen are temporal, but the things which are not seen are eternal."

—2 Corinthians, 4:18

When the omelet in mind is eternal life, is there any possible limit to how many temporal eggs can be broken? If there's one thing I've learned via all of this research it is that, the more awful the actions being implemented are, the more elaborate and profound the justifications tend to be.

Most people who enjoy eating meat would be appalled to see the conditions necessary for getting that meat into their bellies. Many of them might even become vegetarians, at least for a spell (I know I did). Just so, many of us consciously choose not to look at or dwell on certain social realities because we know they are going to make it harder for us to continue doing the things we enjoy. If we knew the truth about what makes our current civilization run, how many of us would be unable to continue to support it—or be supported by it? And what then, when there doesn't appear to be any viable alternative to civilization?

151

Perhaps the hardest thing to imagine about the secret life of the cryptocracy is that it isn't a subculture at all: it's a superculture. It's an underworld that rules over each and every one of us, and trying to see it is like trying to imagine a fifth dimension from the perspective of a fourth. Yet we also belong to this parallel world and it has always been there, acting on us in ways both invisible and oppressive—oppressive most of all *because* invisible. For what we fail to see, continues indefinitely.

If we want to pull on the string of child sexual abuse to try to remove it from our lives, are we prepared to watch as our entire social tapestry comes undone? If traumatized children grow up to be adults; if they never address, integrate, or heal their early experiences of abuse, there's a good chance they will end up unconsciously acting out those internal nightmare scenarios on their partners or their children—or on other people's children. They might have no memory of the actual events. They may have no conscious awareness of the waking nightmares which the events caused. But the feelings still trapped in their bodies may be acute enough to drive them to commit unimaginable acts in an unconscious attempt to find relief. And then, to spin elaborate mythical, ideological justifications for them.

What would be the potential, exponential escalation rate of such an equation? Would it resemble some form of multigenerational ritual abuse that forms the hidden under layer—and the backbone—of our present culture? The adult horror shows of occult-style ritual abuse are like the dark side of "creative self-expression": destructive self-repression. And yet they also have a creative, theatrical component, fueled by the same unconscious trauma as dark fairy tales or cathartic works of art. It's nearly impossible to delineate where one ends and the other begins, because it is a continuum and there *is* no actual cut-off point. These horror shows are being both openly and secretly enacted via fantasy and reality. This liminal realm of dissociation is an eerie conflation of fantasy and reality, culture and abuse. It is abuse culture: abuse that is culturally conditioned, and a culture that is fundamentally abusive.

*

"There are large numbers of people, I'm afraid, who enjoy inflicting misery on others. And when you unite that kind of sadism to a sense ... of messianic purpose, then obviously it's a very unpleasant combination .... I think there are social conditions which either encourage or discourage it but you will never eliminate this kind of behavior altogether .... And if I take my own society, I think we've done everything possible to encourage it."

—Theodore Dalrymple, *YouTube*, 2015

Referring to the open-source standards of Wikipedia, pedophilia is a single designator for an extremely wide spectrum of behaviors, ranging from the pathetic (and relatively harmless) to the most heinous and destructive acts human beings are capable of committing. The word pedophilia comes from the Greek: παῖς, παιδός (*paîs, paidós*), meaning "child," and φιλία (philía), "friendly love" or "friendship." Pedophilia is used for individuals with a primary or exclusive sexual interest in prepubescent children aged thirteen or younger. *Nepiophilia* (from the Greek: νήπιος (népios) meaning "infant" or "child" (which in turn derives from *ne-* and *epos* meaning "not speaking"), sometimes called *infantophilia*, is a subtype of pedophilia used to refer to a sexual preference for infants and toddlers (children under age five). *Hebephilia* is defined as individuals with a primary or exclusive sexual interest in eleven- to fourteen-year-old pubescents. Pedophilia supposedly emerges before or during puberty, and is said to be stable over time. It is defined as "self-discovered, not chosen," and has been described as "a disorder of sexual preference," and as "phenomenologically similar to a heterosexual or homosexual orientation." What currently keeps pedophilia mostly grouped with other "mental disorders" (unlike homosexuality) is primarily the recognition of the *harm* that pedophilic acts cause to children. Yet since the harm is often psychological in nature, this makes it by definition subjective, and hence difficult to pin down.

In fact, the word "pedophilia," in the context it's usually associated with (that of child sexual abuse), is something of a misnomer. The word means child-*love*, and yet we would hardly call someone who rapes women a woman-lover, so a better word for the sort of atrocities which this present work is addressing would be *misopedia*, meaning the hatred of children. Instead, a sexual proclivity or disorder (the desire for children) has been conflated with a criminal act (child abuse), to the point that, to most people, the word pedophile means someone who abuses children and, vice versa, anyone who abuses children is automatically identified as a pedophile. It's likely, however, that many child abusers aren't pedophiles, in the sense of being irresistibly attracted to children, just as many people who are attracted to children do not act on it. The former class—child sexual abusers who are not pedophiles—are known as "situational offenders."

> This category refers to individuals who do not display any distin-
> guishable sexual preference for children or adolescents but who
> will engage in the sexual exploitation of children if and when they
> find themselves in situations where a child is readily available for
> sexual use. "Situational sex offenders" frequently molest readily
> available children to whom they have easy access, such as their
> own or those they may live with or have control over .... It has been
> posited that the majority of perpetrators of child sexual exploita-
> tion fall into the category of situational offenders [and] that violent
> sexual offenses against children are much more likely to be com-
> mitted by non-pedophiles than by pedophiles. This clearly speaks
> to the very different motivations for offending between situational
> offenders—most likely frustration and anger, leading to a violent
> offense—and preferential offenders, or pedophiles—a misguided
> "love" and the notion that the child welcomes the sexual experi-
> ence. (Wiggin, 2016)

Such data indicates that, in cases of the sexual molestation of children, significantly fewer are committed by pedophiles—that is, people with a strong sexual preference for children, whether or not they act on it—than by situational offenders, or non-pedophiles, the figures oscillating between 16 percent and 40 percent (ibid.). So why the conflation of terms?

Whatever the motivation for it, the result has been not to increase awareness of the reality of child sexual abuse, but to narrow our perceptions around it and close down our ability to question and explore it. Reducing a complex reality to a social and moral absolute has helped to obscure a spectrum so wide and deep that it potentially includes everyone raised in our current society (and probably throughout history too). When something is as pervasive and endemic as traumatic child sexual abuse, can it even be called aberrational?

The law of the jungle is never more inconveniently at odds with the law of the state than when it comes to the question of sexual readiness. At first pass, it seems sensible to use the criterion of what causes *harm* to another to define what constitutes a sexual disorder (in this case pedophilia, as opposed to hebephilia, which while illegal and overlapping with pedophilia, is not viewed as a sexual disorder). But, as with homosexuality (or for that matter, with fully adult sexuality), the question of harm is both wide and deep.

It's noteworthy that people are talking a lot about pedophilia today but not so much about incest (which has always been rife in society). The two overlap without being synonymous, and though it's likely the majority of child sexual abuse is committed by parents, uncles and aunts, older siblings, and other family members, the kind of pedophile we hear most about is either the "stranger danger" of lone predators stalking other people's children or, more recently, that of politicians, DJs, and other high-profile public figures abusing children in a systematic, organized, and institutionally protected fashion. In these latter cases, the parents are often complicit with the abuse, to whatever degree, if not actually participating in it. (Strictly speaking, parents are always somewhat responsible for the abuse of their children, if only due to neglect.) One thing we almost never hear about is mothers who sexually abuse their children; yet this happens too, and in the available testimonies of ritual abuse, it seems almost as common as abuse by fathers. (According to author and therapist Alison Miller, mothers belonging to multigenerational organized abuse cults are taught to sexually abuse their children as infants.)

When it comes to organized sexual child abuse by the rich and powerful, as shocking as these stories are, they at least place the abuse outside what most people consider their own communities and, most important, their own homes. Yet what seems to be involved in these cases is not so much pedophilia as sadism. Since there are forms of sexual child abuse that are not sadistic, and forms of sadism that don't involve children, the two shouldn't be conflated, any more than "regular" (adult consensual) sex and sadism should be. Sadism spans the entire spectrum of human sexuality: It can inform all types of human relations, whether heterosexual, homosexual, pedophilic, or whatever else is on the menu these days. The use of sex or violence as a means to dominate others is at base of the sadistic urge, and dominating a child is a lot easier than dominating an adult. Those who have an unhealthy desire to use sex as a means of having power over and causing pain to others are likely to be drawn to children as victims: not because they are pedophiles but because they are sadists.

The clinical psychologist Dr. Lynn Daugherty, author of the 1984 book *Why Me? Help for Victims of Child Sexual Abuse (Even If They Are Adults*

Now), refers to situational sex offenders as "regressed child molesters" and describes them as:

> ... people who have wives or partners whom they are sexually active with, but who still abuse their own children. When this type of man comes under tremendous stress, he degenerates to touching or having sex with the child .... These men are often controlling, and may feel that their life is out of control. The only way to regain power is to assault a vulnerable child who cannot fight back .... Situational child molesters ... are also more likely to use force. The abuse of the child might only materialize in times of high stress .... "Regressed child molesters" could account for why so many accusers in cases of repressed memory came from a middle or upper class home where everything appeared "normal" to outside observers. (ESATDT, 2012)

With all this in mind, it may be that the problem being addressed, or rather not addressed, is less pedophilia *per se* than sadistic pedophilia, which is part of a larger problem of sadism, *per se*, and of the more destructive kinds of narcissism or solipsistic self-regard. If we dare to journey deeper still, we may be compelled to look at traumatized sexuality in all its forms, which is to say, a libido that has been polluted and distorted by sexual trauma of one sort or another. This could even include birth trauma and emotional incest, both of which are probably so common in Western families as to be pretty much the rule. So where does normality end, and abomination begin?

Such indifference to the finer points of sexual perversion and its relation to childhood trauma obviously makes life a lot harder for someone who is sexually confused or dysfunctional, and who may have certain desires that take them dangerously close to being socially condemned as a pervert. It also makes things easier for acting pedophiles and other sexual predators to slip through the net in all the confusion (look at the McMartin preschool case, which Ross E. Cheit, 2014, persuasively demonstrated was very far from mere Christian hysteria). This isn't a question of rational processes so much as emotional reactions, social contagion, and mimetic violence. Once a community is stirred into a panic-frenzy at the suspicion of inhuman predators in its midst, it invariably spills out onto more innocent bystanders. Even someone who tries to consider the perspective of the alleged pedophile can become suspect; even someone who isn't expressing what's seen as a suitable level of outrage and condemnation. Since people within a community know this instinctively, they are likely to increase their own ire to signal to others that they are "kosher." This makes escalation inevitable.

And of all of these concerned citizens, what percentage of them was sexually abused as children (with or without memory of it)? What percentage is interfering with their own children—or with someone else's? Doesn't it stand to reason that, in a small community, child abusers would be among the loudest voices decrying child abuse? It's easy to get up in arms about some newcomer in town nobody much likes, or about some distant celebrity; but what about when it's a spouse, a brother, an aunt, a mother or father? Then the standard operating procedure is to say nothing and pretend the abuse is not happening or convince oneself it isn't. This isn't so simple a matter as denial—or rather denial is anything but a simple matter. In my own experience, when abuse is occurring in a domestic or "local" context, the most common response is *not to see it* at all. When the suggestion arises that people we love and trust—or at least think favorably of—are committing acts we are socially conditioned to see as "monstrous," the cognitive dissonance may be too great and lead to our dismissing the evidence of our senses. This is another consequence of demonizing pedophiles: If our lived impression of a family member or neighbor is that they are very far from being monsters, then they must be incapable of committing the monstrous acts which the evidence suggest they are committing. Much easier by far is to accuse the victim of lying, fabricating, or being deluded.

There might even be a correlation between the denial of abuse happening in one's own family, or among trusted community members, and the ferocity of condemnation—the demonization—of child abuse in the abstract, and of abusers (or possible abusers) identified (rightly or wrongly) outside one's immediate circle. As Michael Lesher notes in *Sexual Abuse, Shonda and Concealment in Orthodox Jewish Communities*, child molestation is *condemned in the abstract but tolerated in actuality*. It is condemned abstractly partially *because* it is tolerated in actuality: because we judge and reject most fiercely in others what we cannot bear to see in ourselves. This makes condemnation of abstract child molestation a kind of *safety valve* that allows us to continue tolerating it in actuality.

Moral outrage at child sexual abuse may be the flip side of the desire to de-pathologize and normalize it, if only because moral outrage obliterates all nuance. Along with it, the possibility for compassion and deeper understanding is reduced, and dehumanization occurs. This then gives rise to a compensatory "tolerance" response: since not *all* pedophiles can be branded as "monsters" who need to be castrated or destroyed (or even as child molesters), painting them with such a broad brush stroke potentially places pedophilia in the category of misunderstood minority, and so strengthens the case for normalization.

*

> "[T]he 'need for meaning' can just as easily incorporate envy, violence, and hate. The 'warmth' of common identity can be generated through the shared 'pleasures' of persecution, gang rape or the 'joy of killing.'"
>
> —Sara Scott, *The Politics and Experience of Ritual Abuse: Beyond Disbelief* (p. 96)

Apparently, one primary reason most people dismiss the subject of organized ritual abuse is because of the connection with occultism, specifically with Satanism. Our modern materialist bent "instinctively" (unthinkingly) rejects anything that smacks of mysticism or religiosity as not credible. Add to this the strong association with mobs of hysterical, moralistic Christians, and a subject that was already highly unappetizing can all-too-easily be deemed "beyond the pale." The notion that ritual abuse of children (which is often associated with satanic imagery and ideology) can all be explained by mass hysteria, "satanic panic," and "false memory syndrome" is now widely believed. It has even been recently promoted—unconvincingly—in an execrable piece of Hollywood propaganda, *Repression*, starring Ethan Hawke. This belief is "supported" by (and supports) the equally erroneous belief that no evidence has ever been found for ritual child abuse. The truth is that the evidence is quite overwhelming, but that it has been almost entirely buried by a counter-narrative generated by mainstream media (that of a "witch hunt" driven by hysterical Christians, delusional would-be victims, and unethical therapists). Phrases such as "no proof," "just a rumor," and "satanic panic" work like a mantra which people pick up and, after hearing it and repeating it for long enough, may end up believing. Or perhaps it is more accurate to say—since I think most people *are* aware to some degree of what is occurring—that, since the dominant narrative signals "no proof" and that only the hysterical and the gullible believe such stories, people meekly go along with this assertion and choose not to speak about their own beliefs or experiences. As Sara Scott writes in *The Politics and Experience of Ritual Abuse*: "Much of the literature describing ritual abuse as a moral panic itself reads like moral panic" (p. 48). Yet statistics at the very least throw into question the ease of such dismissals:

> Bottoms, Shaver and Goodman found in their 1993 study evaluating ritual abuse claims that in 2,292 alleged ritual abuse cases, 15% of the perpetrators in adult cases and 30% of the perpetrators in child cases *confessed to the abuse*. "In a survey of 2,709 members of the American Psychological Association, it was found that 30 percent of these professionals had seen cases of ritual or religion-related abuse (Bottoms, Shaver & Goodman, 1991). Of those psychologists who have seen cases of ritual abuse, 93 percent believed that the reported harm took place and 93 percent believed that the alleged ritualism occurred. [Nancy Perry, 1992] conducted a national survey of therapists who work with clients with dissociative disorders and she found that 88 percent of the 1,185 respondents indicated "belief in ritual abuse, involving mind control and programming." Recently an online survey of over one thousand people answered questions about ritual abuse and extreme abuse crimes. In a summary of the survey, it was found that ritual abuse/mind control is a global phenomenon .... Stephen Kent, Professor in the Department of Sociology at the University of Alberta in Edmonton, believes that intergenerational satanic accounts are possible and that rituals related to them may come from a deviant interpretation of religious texts. (*Child Abuse Wiki*, 2012, emphasis added)

The nonexplanatory explanation of "satanic panic" is so effective because it itself requires no proof, and no further extrapolation. It essentially argues that, since crimes of organized ritual abuse are impossible, all reports, allegations, and even confessions, must be dismissed as hysteria. The very extremity of organized ritual abuse provides a "natural" cover for it. Such crimes are unthinkable to most "sophisticated" people, for one reason or another (though apparently not to Christians). And if we are unable to think about something, how can we expect to reach any reasonable conclusion about it? As Sara Scott writes, "The possibility that there may be *both* unwarranted panic about 'satanism' or ritual abuse in specific contexts *and* real experiences of ritual abuse (or even satanic ritual abuse) seems not to have been considered" (2001, p. 44). Simply put, the preferred notion that moral panic can explain *all* accounts of ritual abuse effectively banishes the less appealing possibility that at least *some* of the moral panic might be accounted for by a very real phenomenon, that of organized ritual abuse.

This current work is not based on the assumption that all accounts of organized ritual abuse are accurate (something that would be impossible to determine), but on the understanding that *at least some of them* have been proven (beyond reasonable doubt, e.g., Colin Batley, see next chapter) to be true, first of all, and secondly, that many people *believe* these accounts to be true, including thousands of people who (as victims of organized ritual abuse) "know" they are true. In this latter, obviously most essential group, it is possible a) they are correct; b) they are lying for some unknown purpose; c) they are deluded in ways that have not yet been explained by psychology or science. Occam's razor points to the first option, though not necessarily for everyone.

This same breakdown can be applied to many, perhaps even *as* many, believers in alien abduction, though one key difference here is that accounts of alien abduction are far less horrendous and appalling than those of organized ritual abuse (ORA), hence it is easier to imagine them as some sort of dissociative fantasy designed to protect the person from a more unpleasant reality. It would be difficult to argue this about ORA, since many of the accounts are the very definition of horror, horror that in fact is beyond most people's ability *to* imagine. Despite this we may encounter "arguments" that "a patient was so disturbed that a beloved grandmother would read scary detective magazines to her that she would rather believe and report a screen fantasy that she herself, as a young child, had witnessed or passively participated in the slaying of twelve children from her Sunday school." By such reasoning, the whole meaning and function of dissociative fantasy is inverted and rendered absurd. This seems transparently a question of denial at work, by which a supposed investigator prefers to believe that such horrendous accounts must be the stuff of fantasy precisely *because* they are so awful. This is an understandable reaction, but hardly a defensible one.

My approach here is not so much to prove that ORA exists, because I think in one form or another the proof has already been established. Rather my intention is to seek out a context in which these sorts of unspeakably horrible activities, if they *are* occurring, can be better understood. In other words, if the primary resistance to believing these stories is that they "do not make sense" within the context of what we think we know about our world, about human beings, society, religious worship, and violent abuse, then, rather than throwing out the stories, perhaps it is time to question our assumptions about these things. Put more simply still, if these accounts are *at all true*, what do they indicate about our world, about human beings and human society and the ways in which we have misperceived them, and therefore ourselves?

CHAPTER XX

None dare call it insanity: Crowley, occultism, and child sacrifice

"Yea, though I walk through the valley of the shadow of death, I shall fear no evil, for I am the meanest motherfucker in the valley."

—Anonymous

There's a saying that, once a person makes a pact with the forces of the occult, there is no getting out of it. Sooner or later, these forces will come to collect their due. Personally, I know this to be true, though not necessarily in the way the superstitious might think. If we wake the sleeping dogs of the unconscious and then close the door on them, we should not expect them to go back to sleep. Once stirred, the dogs must be released, whether to be tamed, destroyed, or to destroy the one who releases them.

The second part of this work began as an attempt to demonstrate two things. First, that Aleister Crowley—perhaps in equal parts revered as a holy sage and reviled as a diabolic scourge—both advocated and was involved in the ritualistic sexual abuse, and possibly murder, of children (as well as the torture of animals) for "magickal" purposes.

Second, that such activities are intrinsic to the occult philosophies and related social movements which Crowley participated in and which he helped make so widespread today.

It became clear to me early on that this would not work as simply a "hit piece" aimed to undermine one man's reputation. That might be my first conscious desire but underneath that was a deeper, darker, subtler, and more meaningful one: my desire to identify and extricate all the ways in which Crowley's influence—the beliefs he propagated—shaped my psychological development and behaviors throughout my adult life. To the extent that Crowley discovered and developed magickal and mystical ideas (including the most abhorrent ones he was able to conjure) to solidify his identity as "the Beast," and then generated the corresponding "confirmation" experiences to build an iron fortress on his island of "Ipsissimus," I was drawn to his legacy with the exact same ends in mind.

As with most, if not all, of the literary projects I've embarked on in the past several years, this present one has come about only partly by conscious choice. Mostly it's emerging as a reluctant response to unconscious forces I unwittingly unleashed within myself, forces that are now demanding my attention. This is something like how a man might stumble from bed and into his living room after being awoken by fierce winds that have blown his front door wide open. He might start the process half asleep and somnambulant; but by the time he gets to the door and closes it, he is fully aware of what he is doing there.

At this point in my life, it's tempting to wish I'd never *heard* of Aleister Crowley. But since that's an impossibility, it's also an infantile wish. What it leaves is the possibility of fully understanding what "Aleister Crowley" means to me. Rejecting "Satan" comes down to one thing and one thing only: taking full responsibility for my own affinities with the darkness.

The question that came to me, while undergoing the unpleasant task of reading through Crowley's journals was: Why take Crowley seriously at all? The answer is really a variation of the same question: because so many people *did* take Crowley seriously and continue to do so. Crowley's influence on Western culture is incalculable, so we may as well ask why take Hitler seriously when he was so obviously "insane." The point isn't how sane or insane a person is by the usual psychological criteria, or how demented their beliefs might seem to us.

The point is how well these beliefs have communicated and *how much they have been imitated.*

John Harrington wrote, "Treason doth never prosper: what's the reason? Why, if it prosper, none dare call it treason." Insanity that's communicated in such a way as to inspire mimesis eventually becomes something that can't be called insanity. If not normalized, at the very least it becomes the basis for a religious (or other) sort of social "movement." When insanity prospers, none dare call it insanity. What's clear from my own case is that Crowley's particular brand of insanity, his visions, and his goals, *are* highly infectious.

Aleister Crowley is of interest—and of huge, though perhaps lamentable, social importance—because his work literally spells out some of the major lynchpins of "occultic" beliefs in the nineteenth, twentieth, and now twenty-first centuries. The degree to which he merely reintroduced existing beliefs, as opposed to formulated new ones, is beyond the scope of this exploration. Suffice it to say that these beliefs have persisted at least for the past hundred years or so, and that they continue to inspire people to act on them. As such, these beliefs have to be considered real, practical, and useful, as beliefs, though the question of useful *to whom* and *for what* is another matter, and one of the primary questions of this investigation.

Crowley's claim was that the end goal—the Great Work—was the enlightenment of humanity. This is a convenient claim (if grandiose to the point of madness), because such a goal can be made to justify any and all means imaginable, most especially when morality (restriction) is considered the primary obstacle to achieving it. There's really no way to analyze the validity of the goal (though we can speculate as to how effective Crowley and his belief system have proven to be). What *can* be analyzed are Crowley's own actions, the ways in which they were a natural continuation of his beliefs (how the beliefs were the rationale or rationalization for his actions), and what some of the consequences might have *been,* for Crowley and others—including those who have followed in his footsteps to whatever degree. I am not going to argue that such beliefs are evidence of derangement, but rather something closer to the reverse: Whether or not there is truth in these beliefs, the nature of them means they are likely—I would say bound—to lead to *some degree of derangement.*

*

"For the highest spiritual working one must accordingly choose that victim which contains the greatest and purest force. A male child of perfect innocence and high intelligence is the most satis-factory and suitable victim."

—Aleister Crowley, *Magick in Theory and Practice*

The above quote (from chapter twelve of probably Crowley's most widely read book) has a footnote that reads: "It appears from the Magical Records of Frater Perdurabo that He made this particular sacrifice on an average about 150 times every year between 1912 e.v. and 1928" (1991, p. 95). Crowley later claimed that this comment about performing child-sacrificial rituals 150 times a year for sixteen years was *a joke-reference to masturbation*, made necessary by the restrictions of the time which made it acceptable to write of child murder but not of autoerotic stimulation. Once upon a time, when I knew considerably less about these things, I took Crowley at his word. The official interpretation of Crowley's coded language was later added to the text at the insistence of Martha Kunzel, a Crowley disciple and high-ranking member of the German Ordo Templi Orientis. (In passing, the reader may note how it invokes my brother's "confession" of aborting his own inner child):

It is the sacrifice of oneself spiritually. And the intelligence and innocence of that male child are the perfect understanding of the Magician, his one aim, without lust of result. And male he must be, because what he sacrifices is not the material blood, but his creative power. (Duquette, 2003)

Nonetheless, the alleged "codified" joke-claim is embedded within sur-rounding text that is far from satirical:

It would be unwise to condemn as irrational the practice of those savages who tear the heart and liver from an adversary, and devour them while yet warm. In any case it was the theory of the ancient Magicians, that any living being is a storehouse of energy varying in quantity according to the size and health of the animal, and in quality according to its mental and moral character. At the death of the animal this energy is liberated suddenly. [F]or nearly all pur-poses human sacrifice is the best .... *Experience here as elsewhere is the best teacher.* In the Sacrifice during Invocation, however, it may be said without fear of contradiction that the death of the victim should coincide with the supreme invocation. (Crowley, 1991, p. 96, emphasis added)

Author and Crowley-ite, Lon Milo Duquette explained away the infamous chapter as follows:

Crowley clothed many of his teachings in the thin veil of sensational titillation. By doing so he assured himself that one, his works would only be appreciated by the few individuals capable of doing so, and two, his works would continue to generate interest and be published by and for the benefit of both his admirers and his enemies long after death. He did not—I repeat—did *not*—perform or advocate human sacrifice. He was often guilty, however, of the crime of poor judgment. Like all of us, Crowley had many flaws and shortcomings. The greatest of those, in my opinion, was his inability to understand that everyone else in the world was not as educated and clever as he. It is clear, even in his earliest works, he often took fiendish delight in terrifying those who were either too lazy, too bigoted, or too slow-witted to understand him …. Such is the case when he wrote about sex magick. First of all, he felt bound by various oaths not to openly reveal certain secrets of sexual magick. Secondly, in the years he was writing on these subjects, one could actually be arrested for writing too explicitly about sexual matters. Unfortunately, in part 3, chapter 12 of *Magick: Book Four, Liber ABA*, where Crowley attempts to discuss theories and techniques of sexual magick, it seem he was not satisfied with being simply subtle; he went out of his way to be scandalously misunderstood. For perhaps a score of initiates on the face of the Earth at that time, chapter 12 was an informative (and in places hilarious) essay on the theory and practice of sex magick. Among other fool traps, he uses the words "blood" and "death" and "kill" to replace the words "semen" and "ecstasy" and "ejaculation." To the unwary, the entire chapter reads like one big instruction manual on human and animal sacrifice. Big joke!

As Duquette allows, as a "joke," it was in the worst possible taste and context. If Crowley wanted to refer to masturbation without risking having his book banned, there are dozens of ways he could have done so without advocating ritual child sacrifice. (In fact this "explanation" from Duquette is dubious at best, because Crowley didn't flinch from writing about his penchant for buggery—and even pederasty—on other occasions.[1]) As it is, how many people who read this chapter fell into Crowley's "fool traps" and took the prescriptions both literally and seriously? Besides avoidance of a scandal (something Crowley was hardly averse to), this was apparently (in Duquette's view at least) the whole *point* of the "joke." It was a joke *on* the undiscerning reader (and presumably British censors), a wink and a nudge aimed at twenty or so "initiates" on the planet!

It's interesting how Duquette argues that Crowley might have been using one kind of coded, concealed language to communicate magickal truths in order to refute the idea that he was using *another* kind of code, to communicate *another* set of magickal truths. The logical deduction is that it was not a matter of *either* sex magick *or* ritual sacrifice, but of both/and. And this is precisely what the text communicates. And for all his finger-wagging, Duquette conveniently sidesteps the question of how many times Crowley's "joke" might have been *acted on* since it was first printed in 1930. If Crowley was relatively unsuccessful as an author during his own life (despite being known as "the wickedest man in the world"), it was not through lack of trying. He believed he was a Grand Magus and the prophet of a New Aeon, and is now seen that way by hundreds of thousands of people (Duquette presumably among them). Such far-reaching influence was Crowley's primary goal, so he could hardly not have known, or at least hoped, that his "joke" would someday inspire hundreds, perhaps thousands, of readers—not just to moral indignation, but to loyal imitation.

From what I've come to understand after several years looking into the possibility of large-scale, systemic, ritual abuse of children, in the UK and elsewhere, one of the standard methods of perpetrators is to make "jokes" about what they do. C. S. Lewis even included a description of this method among the demons' arsenal in *The Screwtape Letters*: "A thousand bawdy, or even blasphemous, jokes do not help towards a man's damnation so much as his discovery that almost anything he wants to do can be done, not only without the disapproval but with the admiration of his fellows, if only it can get itself treated as a Joke" (2002, pp. 55–56). Jimmy Savile must have learned from Screwtape: He spoke and wrote about his abuse of minors in such a brazen and shameless way that only those in the know could ever imagine it was anything *but* a joke. Those who are in the know—and/or who are similarly inclined—recognize the tells, and signal back. All others are fooled. Of course, if all there was to go on were this Crowley passage and the "joke" footnote, it would be rash to presume anything but gross irresponsibility on Crowley's part. But there is considerably more.

The other thing Duquette leaves entirely alone is the possibility that there might be (and have been in Crowley's time) initiates who still practice animal, human, and child sacrifice for magical purposes, and that Crowley might just as likely have been signaling to them as to high adepts of sex magick, and for the same reason: because *he was one himself.* The only reason not to address this possibility is the unquestioned assumption that such practices are by definition primitive, atavistic, outdated, and therefore beneath the capacities of any civilized twentieth-century magician. In other words, that, since such rituals no longer happen anymore, Crowley could not possibly have been referring to *that* sort of "magick." But while the intelligentsia knowingly chuckle, the less sophisticated take a shovel as a digging instrument, and use it.

One person who has testified to Crowley's profound influence on programs of ritual abuse is survivor Kathleen Sullivan, who told researcher Jeff Wells:

> [M]ost of the Nazi immigrants I met as a child were fervent devotees of a religion that Hitler also seemed to strongly adhere to .... Unfortunately, their religious practices included those from ancient Egypt, freemasonry, the Kabala, and sometimes practices promoted by Great Britain's Aleister Crowley. Those practices are especially bestial and dangerous—especially for children .... My father, who was my primary mental programmer and tormentor, was big into the teachings and practices of Aleister Crowley. Dad incorporated them into his extremely gory, murderous occult rituals—particularly in the 60's. (Wells, 2005)

*

> "The best blood is of the moon, monthly: then the fresh blood of a child."
>
> —*The Book of the Law*, III:24

For the benefit of any readers who remain skeptical, regarding Crowley's complicity with—or at least accountability for—organized ritual abuse, a few detailed examples may be in order. First off, there is the fairly well-known (though little-publicized) 1969 case of the Solar Lodge, a splinter group of the Ordo Templi Orientis based in California. The O.T.O. is an international occultist organization founded at the beginning of the twentieth century by German occultists which was later reorganized around the Law of Thelema under the leadership of Crowley. The Solar Lodge case of 1969 is known as "the Boy in the Box." (Curiously enough, this is also the title Whitley Strieber used when first disclosing his childhood experiences of government mind control, in Texas in the early 1950s.[2]) A case of severe child endangerment, charges were filed against thirteen members of the Solar Lodge after their California ranch was raided by deputies of the Riverside County Sheriff's Department, on July 26, 1969. Police found six-year-old Anthony Saul Gibbons chained inside a six-foot by six-foot box (that's 6-6-6), supposedly as punishment for starting a fire. There were "'indications' Anthony was kept in the crate since June 1st—56 days" (The Bulletin, 1969).

The police report from the time described the appalling conditions of the boy's confinement, complete with nauseating stench and swarming flies. (The temperature during his confinement was as high as 117 degrees.) Apparently the reason for the boy's confinement was punishment for burning down a Quonset hut at the commune, with many of the cult's belongings and two goats also destroyed by the fire. (It was not reported to authorities.) O.T.O. members tortured the child by holding lit matches to his hand beating him "all day" with bamboo sticks. During a meeting at the O.T.O. Temple in Los Angeles, Jean Brayton "told those present that ... when it was convenient, she was going to give Saul LSD and set fire to the structure in which he was chained and give him just enough chain to get out of reach of the fire." No one, including the boy's mother (Beverley Gibbons), had any objections. One member suggested killing the child. The mother allegedly stated that it was a question of "sacrificing one to save many" (Koenig, 1999/2011). When a former member of the Solar Lodge, Candace Reos, was questioned by the police in 1969, she stated that "Brayton practised thought-control on the Lodge's members; one member ... was ordered to curb his sexual desires by cutting his wrists every time he was aroused." When Reos became pregnant, she claimed,

> Brayton was outraged, and told Reos that she would have to train
> herself to hate the unborn child. Reos went on that the children of
> the group's forty-three members were kept apart from their parents,
> and received special "training" that was given in "very severe

tones." She added that "there was a lot of spanking involved, and a lot of being enclosed in dark rooms." The teacher's punishments "left welts," and the Order parents themselves were sometimes ordered to beat their own children. (ibid.)

All of this is heavily reminiscent of Strieber's fragmented memories of military-based child abuse that included keeping children in cages, "under intense pressure, abused both physically and emotionally, until, as a defense mechanism, the child developed a second personality that the first was not aware of" (Strieber, 2003). In a word, trauma-based mind control within the context of cult activities (and, in the case of the Solar Lodge, clearly inspired by Crowley's writings).

Then there is the UK case of Colin Batley, which went to trial in 2011. In court, Batley was described as "active as a molester and rapist of children and young people for more than three decades." Batley's cult "lived in the same cul-de-sac, took part in a catalogue of abuse against children and young adults," and according to victims "used occult writings and practices to 'brainwash' them, and justify their abuse." "It is likely that you have dedicated your life since you were twelve years old to satisfying your sexual urges by whatever means at your disposal," the judge said in court. The judge "attacked the works of occultist Aleister Crowley, which inspired the Kidwelly cult. Batley and the others were said to have used Crowley's *The Book of the Law*—which praises prostitution and free sex—as a guide for their own actions." He told Batley that "he had used the occult to manipulate and control his victims" (*BBC News*, 2011b). One of Batley's victims told the court that she became pregnant as a young teenager, and "Batley told her the unborn baby was a 'child of the occult' and threatened to kill her if she spoke out" (*BBC News*, 2011a).

Defenders of Crowley's work—and of occultism in general—can always say this is simply a case of ignorant people misunderstanding and misapplying esoteric knowledge and due to their own pathologies, which to some extent is doubtless true. Far more people have been inspired by the Holy Bible to commit atrocities than have by Crowley. But in the case of the Bible, a *willed inversion* of the meanings is often involved in "satanic" practices. With Crowley, it seems more as if his works have been taken and used as *manuals*, which, after all, is how Crowley presented them ("Magick in Theory *and* Practice"). Nor is the Batley case an isolated one. According to Australian criminologist Michael Salter, "Crowley's literature has been widely linked to the practice of ritualistic abuse by survivors and their advocates, who in turn have been accused by occult groups of religious persecution" (2013, p. 38). In 2006, an Australian branch of the O.T.O. was embroiled in a brief scandal revolving around accusation of ritual child abuse. The charges came from Dr. Reina Michaelson in Victoria, founder of the Child Sexual Abuse Prevention Program, who accused the O.T.O. of "hosting parties at which naked children acted as waiters and at which members had sex with and murdered children" (Zwartz, 2006).

Michaelson was a consultant to UNICEF who completed a major research project in Vietnam on child trafficking, child labor, child prostitution, and child pornography[3]—hardly someone to make frivolous or hysterical accusations. A website repeated these charges without Michaelson's awareness or permission and the O.T.O. filed a complaint against it. Ironically, the complaint contains the fullest description of Michaelson's charges that is currently online, which suggests that either the O.T.O. members were clueless as to the principles of public relations, or that, since they were absolved from any legal repercussions, they didn't care who knew about the allegations. According to the O.T.O.'s complaint, "Michaelson said it was not a religion but a child pornography and pedophile ring, that its members practised trauma-based mind control, sexual abuse and satanic rituals to discourage its victims from complaining to the authorities, and that it condoned kidnapping street children and babies and children from orphanages for sex and sacrifice in religious rituals." The article suggested that "senior politicians and television celebrities are part of a top-level pedophile ring and have been protected by some police [and that] some members of the ring pretended to support Dr. Michaelson's campaign and became board members of her group to subvert it from within" (ibid.).

Considering her reputation and the seriousness of the charges, you would think Michaelson's claims would at least have been investigated; yet I found no evidence for it and the story has been largely buried. Only the previous year, Michaelson had called for a royal commission "to investigate her claims that Victoria Police did not properly investigate pedophile ring allegations." The O.T.O. case was settled out of court in November 2006, and the offending website was taken down in 2008, though copies of the article continue to circulate on the Net.

Within the context of the evidence presented in Part I of this work, Michaelson's charges are not only credible but depressingly familiar. They might even be described as "standard operating procedure."

CHAPTER XXI

Island of the Ipsissimus: the Abbey of Thelema

"My sole duty is then to make myself, body and mind, the perfect weapon."

—Aleister Crowley, *The Magickal Record of the Beast 666* (p. 216)

I don't remember when I first read *Magick in Theory and Practice*, when I first hit on that passage, or what I thought of it. I do know that, when I read Crowley's "explanation" of it as joke-code for masturbation, I accepted it without question. The idea that Crowley might actually have committed child sacrifice—even once, never mind hundreds of times—seemed absurd to me, the combined product of Christian hysteria and Crowley's own devilish humor. How was I so easily led to this conclusion? I think it was a combination of two factors: first, I was blissfully unaware of how endemic this sort of ritualistic violence is to our culture; second, I was largely taken in by Crowley's intelligence, insights, and spiritual charisma. I believed he was being scapegoated by ignorant people who conflated occultism with Satanism. His genuine (if misguided) bid for sexual and spiritual liberation was all-too-easy for the uninitiated to confuse with human depravity. While I had no trouble believing Crowley conspired with Hitler (as I speculated freely about in one of my earlier books), something as garish as child sacrifice seemed too … profane and unimaginative for someone like Crowley; too predictable.

The most damning evidence I found for Crowley's involvement in the sexual abuse of children pertains to the period in the early 1920s, when Crowley (then in his mid-forties) moved to Italy and set up the Abbey of Thelema in Cefalù.[1] He brought two women with him, Leah Hirsig and Ninette Shumway (her magical name was Sister Cypris, after Aphrodite), and both of them allegedly became pregnant by Crowley at the Abbey. Hirsig had a miscarriage, but Shumway gave birth to a daughter in late 1920, named Astarte Lulu Panthea. On first arriving in Sicily, Hirsig brought with her a two-year-old son named Hansi, and Shumway a three-year-old son named Howard. Crowley (who was not their father) nicknamed them Dionysus and Hermes, respectively.

> In 1921 Leah Hirsig writes in her diary: "I dedicate myself wholly to the great work. I will work for wickedness. I will kill my heart. I will be shameless before all men. I will freely prostitute my body to all creatures." In January 1920, Crowley moved to Paris with Leah Hirsig; they were soon joined in a *ménage à trois* by Ninette Shumway, and also by Leah's newborn daughter Anne "Poupée" Leah. Crowley offered a libertine education for the children, allowing them to play all day and witness acts of sex magic. (*The Wonders of Sicily*, 2015)

This last claim is backed up by many other sources, including Crowley's own writings, such as in *The New and Old Commentaries to Liber AL vel Legis*, The Book of the Law:

> The Beast 666 ordains by His authority that every man, and every woman, and every intermediately-sexed individual [Uranian? Crowley here seems to be anticipating the transgender phenomenon by decades], shall be absolutely free to interpret and communicate Self by means of any sexual practices soever, whether direct or indirect, rational or symbolic, physiologically, legally, ethically, or religiously approved or no, provided only that all parties to any act are fully aware of all implications and responsibilities thereof, and heartily agree thereto …. Moreover, the Beast 666 adviseth that all children shall be accustomed from infancy to witness every type of sexual act, as also the process of birth, lest falsehood

fog, and mystery stupefy, their minds, whose error else might thwart and misdirect the growth of their subconscious system of soul-symbolism. (1975, p. 46)

In Crowley's *Confessions*, he writes, "*The Book of the Law* solves the sexual problem completely. Each individual has an absolute right to satisfy his sexual instinct as is physiologically proper for him" (1989, pp. 874–875). On the other hand, in his commentaries he also wrote that "[A]cts invasive of another individual's equal rights are implicitly self-aggressions …. Such acts as rape, and the assault or seduction of infants, may therefore be justly regarded as offences against the Law of Liberty, and repressed in the interests of that Law" (1975, p. 43). In the same work, however, he allows that, "Physical constraint, up to a certain point, is not so seriously wrong … Some of the most passionate and permanent attachments have begun with rape … Similarly, murder of a faithless partner is ethically excusable, in a certain sense; for there may be some stars whose Nature is extreme violence" (ibid., p. 28). When faced with a nonresponsive woman, Crowley advises, a man's "proper course is to choke her into compliance, which is what she wants, anyhow" (ibid., p. 126).

In a 1938 radio interview transcribed in *Real Action for Men* some two decades later, Crowley bragged about raping a young woman at knifepoint when he was fourteen. He described it as "the day I became a man":

> I was 14 and rather big for my age, also not a little precocious, as you will see. We had a scullery maid. She was a lusty wench of 19, and she had been tormenting me for a long time. She would spy on me in my bath, sneak into my bedroom early in the morning and tickle me under the covers, lift her skirts at me, and in general do her best to arouse the young man in the boy of 14. She succeeded. I took these gestures to be frankly insistent invitations, and I attempted to accept. But she played coy and shoved me away. After a few such rejections and her tantalizing fraud continuing, I caught her alone one morning in the scullery when all the house was away somewhere. What I was unable to accomplish by sheer muscular power, I managed by the ever-so gentle pressure of boning knife to throat, and thus this treacherous lass of 19 got her come-uppance from a mere stripling of 14. (Burke, 1957)

Crowley refers to this incident obliquely in his *Confessions*, without describing it as a rape and focusing primarily on two things: his cunning in enlisting a local tobacconist to provide an alibi when the maid leveled charges against him; and absolving himself of all responsibility for his actions by blaming them on the repressive *Christian* attitudes towards sex prevalent at that time. "The individual is not to blame for the crime and insanity which are the explosions consequent on the clogging of the safety valve. The fault lies with the engineer."[2]

Crowley's avocation of total sexual freedom and a shedding of *all* inhibitions was central both to his life and his mission. Until recently, I never thought much about whether that could include sex with children. To this day, I am still wrestling with how easily this aspect of our culture conceals itself and how unconsciously complicit we are with keeping it concealed. Since an open practice and endorsement of sex with children is unthinkable to us, we can't think about it. So when we see evidence for it (as everyone who knew Jimmy Savile did), our tendency is simply not to believe it and to assume it must be evidence for *something else*. Now that I have seen this mechanism and how it works, it's hard for me not to imagine that I see it everywhere.

Crowley's credo included satisfying all sexual desires, combined with an insistence that any kind of sexual repression distorts the essential (sexual) nature of children. So how exactly did Crowley draw the line, once these "instincts" were in play, between allowing children to watch adults engaging in sex acts and allowing, or encouraging, them to *participate*? The only way to prevent this from happening would be to make that line both very clear and very firm. There is nothing of the sort, either in Crowley's prescriptions (and proscriptions), or in the accounts of what occurred during his time at the Abbey.

*

> "[T]he Antichrist must surely be the most 'deluded' of all beings."
>
> —Rene Guénon, *The Reign of Quantity*

It was also during this period (1920–21) that Crowley's disciple Raoul Loveday moved to the Cefalù Abbey with his wife Betty May. While Loveday was devoted to Crowley, Loveday's wife apparently detested

Crowley, and went on to make a series of denunciations of what occurred at the abbey. She claimed they were required to cut themselves with razors every time they used the pronoun "I" (a fairly well-known magical practice and one Crowley almost certainly prescribed). She also claimed that Loveday was made to drink the blood of a sacrificed cat (probably true). It was largely May's complaints to the British press, on her return from Italy, that led to Crowley's being labeled "the wickedest man in the world." Supposedly Crowley was unable to afford the legal fees to sue the press, as a result of which the stories were picked up by newspapers in North America and throughout Europe. In April 1923, Mussolini's government forced Crowley to leave Italy, though whether this was due to the stories of sexual depravity or because of Crowley's affiliations with British intelligence, or both, is hard to say (or to the creation of anti-fascist propaganda, see Pasi, 2014, p. 127). Whatever the case, the abbey closed. Loveday died from a liver infection in February 1923, supposedly due to drinking from a local polluted stream, though one has to wonder about that ritual.

In *A History of Orgies*, Burgo Partridge confirms May's account and adds to it:

> Inside the abbey, the Beast ruled with a rod of iron. His women had to dye their hair alternately crimson and black. The verbal use of the first person singular was prohibited, and punished by self-inflicted wounds. Drugs lay about the house. Even Crowley's son, aged five [Partridge means Hansi], was an addict. This child remarked to the outraged Betty: "You must leave me alone! I am beast number two, and can shatter you!" (1960, p. 218)

(On the following page, Partridge describes the killing of the cat and the drinking of its blood.) In her diary, May claimed that

> The children [at the abbey] were allowed to run free, even being allowed to witness the sexual relations of the residents. Crowley believed this would alleviate any "repression" the children could develop. The children received almost no discipline and problems soon arose, the Scarlet woman's child Hansi [Hirsig's son] contracted the cigarette habit at the age of five and was such a "fiend" you never saw him without one in his mouth.

The belief that May exaggerated her claims, combined with the well-known prurience of the British press in publishing the most sensationalist scandals it could find (or fabricate) about Crowley, have allowed most Crowley students to dismiss these charges as yellow journalism. Yet the facts suggest that May's charges were the *least* of what was occurring at the abbey. In her memoir, *The Laughing Torso*, Welsh artist and painter Nina Hamnett, who was briefly Crowley's lover as well as Roger Fry's (and close friends with Augustus John), writes of black magic at Cefalù and mentions how "one day a baby was said to have disappeared mysteriously" (1932, p. 173). Crowley attempted to sue Hamnett for defamation but the court ruled against him due to the undeniable evidence regarding "black magic" practices at the abbey. This incident is mostly reported by Crowley biographers to show how he lost the case because of general Christian hysteria, not because of any evidence of a missing baby. This latter question is never raised, perhaps because it's assumed there were no babies to go missing and Hamnett's claims were simply the result of superstitious villagers confabulating tales. (Hirsig's and Crowley's second child reportedly miscarried after the death of Poupée, so it's possible the child was sacrificed and the miscarriage was a cover story designed to conceal this intention.)

In Crowley's diary entry, from August 12, 1920, reprinted in *The Magickal Record of the Beast 666* (edited by John Symonds and Kenneth Grant), Crowley wrote about his "Scarlet woman":

> Her breasts itch with lust of Incest. She hath given Her two-year bastard boy to Her lewd lover's whim of sodomy, hath taught him speech and act, things infinitely abhorred, with Her own beastly carcass. She hath tongued Her five-month girl, and asked its father to deflower it. She hath wished Her Beast to rape Her rotten old mother—so far is woman clean of Her! Then Her blood is grown icy hard and cold with hate; and her eyes gleam as Her ears ring with a chime of wedding bells, dirty words, or vibrate, cat-gut fashion, to the thin shrieks of a young child that Her Beast-God-Slave-Mate is torturing for Her pleasure—ay! and his own, since of Her Cup he drank, and of Her soul he breathed. (1972, pp. 251–252)

The passage describes the sodomizing of a two-year-old boy; the oral abuse of a five-month baby girl; the invitation to rape the same infant; and the sadistic torture of at least one of these children. Apparently, this material is not considered worthy of serious consideration (as anything but a poetic flight of fantasy) by Crowley scholars, or by those who practice and propagate his magickal doctrines in one form or another. I have yet to hear a credible argument for this passage being an obvious literary fantasy rather than a confession, however. Once again, it may be worth drawing parallels with Jimmy Savile, who admitted to a number of crimes in his autobiography *As it Happens*, none of which were picked up for almost forty years, by which time he was dead. I doubt if anything would have come out about Savile except for the growing number of victims who came forward and testified to the abuse they suffered at his hands. Nothing of the kind has happened in the case of Crowley, who died in 1947 in relative obscurity. In fact, where Savile was seen as a philanthropist and cultural hero in life, and a monster after his death, Crowley's arc has been the reverse.

One of the reasons Savile's victims were willing and able to come forward in 2012 was that they became aware of each other via the internet, and were emboldened to speak out. There was nothing of the sort in place after Crowley died, or for another several decades. Now such possibilities exist, the youngest of his possible victims would be seventy, and any living victims from the Abbey of Thelema period would be in their nineties. Add to this the fact that, unlike Savile, Crowley left a literary estate that has proven to be a considerable financial benefit to all kinds of people, giving rise to a bona fide (if marginal) religion, and it's easy to see how vested interests in keeping Crowley's name and reputation relatively untarnished are, shall we say, legion.

CHAPTER XXII

To the assault! or: why *should* we take Crowley seriously?

"I myself think that the spiritual idea of revolt against restrictions is the father of the act. It is a ceremonial protest against American Ideals."

—Aleister Crowley, *The Magickal Record of the Beast 666* (p. 257)

Shortly after I started work on this piece and it began to expand outward in every direction, I came across a recent, self-published work by Richard T. Cole called *Liber L Vel Bogus*. Cole's book purports to offer proof of the falseness of Crowley's "reception narrative" around *The Book of the Law*. What struck me most about it, however, was that he singles out the same journal entry from August 12, 1920, as *a turning point* in Crowley's trajectory:

I believe that Crowley's singularly infamous (in consequence of its immortalisation on page 251 of Grant and Symonds *The Magical Record of The Beast 666*) diary entry represents the pivotal moment of his life. Not in consequence of alleged child abuse overtones. Rather, because at that moment Crowley glimpsed the extent of an almost immeasurable divergence between the hypothetical "ideal" of his construct, Thelema (as depicted in *The Diary of a Drug Fiend*), and its comprehensively grim reality—An insight that undoubtedly terrified him.

Although Cole doesn't devote any time to exploring whether the journal account implies *actual* child abuse (he dismisses it as porn by Hirsig to inspire Crowley's lust), he does substantiate the reality of these passages by pointing out a couple of entries before and after the notorious passage, entries which, in my squinty-eyed Crowley-fatigue, I had managed to miss. Cole writes:

> At 8:46 AM, Crowley decides it's time to quit stalling and "get to the point."—He writes, "*To the assault!*" Even so, his final dash at the summit takes a long, circuitous route. Pushing off with a confidence boosting assertion that his literary powers surpass those of Keats and Shakespeare, Crowley then launches into a sustained tirade against himself! Each subsequent paragraph exposes deeper layers of self-contempt, loathing and disgust. After spewing two pages of almost unreadable bile over his own character and life Crowley succeeds in whipping himself into enough of a (cocaine-fueled) frenzy to dare expose the raw nerve he's been tentatively prodding for nearly nine hours.

There then follows the infamous passage, which Cole quotes in full, and then adds his own commentary:

> Three days later, at 9 PM on 15 August, Crowley writes, "*Everybody sick or damaged; all a mess.*" An observation made only four months into his grand experiment and, as those with an interest are aware, the "mess" didn't improve. In fact, things got worse, much worse. By the time Crowley was forcibly ejected from Sicily (April 1923), his dream of launching Thelema as a New World religion was dead and buried beside the corpses of his two children and devoted disciple Raoul Loveday ... In the months following his expulsion, Crowley considered suicide and—unbelievably—reverting to Christianity!

This reading is very different from the official one—the one propagated by Crowley and picked up by Kenneth Grant and John

Symonds et al.—which is that, by this time, Crowley had attained the grade of "Ipsissimus," or total enlightenment.

*

"Compared to the finite nature of the traumatized soul, the traumatic event seems infinite, all-powerful, and wholly other."
—Greg Mogenson, *A Most Accursed Religion*

While Cole may be right that it's impossible to say with absolute certainty if Crowley committed infant rape and torture anywhere outside of his own drug-soaked visions, what *has* been corroborated by various sources is that he presided over the sacrifice of a cat at the abbey during this same period. Crowley's hagiographer John Symonds wrote about the sacrifice, and Crowley's associate during the period, after he initially denied it, eventually confirmed it. This is reported by Crowley's most recent hagiographer, Richard Kaczynski (the very antithesis of a muckraker), albeit it in an endnote at the back of the book:

> Crowley conceded that a wild cat had caused some damage at the Abbey, but stressed that he certainly never sacrificed it. Neither was he a hater of cats, for Yorke states that, in later years, Crowley kept one as a pet. In a letter to Roger Staples dated September 25, 1963, Yorke wrote, "Symonds is wholly incorrect about the death of Loveday and the sacrificed cat at Cefalù. He would follow the newspaper accounts of the day which were mostly fabrication by Betty May." However, on November 3, 1963, Yorke conceded to Staples (private collection), "The cat was indeed sacrificed. It had been making a nuisance of itself by keeping the Cefalù inhabitants awake at nights. So AC used it for a blood sacrifice .... Loveday made a bosh of cutting its throat and it crawled out of the consecrated circle. Technically this broke the circle and let undesirable elements in. (Kaczynski, 2012, p. 645)

Besides establishing that (whatever Duquette has to say) Crowley didn't draw the line at blood sacrifice, this also shows that he was perfectly capable of lying to conceal some of his more questionable magickal activities—a fact which surely shouldn't come as a surprise to anyone. It also suggests that the "wild" accusations of Betty May might not have been fabrications, or even exaggerations, at all, though to this day they are generally seen as such. Despite the evidence of Crowley's journals, his description of the same period (1920) in his *Confessions* is so anemic that it suggests Crowley never expected his journals to see the light of day, and was confident that his own official version would be the one that survived:

> What struck us as the best joke in the whole article [in a British newspaper] was the description of the abbey as a focus of all possible vices. We were all drug fiends devoting ourselves uninterruptedly to indulgence in all conceivable sexual abominations. [In fact] our morality compared favorably with that of the strictest puritan. The only irregularity that had ever occurred at any time was intercourse between unmarried people, which is, after all, universal in good society, and in our case was untainted by any objectionable features apart from the question of formality .... By this particular period, our conduct was so moral by the strictest standards that it would not be matched by any community of equal numbers in the world. (1989, p. 915)

The question is what sort of morality were Crowley and his followers observing? Thelemic morality, after all, is "do what thou wilt." When Crowley killed a cat, it was part of a Thelemic ritual. It would have been intended with the cool, rational intent that befits an ongoing mystical process of sexual and spiritual transformation (however delusional). So if Crowley was capable of killing a cat for "magickal" reasons, what *else* was he capable of under the guise of similar rationales, and which he would view as Thelemic, and hence highly moral, behavior? Crowley lived for excess, as prescribed by his personal bible: "But exceed! exceed! Strive ever to more." This pattern began early. In Crowley's own *Confessions*, he describes the torture and murder of a cat at the age of fourteen. Crowley prefaces his grisly account with the following disclaimer: "no question of cruelty or sadism arises in the incident which I am about to narrate."

> I had been told "A cat has nine lives." I deduced that it must be practically impossible to kill a cat. As usual, I became full of ambition to perform the feat. (Observe that I took my information

unquestioningly *au pied de la lettre*.) Perhaps through some analogy with the story of Hercules and the hydra, I got it into my head that the nine lives of the cat must be taken more or less simultaneously. I therefore caught a cat, and having administered a large dose of arsenic I chloroformed it, hanged it above the gas jet, stabbed it, cut its throat, smashed its skull and, when it had been pretty thoroughly burnt, drowned it and threw it out of the window that the fall might remove the ninth life. In fact, the operation was successful; I had killed the cat. I remember that all the time I was genuinely sorry for the animal; I simply forced myself to carry out the experiment in the interest of pure science. The combination of innocence, ignorance, knowledge, ingenuity *and high moral principle* seems extraordinary. It is evident that the insanely immoral superstition in which I had been brought up was responsible for so atrocious an absurdity. Again and again we shall see how the imposition of the anti-natural theory and principles of Christianity upon a peculiarly sane, matter-of-fact, reality-facing genius created a conflict whose solution was expressed on the material plane by some extravagant action. (ibid., p. 74, emphasis added)

It's hard to imagine a more questionable passage, as regards Crowley's moral character. Yet *The Confessions* was written in 1923, just after Crowley left Sicily, having *in his own mind claimed the highest possible "grade" of human spiritual evolution*. With a chilling lack of empathy, he describes the sort of behavior known to characterize adolescents who grow up to become violent criminals, even serial killers. His cool ratiocination blames it on an absurd superstition, which he denounces as "insanely immoral," while his torturing a cat is characterized as the result of his prodigious genius and "high moral principle"—unfortunately oppressed by his Christian upbringing. And thirty years later, he was still committing almost identical behavior, and still rationalizing it in the same manner.

*

"Crowley created a blueprint that enabled any initiate or dabbler with some aptitude for dissociation to experiment with magic and occultism and achieve at least psychological results.

> Prior to Crowley, dabblers might be deterred by a total lack of results and go on to dabble in something else. For those who lacked this aptitude, Crowley endorsed the use of drugs for the initial expansion of consciousness."
>
> —Martin H. Katchen, "The History of Satanic Religions"

Without going into the question of what makes a psychopath, what seems more compelling than Crowley's possible pathologies is the question of how such a personality type—without concealing many of his more overtly destructive qualities—could become a figure of the highest cultural significance and be remembered, not as an example of runaway psychopathology, but as one of the great spiritual teachers and pioneers of his time. This isn't merely a case of a few thousand Crowley apologists. It's more complex and mysterious than that.

In the rather salacious (and very brief) Colin Wilson biography, *The Nature of the Beast*, Wilson mentions some Crowley papers cited by Oliver Wilkinson (the son of the Crowley executor, author Louis Wilkinson, a lifelong friend of Crowley's). According to Wilson, "[T]here is a description of [Crowley] tying a negro to a tree, cutting a hole in his stomach, then inserting his penis" (2005, p. 153). With any other subject, I would have expected hordes of researchers to be eager either to prove or disprove a claim of this sort; instead, it has been entirely ignored. How is it possible for a charge of such gravity to have gone unaddressed for this long? I found no mention of it in any other Crowley biography or book on the occult (besides one about Satanism and ritual abuse), and found only a few sites on the entire World Wide Web quoting Wilson's book. These be grave mysteries indeed.

The most recent Crowley biography is *Perdurabo: The Life of Aleister Crowley* by Richard Kaczynski (who is also staff affiliate at Yale University's Department of Psychiatry), and it issues from the leading New Age publisher, North Atlantic Books. In it, there is no mention of tree-bound Negroes, teenage cat murders, his raping the family servant at knifepoint, or of the most damning 1920 journal entries that suggest a predilection for, and avocation of, child rape. The Cefalù cat sacrifice is described in a single paragraph with an endnote. The author skirts the question of Crowley's being sodomized as an adolescent. He also takes him at his word when he writes that Crowley had "a happy boyhood through age ten" (2012, p. 14)! Yet boys who have happy childhoods do not rape servants or violently kill cats (unless they are born

psychopaths). The biography reads more like a novel than an exploration, repeatedly regurgitating Crowley's version of events as a linear
narrative that precludes any doubts as to the reliability of the narrator.
Kaczynski winds up his 562-page nonfiction narrative with a paragraph
about Crowley's enduring spirit:

> Crowley's admirers have grown steadily in number since the 1970s,
> and it's easy to see why. He was a fascinating mix of titillation, mys-
> tery and discovery, eccentricity and substance; a misfit in his own
> time but a forebear of social changes that would not occur until well
> after his death. Half a century before Timothy Leary told the flower
> children to "Tune in, turn on, drop out," AC had experimented
> with drugs as an adjunct to consciousness expansion. By the time
> the Beatles had discovered meditation as a consciousness-altering
> alternative to drugs, Frater Perdurabo had already been there too.
> When the birth control pill sexually liberated a generation, they
> found the Beast had kept a light on in the window. And before the
> 1980s were dubbed the "Me Generation," the prophet To Mega
> Therion had made a religion out of individuality. Rock music offers
> a prime example of AC's persistent presence in our culture, as he
> has been embraced by psychedelic rock in the 1960s, hard rock in
> the 1970s, heavy metal in the 1980s, goth and industrial music in
> the 1990s, and progressive metal in the twenty-first century. In our
> jaded modern age, magick offers an opportunity for adventure
> and discovery in the only uncharted domain that doesn't require a
> space shuttle: the spirit. Crowley may be gone, but look around: the
> spirit of Frater Perdurabo endures.[1]

Is it any wonder, with PR management like this? There is no question at
all, in Kaczynski's lionizing of Crowley, that the values that have been
"sold" to us—drug use, the Pill, sexual liberation, pop and rock music,
individualism—are anything but positive. Nor is there any question
that they are the expression of a genuine spiritual transformation and
not part of cynical social manipulation. Seventy years after his death,
the transgressive, pleasure-seeking, "spiritually liberating" (and ego-
aggrandizing) values exemplified by Crowley's life are almost universally accepted components of the "enlightened" neoliberal lifestyle.

It's worth pausing a moment here to mention that, on *Late Night
America* in 1980, Timothy Leary described himself as "an admirer of

Aleister Crowley" who was "carrying on much of the work that he started over a hundred years ago." Leary continued: "I think the Sixties themselves, you know, Crowley said, he was in favor of finding your own self, and 'Do what thou wilt shall be the whole of the law!'—under love! It was a very powerful statement. I'm sorry he isn't around now to appreciate the glories that he started." (Leary cites Crowley wrongly here, intentionally or not: Thelemic law, significantly, is "love under will," not will under love.)

> The irony of this, though, is that Leary didn't drop out or subvert authority. Much like the way the CIA funded abstract expressionism, Leary was doing research at an ever-prestigious Ivy League college [Harvard] which consisted of experimenting on prisoners (see the Concord Prison Experiment). This isn't all that different than in the 1950s when the CIA launched Project MKULTRA, which administered LSD to unwitting participants as a means toward experimenting with mind control. In fact, prior to meeting Leary, in 1959 [beat poet Allen] Ginsberg participated in experimental studies of LSD at Stanford University, which it turned out were administered by psychologists working for the CIA to develop mind-control drugs. Leary also began experimenting on writers. (Nikolopoulos, 2014)

Leary got his career start when he was discovered by Mary Pinchot Meyer in 1961. She was having an affair with John F. Kennedy at the time, and allegedly recruited Leary to dose the president with LSD. Previously, Pinchot Meyer had been married to Cord Meyer, and Meyer worked under Allen Dulles in the CIA from 1951 to 1977. According to Howard Hunt's son, Meyer was involved in the assassination of Kennedy. After the assassination, Pinchot Meyer told Leary that it was a conspiracy. She was murdered in highly unusual circumstances in late 1964. According to Leary's recollection of meeting Pinchot Meyer (1990, pp. 154–156), she revealed to him some startling information about the involvement of the CIA in domestic US affairs. She might well have had inside information about this, since her ex-husband Meyer was the "principal operative" of the aforementioned Operation Mockingbird, a plan to secretly influence domestic and foreign media (Goldman, 2015, p. 248). Pinchot Meyer allegedly told Leary that the CIA started the American Veterans Committee, a liberal veterans group that Leary belonged to after the war. She then told him that the CIA "creates the radical journals and student organizations and runs them with deep-cover agents … dissident organizations in academia are also controlled." Not only had the CIA been running left-wing groups as fronts, she said, but Leary himself was "doing exploratory work the CIA tried to do in the 1950s." "Since drug research is of vital importance to the intelligence agencies of this country," she told him, "you'll be allowed to go on with your experiments as long as you keep it quiet."

As it happens—the world of social engineering being such a small one—the Unabomber Ted Kaczynski was also at Harvard during the same period as Leary. In his sophomore year (1959), Kaczynski was recruited for a psychological experiment that lasted three years and involved psychological torment and humiliation. It has been widely speculated that these experiments were contributing factors in Kaczynski's decision (giving him the benefit of autonomy) to become a serial bomber. The behavioral experiments—which had marked parallels to the then-active MKULTRA program—were conducted by Henry Murray, who "is said to have supervised psychoactive drug experiments, including Leary's."

Like his mentor and cultural forerunner Crowley (whose intelligence work may have been as central to his goals as his magickal operations), Leary functioned as both an agent for the intelligence community and a *seemingly* independent cultural pioneer, pushing past the boundaries of social, intellectual, and moral convention, in the ostensible interests of "individual freedom." Researcher Joe Atwill has coined a term for this: "lifetime actor." These are the spies that never come in from the cold. If so, maybe this accounts for the seemingly incomprehensible obtuseness practiced by Crowley biographers, apologists, and endorsers everywhere, as they weave their titillating and relatively untarnished narratives. It's all in the family.[2]

CHAPTER XXIII

Hangdog with a Hard-On

"I never really had any choice about seeking and forging a relationship with Lucifer—a relationship of equals—since I believed He was intent on making my life Hell to make sure I paid him mind. That, I reasoned, was the nature of divine (and satanic) discontent: my awareness of the forces within me caused me to suffer (the damnation of "self"), while simultaneously, my suffering drove me into a fuller awareness of the divine (and satanic) nature of the forces inside me. A soul caught in flames of purgatory that can last a lifetime has no recourse besides endurance …. My body had been designed expressly as a host for a specific force and intelligence, and it was that force alone that could sustain me. If I denied it access (or release) it would have no qualms about destroying me."

—Jasun Horsley, *Hang-Dog with a Hard-On*

Traditionally (or should I say *counter*-traditionally?), pacts with the devil are sealed by some sort of blood oath. This kind of act—whatever our atavistic leanings—has little appeal to our sophisticated twentieth-century sensibilities. If we are going to take the mark of the beast, we first want to be sure the needle has been sterilized. Over the millennia, individuals have most commonly been drawn to Lucifer—or the equivalent force/entity—when seeking that most coveted of human resources: power (and its esoteric brother, knowledge). To this day, even without looking at some of the modernized, sterilized updates, there are rites and ceremonies said to literally bestow superhuman abilities upon those who practice them. All of these rituals are said to exact a price.

I was raised by secular intellectuals who were, if anything, *anti*-Christians, and even when I wandered into the Chapel Perilous of occultism I had little conscious interest in such a mundane goal as worldly power. I was drawn to the idea and archetype of the Fallen Angel in the more romantic spirit of artistic exploration, in the tradition of Byron, Shelley, Poe, Dostoyevsky, or (perhaps the most a propos example) Roman Polanski. There was never any *conscious* emotional motivation for my "pursuit" of knowledge, unless intense curiosity can be considered an emotion. When such an emotional impetus did finally become conscious in me, it came—no doubt tellingly—in the form of rage. I suspect that all powerful drives for power, no matter how well dressed-up in spiritual or philanthropic robes, are fueled by this same basic, primal emotion.

Still, it took me years to even begin to see the unconscious psychological complexes fueling and shaping my conscious interest in, and pursuit of, occultism. In 2011, after a series of catastrophic endings in my life that began with the death of my brother, I put together a "shamanic memoir" that remains mercifully unpublished. I first called it *Confessions of a Sin-Eater*, and then *Hang-Dog with a Hard-On*. During the process of collecting and arranging what I considered my sorcerer's stories, I discovered that the two most obvious themes running through it were sex and cats. The following is from a chapter of that unpublished memoir, called "Anima Enactments: Unholy Pacts, Awkward Facts, & Abandoned Cats."

> What is it about cats that they mean so much to me? It goes all the way back before memory begins. Accounts of my childhood are peppered with incidents involving cats, starting with Cocoa, a cat I allegedly dyed purple (using some kind of powder paint) for my amusement. I also allegedly put Cocoa inside the washing machine, without turning it on (I probably didn't know how to). There may have been more incidents, and the official story about Cocoa was that she ran away due to my treatment of her.
>
> (Recently, while speaking to my sister, she told me that our father was especially fond of cats, something I hadn't known before that

moment, despite his being dead for twelve years. If so, maybe my strange treatment of the family cat was related to this?)

When I was eight or nine (and our father was no longer living with us), I tied our ginger cat, Sophie, to my sister's piano with a piece of string. The knot around the cat's paw was extremely tight and I was aware that she was afraid. I wasn't simply playing (though it may have started out that way), I was tormenting her. As I remember, vaguely, once I realized this I felt ashamed and let her go. (This may be a faulty memory: a friend of my brother's from that time remembers finding the cat and untying her.) In adulthood, almost as if it were payback for those early transgressions, I underwent a string of traumatic events involving cats. A cat my sister and I had when I was twenty, Travis, gave birth to kittens. We were shocked because we were sure Travis was a male (I named him after *Taxi Driver*'s Travis Bickle), and because the vet had already diagnosed "him" with stomach cancer. As if undergoing sexual identity crisis, Travis hid her kittens under the floorboards outside my bedroom and abandoned them. They died there.

There followed a series of traumatic encounters with cats during the ten-year-period leading up to my thirtieth year, culminating in an experience—too long to go into—in which I underwent a personal betrayal by someone who had promised to take care of my cat, Gobbolina (who I had named after a children's book about a witch's cat). In my grief and fury, I performed a ritual that included cutting the palm of my hand to draw blood, and making an oath to "Lucifer." I swore to either rescue my cat or avenge her. As far as I know, this was the first occasion on which I consciously and verbally pledged myself to "the devil," and once again, the incident centered on a cat. (For the concerned reader, I *was* able to rescue her, and no vengeance proved necessary.)

*

"Is a God to live in a dog? No! but the highest are of us. They shall rejoice, our chosen: who sorroweth is not of us."
—*The Book of the Law*, II:19

It was soon after, in my early thirties, that I entered all the way into my own "God complex." Like Crowley, I was convinced I was an avatar of Lucifer/Horus whose task was to bring about the liberation of humanity (Crowley having botched the job). Compared to what is known of Crowley, my own "embodiment" of, or possession by, this God-complex was relatively mild. At its peak, I was taking weekly doses of the powerful hallucinogen salvia divinorum and smoking a fair bit of marijuana and tobacco (but no alcohol or cocaine). I belonged to no occult fraternities, secret societies, or intelligence organizations. I had not channeled a scripture which I·believed to be the Word of the New Aeon, nor had I undergone any initiation rites. While a small group of young people saw me as a shaman and hung around me for hallucinogenic ritual parties, I had no followers as such, and certainly nothing to compare to L. Ron Hubbard, Jack Parsons, or Tom Driberg for disciples. All in all, as an environment for ego inflation, my own experience was less than a *tenth* of what Crowley underwent, over the fifteen or so years leading up to his infamous sojourn in Cefalù. Yet even in such a relatively mild state of archetypal possession, I discovered I was capable of things that are painful to recount.

The period in my life that most closely resembles Crowley's Cefalù period was in the year 2000, the year I turned thirty-three. This was, perhaps not coincidentally, also the year my brother underwent his crucifixion experience in the Philippines, during which he participated in a local Easter tradition and was nailed to a cross (though only his hands, not his feet). I was living in a medium-sized rustic house near Lake Atitlan in Panajachel, Guatemala, with three young Guatemalan women and several cats. While I was not sleeping with any of the women (though I had slept with one of them, once), it was not through lack of trying. Having three beautiful women in my house meant the house was a magnet for several young Guatemalan men (really boys), hence the series of vaguely ritualistic drug parties. All of this came to an explosive climax over a period of several weeks in the summer of 2000. A few notes from my journal at the time will give some idea, both of my circumstances and my headspace at the time.

> Now all these women wish to be seduced by me but of course are committed to never admitting it, since the male in the equation, in order to prove worthy of the challenge, must overcome all obstacles, including total denial. If necessary, he must use force. But if he uses force too soon (i.e., when unnecessary), he will destroy everything, and come off as just another cad, instead of a high sex magician.

... Yesterday was the breakthrough that I have been dreaming of and working towards for around 14 years, ever since I realized that such a thing was even possible. What thing, you ask? To become a fully functional Magician, or Juggler. And the price is not the soul, sold to the devil, but the mind, swallowed up in God. [Salvia divinorum] takes you out of yourself and fills you with Something Else, and You have now become Infinity, and "you" is still there, like a grain of sand in a whirlwind, roughly, and the whirlwind is the new You. And there is a fight at first, and I feel myself resisting Them, as if there was a Them that is not I!

... My greatest dream and worst nightmare come true at the same time. Four women [a fourth, a teenager, arrived briefly but did not stay] in a witchlike state of mutual joy bordering on hysteria, all laughing insanely as they beg, cajole, hound, and entice yours truly to dance for them, to let the devil out and satisfy them. CAN YOU IMAGINE THAT? I am happy and proud to say that though I didn't oblige them, exactly, nor did I lose my cool, sweat, blush, stammer, or say anything stupid. That alone I lay claim for as one of my most heroic deeds in this short and crazy life. Lesser men would have committed ego suicide. And that's where we stand, with me not quite ready to quit my day job and become a professional orgasmatron (Ipsissimus), just yet. But it is just a matter of time.

As it happened, what was just a matter of time was my first real psychotic break. A few weeks after this "peak," I assaulted one of the women I was living with, Silvia, out of a combination of sexual frustration and emotional despair. A few days after that, I almost killed an intruding cat with my bare hands. It had been sneaking in at night and eating the food in the kitchen (both my cats' food and my own) and my attempts to scare it away had failed. One night, I snapped and managed to get hold of the cat. I very nearly strangled it to death.

As with my violent enactment with Silvia, while choking the cat I had the powerful sense of being outside of myself, watching as I did something I would "normally"—previously—have been horrified to do. Yet throughout the experience, my main concern was "magical"—I believed I was using the wrong hand (my left, which I considered for healing) to strangle the cat! Following these two back-to-back events,

I knew I was losing my mind. Yet, at the same time as I was appalled, I was also darkly satisfied. Wasn't losing one's mind the *sine qua non* of spiritual liberation? Wasn't this something I had worked long and hard for? Wasn't this what I had secretly strived for, ever since I took those first, irrevocable steps towards forbidden knowledge? Losing the self and losing control were two different things; but when push came to shove, how was I to know the difference? If enlightenment and madness went hand in hand, was I now walking the razor's edge between the two, having come too far to turn back? Was this razor's edge the only way forward? Maybe I had only to stay as close to the edge as possible, and not look down …

These were the kind of thoughts and rationalizations I was using at the time to keep at bay the growing terror of being unmoored from my sense of reality and identity. The experience reached its pinnacle—or nadir—when I underwent a psychedelically induced "Samadhi" experience (as I thought of it at the time), which halfway through flipped over into an overwhelming certainty that I was being damned for all eternity, not just once but repeatedly. I experienced each and every one of my acts as having the power to determine my eternal fate: The smallest infraction or wrong move, and my soul would be hurled into the abyss forever. The experience was so utterly deranging and appalling that it achieved what my psychotic acts had not been able to; it prompted me to swear off psychedelic drugs and reevaluate my "shamanic" path. A few weeks later, I left Guatemala and returned to the UK, by way of Panama.

*

As I wrote about in *Seen and Not Seen* (2015), when I was a teenager, during my formative years of fifteen to twenty, for reasons that were totally obscure to me at the time, I found images of rape and murder sexually stimulating. The more attractive the woman the better, and the more degrading, humiliating, and agonizing her experience, the more it aroused me. These were simulations, not real acts; they were scenes from movies. Yet if I'd had access to scenes of actual rape—the way kids do today—I would probably have watched them.

I am making no defense of this. I am reporting the facts as they are, as grisly and unpleasant *as* they are. Violence and rape erotically depicted was sexually stirring to me, in and of itself; but the most basic factor that caused me sexual excitement was seeing women in pain and terror. I was a closet sadist, and it was only as I turned twenty and began to experience actual, real-life (non-sadistic) sex, or at least to make fumbling and frustrated attempts at it, that I made a heroic effort to put this dark appetite behind me. Not coincidentally, this was also the same period in which my severe physical symptoms began, although it would be twenty years before I was diagnosed with chronic fatigue syndrome. The main reason it took me so long to seek a medical diagnosis was that I was content with my "magical" one, as outlined in the quote that opens this chapter.

My rage against women (though I never thought of it as rage at the time) can, I think reasonably, be traced back to early experiences of my mother. I remember her irrational rages, her intense melancholy and despair, her drunken falls, the smothering affection followed by terrifying coldness, the explosions of vitriol. All of this impacted my psyche to the extent that, in adolescence, I lived in fear of her and at the same time I was a simmering volcano of hostility towards her. Yet my mother was so helplessly unhappy that, when I wasn't consumed by rage or terror, I was oppressed by useless feelings of pity and sadness. Since it wasn't safe to direct my anger *at* her, my sadistic tendencies—which were totally unaccountable to me, proof that I was somehow broken or faulty as a human being—were probably the only safe outlet I had for that rage. They may also have been a way to kill my compassion for my mother, and for myself.

In *Hang-Dog with a Hard-On* I wrote:

> Seeking unconscious revenge against my mother would have been a way to disconnect from my feminine *anima* entirely—to torture and abuse it into shutting down. Having cut off from my own soul in adolescence via a dark predilection for [depictions of] rape and sexual violence, it seems almost inevitable that, in adulthood, I was unconsciously drawn into occultism, and into a bizarre and obsessive courtship with Lucifer. It was the only way for me to approach my disowned feminine side: as something "satanic."

I'm not even sure if I really understand this passage now, but it makes *sense* to me. It comes from a largely intellectual place and yet, at the same time, it speaks to my body. And there may well be something in the correlation I make between Lucifer and matter/*mater*/mother, and between this and how or why I identified my soul as "Luciferic." At the same time—as I became more and more possessed by that "archetype"—it is perhaps no wonder I directed all my unconscious rage outward, rather than inward, against *women and cats*. And while I was sufficiently sobered by the events in Guatemala to stop doing salvia divinorum—to put the brakes on my spirit possession—I continued to self-identify as a Lucifer avatar, and I continued to have power-dreams that confirmed me in this persuasion. Here are a couple of outstanding examples:

As I soar ever closer to the Great Gateway in the Sky [the Sun/ father], I invoke internally the name, "Savitur," the Name of the All and the Naught [a Goddess, hence Mother figure]. This neither quickens nor impedes my progress however; what it does is to give rise to a second God-name, that of "Lucifer" [the son?]. This time there is an instantaneous effect. Suddenly, instead of soaring ever higher towards the Sun, I am plummeting rapidly downward, to Earth. Instead of seeing endless yellow light, what I see now is a silver tube or tunnel, strangely vibrant, almost liquid, more or less EXACTLY as in the movie [*The Matrix*; the imagery also evokes the birth experience.] The silver tunnel is organic and somehow alive ....I am headed for the Labyrinth of the Penumbra (Lovecraftland), beyond all doubt. And as I descend this tube with terrifying speed I am fully aware that, if I hang on long enough, I am heading for a personal encounter with none-other than Satan-Lucifer Himself— head to head, as it were .... As I descend further, I invoke the name of "Lam," and begin also to visualize Him, as drawn by Crowley. If anything, meeting this god-form is even less appealing to me than [meeting] Satan. And though I know I need to encounter Lam in order to access his "Egg" (my astral vehicle, for navigating the lowerworld safely), I am already beginning to anticipate the horri- ble, slavering demon forms that await me once I "arrive" (the lower circle of "hell" = the root or *muladhara* chakra). Since I feel less than adequate to the task, I "wake" instead, i.e., snap back to ordinary consciousness.

I become aware of a split in me. I close my eyes, no longer in the dream, fully lucid now. I am conscious in an unprecedented way of two intelligences co-existing within me. One is my ordinary self, the other is "Lucifer." I see dark thunder clouds gathering and

I feel a great sorrow. I know that Lucifer-consciousness is taking over and that there is nothing I can do about it. It is like a tiny germ within me that has now grown to sufficient size to "eclipse" my previous self, and will soon cause it to disappear entirely. The Lucifer self is infinitely greater, but I am only realizing this, or rather only experiencing it, now it has grown large enough to compete with my conscious self. It will continue to grow, however, until it has taken full possession of my being. I say in my head, something like, "Leave me alone!" But I realize that I don't even know who or what I want to leave me alone (I am not addressing Lucifer). In fact, the cry, more of a whine, makes no sense to me. I hear an inner voice say "Shut up!" in a very sharp voice. (It sounds like my old sorcerer friend, Erik.) Another voice in my head replies, "You shut up!" At that point, I wake.

CHAPTER XXIV

A sodomitic will: from the Crow's mouth

"My will to free mankind is so to speak sodomitic."*
—Aleister Crowley, *The Magickal Record of the Beast 666* (p. 206)

From John Symonds's introduction to *The Magickal Record of the Beast 666*:

> Some portions of these early Crowley diaries are extant; they contain accounts of visions, rituals performed, magical schemes. The visions were either induced by cocaine or were the spontaneous products of his imagination. As visions, they are not impressive, and reveal Crowley's feelings of isolation, guilt and megalomania. One is supposed to take them literally. (Crowley, 1972, p. ix)

From what I read of the 1920 journals, I didn't read anything that stood out as an obvious vision. Admittedly there are long passages filled with religious exhortations and imagery and poetic, philosophical ramblings

---

*When I read this part out loud to my wife in the final stages of prepping the MS, she remarked, "Did he really say that? That's like Whitley's anal probe! 'We're evolving you, we're evolving you!'" (cf. *Prisoner of Infinity*).

that don't *appear* to refer to anything in Crowley's immediate, external life. But what of the passage cited previously, in which Crowley clearly and starkly (albeit in his usual swollen, purple prose) describes the violations of a small child and an infant of only several months, and refers to a child's screams while being tortured? Is this a passage Symonds would have us read as an example of Crowley's "visions [that] are not impressive" but that we are supposed (by Crowley) to take "literally"? If so, what has he based his conclusion on, and why hasn't he shared it with us?

It's worth noting that, as editors, Symonds and Grant are not upholding any kind of academic rigor in presenting Crowley to the world. They are Thelemic believers through and through, and their intention is to expand the Aiwaz industry and extend the reach of Thelema to new generations of readers. A footnote refers to Crowley's "immediately previous incarnation" as Eliphas Levi as a fact, not as the magickal belief of one man. Aiwaz is described as Crowley's Holy Guardian Angel with the same unquestioning certainty. And so on. At the same time, despite heavy footnoting throughout the book, there is no footnote for the passage describing the child rapes. Yet, since it is more or less part of a continuous stream of Crowley's journalistic descriptions of sex magick practices, cocaine use, and invocations, there is no *obvious* reason to consider it a vision rather than the shocking denouement of a long and protracted account of the events of that day and night. The only tangible reason I can think of is that it includes criminal actions that, one might argue, even Crowley would draw the line at committing, much less recording in his journal. On the other hand, Crowley refers to himself throughout this passage in the third person, which does suggest a form of dissociation (as well as the usual self-aggrandizement) characteristic of dream-vision. But it might also characterize a barbaric act that was only possible *in tandem with* a severe case of dissociation.

In fact, Crowley refers to himself in the third person—as The Beast and other names—throughout the journals, though generally not while describing his sex magick activities, which tend to be more in keeping with the mundane passages in the journal (those involving daily activities). By his own account, Crowley did not intend these journals to be read by anyone except close associates (those at the abbey, for example). But he would surely have known there was at least the possibility they would someday be published. It might then be asked, would he really have reported such events (which, if literally true, must have contributed to the death of his infant daughter), if they were more than mere fantasy? On the other hand, would he have been able *not* to include them, when part of the reason for freely expressing his "sexual instincts" outside of any moral framework was to rid himself of every last trace of inhibition? Could Crowley rationalize censoring himself in his magickal diary without compromising the integrity of his mission?

One way around this conundrum could have been to describe his more serious transgressive acts in poetic language—just as Savile recounted some of his "peccadilloes" in a ribald tone—and so have it both ways. Doing so would minimize the risk of any legal procedures or of compromising his reputation after his death. This latter consideration is something Crowley admits, in the journal, as being among his primary concerns. At the same time, he would be staying true to the spirit of his confessional writing discipline. It's also almost guaranteed that, if these sorts of acts *did* occur, they occurred in a drug-fueled trance in which Crowley *was* dissociated. The "transcendence" of personal identity, after all, was very much the point of these kinds of taboo-breaking rituals. So what *does* Crowley clearly (i.e., without the veil of poetry) admit to in his accounts?

For the entry of April 5, 1920, he writes a single line: "Fiddled and spanked children; a rotten day, but I found a wonderful ugly girl with a big mouth" (1972, p. 105). As far as I can tell, this is before Hirsig's arrival, which raises the question of whose children Crowley was "fiddling," never mind the choice of such a highly suggestive word. Once again, there is no footnote from Symonds or Grant to help the reader.

For July 22, 1921, Crowley mentions "our sterile and most blasphemous Abortion-slime, the God-Babe Eucharist." A footnote helpfully explains: "For his Eucharist, Crowley takes elements that are abhorrent to Christians, dead matter, hence 'blasphemous Abortion-slime' and so on" (ibid., p. 231n.). Elsewhere, there are references to Crowley's penchant for devouring human feces and having others do the same (something my brother admits to in his memoir). On July 28 Crowley writes: "Hansi, cocaineless, was very ill with fever. Poupée, snowless and fever-free, sweats over-much and seems uncomfortable all round" (ibid., p. 236). Why did Crowley find it necessary to state that a two-year-old boy and a several-month-old baby girl were not drugged with cocaine? Is it because on other occasions they were, and perhaps that they were suffering withdrawal symptoms? That Hansi was included in at least some of the rituals is implied by an entry from the afore-cited

all-night session of August 12, 1920: "I came in to perform the pentagram ritual etc., like Hansi's Big Lion, and went all but insane—yet
superbly under control—with the attainment of ecstasy, singing and
shouting the words, many of the Barbarous Names new-forged on my
soul's anvil" (ibid., p. 249).

Considering everything we know about the circumstances that surrounded the cocaine-fueled, Barbarous-Named, anvil-psyche of Aleister
Crowley, during this most hellacious period in a life overflowing with
appalling excess, somehow his prideful assertion of being "superbly
under control" fails to reassure.

*

> "Satan I'll be, by favor of our Lord."
> —Aleister Crowley, *The Magickal Record of the Beast 666* (p. 239)

A significant portion of the journals is devoted to Crowley's use of
cocaine. In today's post-countercultural climate (something we have
Crowley's influence to thank for, to a significant degree), Crowley's
excessive use of drugs is easy to overlook when it comes to determin-
ing his sanity and moral capacity—by which I mean the psychological limits to his behavior (assuming there were any). Crowley insists
the cocaine did not harm him, or that it was immaterial if it did. "I have
been taking Cocaine from time to time," he writes, "and I don't care
whether it has hurt me, if it has made me for the time a scribe more
worthy of Him" (ibid., pp. 216–217).

This is hardly surprising. Crowley's sacred screed, *Liber Al*, pre-
scribes indifference to the deleterious effects of substance abuse; in fact,
it denies such effects exist:

> I am the Snake that giveth Knowledge & Delight and bright glory,
> and stir the hearts of men with drunkenness. *To worship me take wine
> and strange drugs whereof I will tell my prophet, & be drunk thereof! They
> shall not harm ye at all. It is a lie, this folly against self. The exposure of
> innocence is a lie.* Be strong, o man! lust, enjoy all things of sense
> and rapture: fear not that any God shall deny thee for this." (II:22,
> emphasis added)

Since Crowley's day, there have been a number of studies on the effects
of cocaine, and none of them indicate that it is even remotely "harmless."

Cocaine has numerous effects on important neurotransmitters in the brain, the most dramatic being an increase in the release of dopamine, the primary neurotransmitter involved in the brain's pleasure centers. Excessive dopamine levels have been

> associated with anger, aggressiveness, hallucinations, delusions .... cocaine-induced mood disorder, cocaine-induced anxiety disorder, cocaine-induced sexual dysfunction, and cocaine-induced sleep disorder .... While voluntary use almost always occurs the first time cocaine is tried, cocaine dependence involving compulsive use frequently follows. This compulsive use is often biologically based, yet many clinicians mistakenly believe the cocaine user can stop using the drug whenever he or she wants. (Morton, 1999)

Paranoia and suspiciousness are characteristic of frequent cocaine use (particularly binge use), and they are often the initial symptoms of full-blown psychosis. Paranoia has been estimated as occurring in as high a proportion as 84 percent of cocaine users, and psychosis, including hallucinations and delusions, has been attributed to between 29 percent and 53 percent of users (all symptoms possibly related to an imbalance of dopamine). Around 50 percent of cocaine users suffering these symptoms are known to commit cocaine-related violence. Violent behavior associated with cocaine use "is predictable based on the effects cocaine has on neurotransmitter dysfunction [that] might provoke aggression, hyperactivity, impaired judgment, and paranoia ... 'fight-or-flight' behavior, [and becoming] hyperalert and 'armed to the outside world.'" Cocaine users suffering these symptoms tend to interpret rapid or unexpected movements by people around them as "hostile," and all of these factors "contribute to a cocaine-violence connection."

Cocaine also causes "problems with thinking logically ... impaired executive functioning (decision making, judgment, attention/planning/mental flexibility) [due to loss of the] functional integrity of the prefrontal lobe [which] regulates impulse control. The resultant effects would be poor judgment in an individual experiencing impulsivity in the face of severe cocaine craving." Then there is delirium, "a potentially fatal syndrome marked by severe, fluctuating confusion and autonomic nervous system instability (such as severe blood pressure changes, pulse changes, and sweating)" (similar symptoms to those which Crowley describes the children suffering). Delirium is "accompanied by psychotic symptoms (such as paranoia, hallucinations, delusions,

206 THE VICE OF KINGS

and agitated behavior). One report noted that seven individuals with fatal cocaine intoxication developed an excited delirium with intense paranoia and bizarre and violent behavior, requiring forcible restraint (Morton, 1999).

Nor was this unknown in 1920: While Freud prescribed cocaine to some of his patients (and even used it himself), "cocaine psychosis" was first described by him in 1884, "when a patient given cocaine over a period of weeks described swirling white snakes, the sounds of voices and intense paranoia" (Kerr, 1987). Yet Crowley had his own bible to override such concerns, and he claimed to keep his drug use at all times within the context of a magickal discipline. He insisted he never became addicted to any drug and only ever used them for "higher" purposes, that is, while doing his True Will. (This is something I doubt even Crowley's most fervent advocates really believe, considering that Crowley died a heroin addict.) Like all good rationalizers, Crowley leaves aside the question of whether his excessive drug-use might be sourced in his own psychology, in neurotic patterns of dependency laid down by early trauma. If it were, then the magickal belief system that advocated such excess would also be sourced in those same traumatic imprints, albeit *taking the form of archetypal forces commanding him from the outside.* Crowley's diseases, in other words, would have become his gods—and by extension, those of countless others.

Such a possibility appears to have been successfully banished by the power of Crowley's convictions and, as with all good cult leaders, by those who followed after him (myself included). Yet it would be a mistake to make this necessarily a question of either/or. If our gods are our diseases, then our diseases are our gods, and so on. But the question that arises, if we at least allow for both disease *and* god at work, is this: In what ways was Crowley's cocaine use affecting him physically and psychologically that he was *not* aware of? Most recovered alcoholics will tell you that the booze tells its own story, a story in which it invariably casts itself in the role of hero. In this story, booze is never seen as a life-destroying poison but as a soul-rescuer, a Dionysian agent of awakening. Give in to that whisper and before long the alcoholic is literally possessed by spirits. Since these spirits by definition are not human (they are plants), their criteria for what is permissible or desirable in order to perpetuate their influence is likewise—other than human. The same thing happened to me with salvia divinorum: At a certain point I became aware that I was "possessed" by the spirit of the plant, and she was constantly calling me to her embrace.

This of course is true of Crowley's imagined "Master," Aiwaz, whom he refers to repeatedly as the Devil, Satan, and "my Lord." Crowley is polluting his body and his psyche with cocaine (it's not clear what the amounts are, but he mentions waking repeatedly with nosebleeds), all under the auspices of selfless service to his Lord and Master Satan. So how *does* the drug affect him? He describes it in quite literally diabolic terms, as an unleashing agent for all the baser urges of the id:

> Cocaine (Leah confirms this) confers a quite peculiar point of view, with a strangely intense and almost drunken pleasure equally unknown to those who have not taken it. This point of view seems to be that of the animal-subconscious; it owns no censor, moral or mental, and may be criminal or insane without qualm. It possesses one, like the "devil" in the old pathologies. (1972, p. 228)

He then provides the caveat that, of course, he would never give in to such urges:

> In me, of course, such tendencies are rudimentary; and the mental and moral inhibitions would cry "Halt! Who goes there?" if I proceeded to externalize one such or to translate it into action; because to do so would need the use of faculties which the sentries Prudence, Righteousness, Honour (and so on) guard for the King-Self by Marshall True-Will's order. (ibid.)

This is a strange, not to say risible, assertion coming from a man who consumes feces as a matter of religious principle. It's also unclear who it's meant to reassure, besides Crowley himself. I say strange, because elsewhere, Crowley makes it clear that his intention is not to inhibit *any* of his baser instincts, but to liberate every last one of them. His methodology is to commit acts of sexual transgression precisely *because* they are loathsome to him and/or the inverse of conventional Christian, *moral* doctrines. So it's not only fair but entirely *necessary* to ask where and how Crowley would choose to draw a line to delineate "criminal" or "insane" behavior. Or why he would draw any line at all, and based on what.

"[W]hen I'm the cocaine-fiend," he writes, "I do my will, even as God doth His, great lust of Act, great lust; no care of Act's result" (ibid., p. 238). To act out of lust without care of result is the same as acting on one's base urges without caring about the consequences. Crowley's idea of surrender to that "higher" will seems to be indistinguishable from, or at one with, giving in to the basest lusts of the body. It entails acting without thought or conscious intention, in ways that are purely instinctive: "insane, yet superbly under control." Crowley tells himself it would never be the animal, only the god, acting through him. Yet the contradictory logic of this model is evident throughout his work—all of which is signed, quite literally, with the name and number of The Beast.

CHAPTER XXV

Necessary offense: the left-hand path and sexual liberation as social engineering

"The ruling ideas of each age have ever been the ideas of its ruling class."

—Karl Marx, *The Communist Manifesto*

On Halloween of 1958, the liberal philosopher Isaiah Berlin gave an inaugural lecture at the University of Oxford during which he said: "Over a hundred years ago, the German poet Heine warned the French not to underestimate the power of ideas: philosophical concepts nurtured in the stillness of a professor's study could destroy a civilization" (Berlin, 1969, p. 119). Is there anything more perniciously far-reaching than a bad idea? And yet bad ideas, like viruses, seem to have a special aptitude for spreading inseparable from their destructive nature. Perhaps this is why, in our present culture, there is nothing quite so coveted as "going viral"?

In *Magia Sexualis: Sex, Magic, and Liberation in Modern Western Esotericism*, Hugh B. Urban (2006) wrote that Crowley "hoped to find in deliberate acts of transgression a radical kind of superhuman power, one that went well beyond the transgressive rites performed by Reuss and the early Ordo Templi Orientis (OTO)—indeed, a power that could explode the boundaries of Western society and open the way for a new era of history."

What I discovered (or became fully aware of) while writing and researching the first part of this book, and while working on *Prisoner of Infinity*, was how and why occultism seems to overlap at every turn with the sexual abuse of children. My tentative conclusion has been that the pursuit of occult power appears to stem—frequently if not exclusively—from an early, formative experience of powerlessness, one which aspirants are eventually (unconsciously) compelled to *reenact* in some form or another. Reenactment compulsion is a difficult subject to sum up, and I refer the reader to *Prisoner of Infinity* for a full exploration of this phenomenon. But suffice it to say that, since all infants experience being powerless to some degree, for that early imprint to be profound enough to create a Crowley—or even a Horsley—it must be severely traumatic. The primary way such a severely traumatized psyche attempts to heal itself is through *unconscious reenactment*—that's to say, by bringing the trauma-affect into consciousness through *reenacting it,* usually without being aware of doing so. Hence we have conscious beliefs, methods, and goals arising behind which is the unconscious drive to reenact buried trauma and so make it conscious. If occultism as a system is a set of beliefs, methods, and goals geared towards this end, it would follow that, at least *some* of the time (i.e., if pursued fiercely and unconsciously enough), it would lead to some sort of ritualized child abuse (i.e., a literal reenactment).

Crowley's desire to attain spiritual and psychological freedom from all restraints and inhibitions was apparently a quest for liberation from the tyranny of identity (to become an "Ipsissimus"). So when do we exist without an identity except as little children? Yet to be as little children to enter the kingdom of heaven—to be psychically open, to have a clean slate—means reexperiencing the powerlessness and corresponding trauma that first tore heaven from us. Is there a way to regain that child state without undergoing the corresponding vulnerability and distress *of* it? I think this is precisely the goal of occultism, and that ritually abusing children is the logical and inevitable outcome of such a pursuit, because it is a way to psychically *possess* that lost innocence through force of will, rather than through surrender. Yet to possess an innocent is to destroy its innocence. This means that, unconsciously, the goal is actually *to eradicate all vestigial memory of innocence,* and of powerlessness, from the seeker's own body and psyche. The occultist then achieves "the pinnacles of power" and gets to "surpass the stars."[1] He becomes a crowned child and conquering lord.

The key passage quoted from Crowley's 1920 journal clearly describes a vision, a fantasy, or an actual event during which Crowley ("her lewd lover") sodomizes Hirsig's small child (Hansi, or "Dionysus"). It states that Hirsig invited Crowley to "deflower" their infant daughter, Anne Leah ("Poupée," born in late February of 1920). If such an act, or some variation of it, really occurred, it would have been at least partially responsible for the child's death, less than two months later on October 14. (Poupée's death was apparently so traumatic for Hirsig that she miscarried six days later, while three months pregnant with another child by Crowley.)

As evidence, this may be far from conclusive. But it does raise the question as to whether Crowley, in his enflamed quest for total liberation of the instincts, would have drawn a clear, hard line at sexual child abuse, and if so, based on what criteria. While he clearly prohibits "the seduction of infants" in his commentaries, at the same time, the Law of Thelema was opposed to "Christian hypocrisy" and encouraged introducing children to (adult) sexuality at the first opportunity. The question must then be asked, what constitutes "seduction," and at what precise age did Crowley consider children ready for active participation in sex? (The Paedophile Information Exchange lobbied to reduce the age of consent to four.)

It's reasonable to expect Crowley to have been absolutely clear about this; yet, as far as I know, Crowley never stipulated a Thelemic age of consent. His admonishment against child-sex refers expressly to *infants*, so when does an infant cease to be an infant? The word comes from the Latin word *infans*, meaning "unable to speak" or "speechless." Applied to humans, the term is more or less synonymous with baby, that is, between the ages of a day and a year. Crowley was an etymologist who spoke several languages (including Latin) and who took great care in his use of words. He chose them consciously, with deliberate intent. The implication, to me at least, is that the seduction of post-infants (i.e., toddlers) is *not* prohibited by Thelema. At the very least, this question has to remain open, because Crowley himself left it that way. It's also worth noting that Crowley's proscription against the seduction of infants was written *after* the death of his infant daughter at Cefalù.

A cursory look at the evidence shows that Crowley had means, motive, and opportunity for child "seductions." Both his magickal philosophy and his sexual "instincts" suggest that sexually "initiating" children was within the range of his interests (motive). The circumstances of his life show both the means and the opportunity to do so. Most damning of all, there are his admissions, as well as the testimony of others present at the time. The mystery then becomes not so much, "Did Crowley have or encourage sex with children?" but "How is it possible for his many defenders to dismiss—or simply ignore—all of the evidence that he did?" The best argument offered seems to be that he was "only joking," that he was exaggerating for effect. It's also been argued that Crowley couldn't have got away with such criminal acts, and that they would have come to light by now. The flip side of this circular argument is that nothing has come to light because nothing ever happened. Yet, as with Alfred Kinsey, whose reputation in the mainstream is miraculously still intact, or Jimmy Savile, whose reputation held out until after his death ("It was good while it lasted"[2]), it is less a question of the lack of evidence than the fact it has been successfully marginalized, *just as if* it were based on nothing but hearsay, hysteria, and rumor.

Mark Twain once wrote that it is a lot easier to fool people than to show them they have been fooled. This relates to the psychology of prior investment. Both Savile and Kinsey were national heroes and it is extremely uncomfortable to see our heroes revealed as villains in disguise, or to even begin to suspect that the pillars of society are rotten to the core. If we have bought stocks in a company, we don't want to hear that the company might be crooked or bankrupt. We prefer *not* to see the evidence. We will even keep on investing to reinforce our belief in the company, all the way until the collapse.

This is also how glamor magic works. Part of the strange obfuscation that keeps the truth about Crowley from being seen is due to the mistaken idea that his sexual philosophy was somehow groundbreaking, daring, visionary, and unique to him—while at the same time, that he was part of something liberating and *good* (like Kinsey). In fact, the basic ideas of "sexual liberation" which Crowley both preached and practiced—the breaking of taboos as a supposed means to social and spiritual emancipation—can be traced, in a more or less unbroken line, through Western history. Nor is it by any means exclusive, or even primary, to social outliers or cultural pioneers. On the contrary, the breaking of taboos is a consistent practice of the ruling class and always has been. Those who create the laws and social mores are by definition not bound by them. Introducing these same "revolutionary" ideas to the masses in concealed and controlled ways may simply be part of the social engineering racket.

If we look at the twentieth century alone, the idea of sexualized children, and a belief in the benefits of adult-child sex, can be found in areas as seemingly diverse as:

- Freud's theories, and his insistence that children's accounts of being sexually abused were based in their own fantasy life and secret desires, more than on actual events.
- Early psychosexual research in the UK by Havelock Ellis and the Fabian Society (and later via the Tavistock Institute).
- Magnus Hirschfeld and the Scientific Humanitarian Committee in Germany, probably the first advocacy for homosexual and transgender rights and later the Institute of Sexual Research.
- The Order of Chaeronea (founded by George Cecil Ives) and the "Uranian" or "third sex" movement.
- Early literary works such as Nabokov's *Lolita* (inspired by Ellis).
- Experiments in progressive schooling initiated by Fabians such as Edward Carpenter and Cecil Reddie.
- The early Wiccan movement (such as the Order of Woodcraft), which Crowley influenced and was directly involved in (he wrote many of the rituals with Gerald Gardener).
- "MKULTRA" mind control experimentation in the US and the UK in the 1950s and beyond. This overlapped with the use of hallucinogens as a means of "liberation," something Crowley was directly involved in.
- Alfred Kinsey's "groundbreaking research," which entailed the controlled sexual abuse of children and the recruitment of child molesters to do it. (Kinsey was also interested in Crowley.)
- The Kinsey-inspired "sexual revolution" and the counterculture which sprung from many or all of these prior (mostly state-funded) "movements." (The Beatles were influenced by Crowley, as was Leary.)
- The *Kinderladen* of 1960s Germany—leftist schools where children were taught, for "political" reasons (i.e., social liberation), to have sex with adults.
- Charles Manson and his "family," who, like Crowley (having doubtless read him), prohibited the discipline of children and included them in group sex play.

- The Paedophile Information Exchange, affiliated with the UK National Council for Civil Liberties; its aim in the 1970s was to reduce or abolish the age of consent so adults and children would be free to "love one another."
- Jimmy Savile, in the 1950s, '60s, '70s, '80s, '90s, and 2000s, whose long career as a child rapist flourished in tandem with his high-level political associations, his "friendship" with the royal family, and his equally long-term, still-undivulged, "charity" work for the UK National Health Service (including Tavistock).

And so on.

By advocating spiritual liberation through taboo-breaking to the uncommon commoner, Crowley opened himself up to demonization from one portion of society (mainly Christians). At the same time, he underwent a corresponding deification by another, so that today he is something of a cultural hero along the lines of Oscar Wilde. In a BBC poll of the 100 "greatest" Britons taken in 2002, Crowley ranked seventy-third, between Henry V and Robert the Bruce. Oscar Wilde was not on the list, and nor was John Keats, D. H. Lawrence, Aldous Huxley, or George Orwell. On the other hand, John Peel (43), Boy George (45), Freddie Mercury (58), and Bob Geldof (75) were, so this gives some idea, not just of the erratic nature of the list, but also of how Crowley's influence extended as far as it did, by spanning both high and low (pop) culture, and even by *bridging the two*.

Crowley was born of upper class stock, and his paternal ancestors were involved in both the railway and ale businesses (the former he had in common with Savile again, the latter with my own family). For all his apparently marginal social status, as we shall see he moved in highly distinguished circles throughout his life. At these higher levels, those of the cultural elite and the ruling class—"the lords of the earth [who] are our kinsfolk"[3]—perhaps he was merely doing his job. By polarizing the collective psyche, he made it easier for social engineers like the Huxleys and the Astors to control it; by dividing the *volk* soul, he made it that much easier to conquer.

This conquering division is in evidence even today. Just try to find someone with whom to discuss Crowley intelligently and impartially. Even ruling out fundamentalist Christian-types (who are pretty much useless for any sort of discussion), those interested in Thelema tend to belong to one of two camps: Either they consider Crowley a cultural pioneer and a progressive; or they are convinced he was a prophet of evil directly involved in high-level mind control and ritual abuse. While I tend to agree with this latter class, the problem is that there isn't much hard evidence for their claims, which makes the lack of coherent, balanced arguments all the more critical. The researchers tend to blur the line between Crowley's teachings having *inspired* satanic groups, and Crowley's direct involvement *with* them—which is a bit like claiming Nietzsche was a Nazi because Hitler embraced his writings. In the other camp, Crowley's defenders—though they often won't admit to it—are already sold on the positive effects of Crowley and his work, overall, and sometimes even offer themselves as proof! They may profess not to care about Crowley's personal qualities or to insist that his many questionable exhortations were either deliberate shock-mongering or else "magickal code" for something else. They may dismiss evidence for the more disturbing aspects of his behavior with the opinion that Crowley was a misunderstood and unjustly maligned character.

Simply stated, there is very little clear, impartial thinking around the man. The mere mention of his name stirs strong feelings and a correspondingly firm position. This leads to polarization, negative identity, and so on. Divide and conquer works not just on groups, but on individual psyches, too. I suspect this is also by design. The cognitive dissonance of trying to hold two conflicting beliefs is a tried-and-true method of thought control (or thought stoppage). Orwell called it doublethink, and CIA anthropologist Gregory Bateson called it "the double-bind." The immoral and even malevolent nature of Crowley's character, life, and teachings (if I may call them that) is very much in plain sight for all to see. Yet it is also at odds with the idea of him as a cultural iconoclast to be respected. As with Jimmy Savile, the toxic nature of Crowley's activities was—and is—an open secret, one that was telegraphed by Crowley himself the moment he adopted the name and number of the Beast. By doing so he cannily anticipated (in fact helped to shape) our current cultural mindset, in which the greatest virtue is the rejection of virtue, because the only measure of character is in becoming whatever we choose to pretend to be, regardless of social context (i.e., the effects we have on others). Crowley both foresaw and helped to create a world in which the words "wicked" and "sick" would become terms of praise rather than consternation or concern, while words such as "moral" or "upstanding" evidence of patriarchal oppression!

However, I suspect there is rather more to it than this. I suspect that cognitive dissonance is not only a means to divide people, internally and externally, or to hijack their faculties for thinking clearly, but to demonically possess them. The brain has a problem with insoluble mysteries or anomalies, and tends to cling to them. This may be a way to create hosts for a mind-virus (a really bad idea) to ensure it be carried far and wide in as short a time as possible. I think that those who do endorse Crowley—or at least persist in maintaining the illusion of a visionary occultist first, a predatory psychopath second (or not at all)—are fully aware of what they are doing. I think they know quite well what Crowley was doing too, but that they believe it is all just in the nature of the Beast. The Left-Hand Path aims to transcend taboo by breaking taboos, to expunge sin from the soul by satiating the soul on sin, which is essentially Lucifer's cry from Hell, "Evil be thou my good." If Crowley believed, and if those who profess to understand him also believe, that his evil was a means to a greater good (i.e., the transcendence of good *and* evil), it is a very small step from here to accepting that his actions and instructions were not evil at all, but a more sophisticated ("encoded") kind of good. For the eyes and ears of the ignorant commoner—the uninitiated, who are nonetheless indispensable to the goals of Thelema—this requires denying even the possibility that Crowley committed acts that are generally seen as evil, despite all the evidence that he did. Among themselves—the intelligentsia and occultism affiliates or apologists—there is perhaps an agreement, as among gentleman, not to linger overmuch on the indelicate nature of the operation—since to do so would suggest faintness of heart—but only to forge onward on the path to freedom, and take Heaven by storm.

These are necessary offenses, after all.

CHAPTER XXVI

A Luciferian Lighthouse: an act of unconscious animal sacrifice

> "We act out what we can't remember."
>
> —Greg Mogenson, *A Most Accursed Religion*

Garbanzo was the cat who found me in Oaxaca in 2004. My girlfriend at the time found him in a shoebox and brought him back to our hostel (the Magic Hostel). As an adult, Garbanzo (an all-black cat) was a surly, highly unusual presence, with a piercing, scorpion-like glare. He rarely purred and he even seemed to dislike being petted. It was as if he resented being treated as a cat. We joked that he was an ex-Nazi, or one of Castaneda's "old seers," doing penance for former crimes.

In the spring of 2006, when he was one and a half, he lost his leg in a battle with a hanging plant. He had been climbing down from a wall and he somehow got his leg caught in the wire around the plant. He hung there for however long it took before the neighbor came and got him down. His leg was broken in three places and the vet assured us it would never heal and would only be dead weight, and that the best recourse was amputation. Garbanzo seemed to adapt to his loss in no time at all, and a short while after the operation (even before his fur had grown back), he was hopping around happily. A few weeks after he lost his leg, Garbanzo suffered an even more severe trauma. The following is taken from my journal at the time:

Garbanzo was attacked by three stray dogs following a three-hour Tarot reading for a fallen sorceress and close friend. I had done a protection ceremony before the reading, but forgot to include Garbanzo in it. That night, while my partner and I were eating, we heard the sound of dogs barking excitedly. I was concerned for Garbanzo, but since there was no sound of cat's hissing or yowling, I assumed he must be safe. Several seconds went by while my partner and I listened. The dogs became more frantic and finally I got up and went out—only to see three dogs throwing Garbanzo around in their teeth like a rag doll.

I beat them off with a piece of fire wood, and we brought Garbanzo inside. He had shat himself, and there was a little blood in it. Otherwise he was dazed but not visibly damaged. He tried to move but couldn't. We called a friend, who called a driver from the Holistica center where my partner and I worked, and we took Garbanzo to a vet's in a nearby town of Antigua, who opened up especially for us. Looking Garbanzo over, the vet was doubtful. He said the skin had been removed from his body, but invisibly so, since the fur wasn't actually torn. Air had entered into the space between the skin and internal organs. Garbanzo looked awful. I knew he might die. The vet said if he made it through the night, he *might* be OK. I have rarely felt such anguish—sadness, grief and rage, all mixed up in black impotent despair. Perhaps the worst part of all was remembering how we had just sat there, eating our food, for those crucial seconds, while the dogs attacked Garbanzo. I ran it over and over in my mind, like a nightmare.

[Garbanzo survived the night, and remained at the vet's under observation.]

A few days after the attack, the day we picked up Garbanzo from the vet's, I bought some poison in Antigua market. It was probably strychnine, judging by the Spanish name. I bought six capsules for a total of around $8; the man who sold them to me explained they were generally used for some wild animal whose name I didn't recognize, like a rat only bigger. He said they would work fine for dogs, and that one capsule would be enough. I wasn't going to take any chances, so I bought six, two for each dog. Later, I realized that I was only certain about identifying two of the dogs. It had all happened so fast that I hadn't really had a chance to see them at all, and was only left with the impression of there being three, that and their colors. However, having seen two or three stray dogs hanging around making noise over the past few days, I could be fairly sure it was the same ones. There were two I was sure of: a small black and brown one, and a large white female I had also seen in the village. If there had been a third dog, I couldn't be sure what it looked like, so there was no way to do anything about it.

The capsules were colored dark and light red. Later, I performed a Mars ritual, consecrating the poison and cementing my intent to destroy the dogs. When I placed the capsules on [Lyn Birkbeck's] *Divine Astrology* card with the Mars symbol, arranging them inside the circle beneath the arrow, I realized the colors of the pills perfectly matched the colors on the card, those pertaining to Mars. Mars is also Horus, God of War and Vengeance; so it was to Him that I first appealed, in preparing to perform the unpleasant but necessary act of destruction .... On Saturday, my partner went to work and I smoked some weed and performed another Mars ceremony, followed immediately after by one to Saturn. This was intended specifically to ensure that my act of violence be leavened and guided by those Karmic principals which Saturn oversees .... If the destruction of these dogs could help with Garbanzo's recovery, then there was no doubt in my mind it would be justified. If the power released by their deaths could be taken up by Garbanzo and used for his healing, this would be a fair and just exchange, a righting of karmic imbalance, and I knew Saturn would help me with such an undertaking. Hence, by stating this as my intent, I could trust that if events went in my favor, it was because the gods had approved my objective.

I sent Garbanzo some Mars energy and surrounded him with crystals and flowers from the garden. He began to knead his blanket and purr, getting sexually aroused as he usually does with his blanket. I advised him to use all that lust energy to heal himself and grow strong again. If Garbanzo could get a hard-on, I figured, then his will to live had not deserted him. It was at this point that Garbanzo began his recovery proper, thank Mars.

After working in the garden a while, I put the poison in a spot where I could see it from inside the garden. Minutes after, I got up and approached the gate, at the precise moment the white dog appeared. It saw me and ran off. I cursed and sat down again. A moment after, the black dog appeared. I watched as he went straight over to the poisoned food and ate it up. I felt relief and satisfaction. Quickly, I put two more capsules inside dog food and placed them in the same spot, hoping to draw the white dog to its doom also. I took up position on a ladder by the fence and watched the two dogs wandering through an overgrown field opposite the house. I'd been told the poison took effect in ten minutes, but I was skeptical. Twenty minutes later, I was still watching the two dogs, with no sign of anything amiss. It began to thunder and the dogs ran out of sight. The thunder grew closer and louder, until it was right over my head, the wrath of the gods. It began to rain. Later, I found out it was also a full moon. Energies were moving. I had the feeling Mars had struck, and that Saturn had come to take the black dog away, that justice was being served. I took the poison away, to wait for another day.

The next morning, I woke to hear the sound of grinding teeth. I looked out the window over the bed, and saw the white dog, lying on our lawn, chewing on the dog food tin, which I had forgotten to put away properly! I got up and went quickly into the garden. The dog saw me and ran off; I got the poisoned food out (which I had hidden the night before) and put it out on the path outside the gate. I waited a while then went to get dressed. When I came back, three or four minutes later, the food was gone. There were no other dogs around, so I was fairly sure it had been the white dog.

That was four days ago. Garbanzo's recovery began right after this .... Assuming I never see either of those demonic mutts again, my guess is the poison did its job and that justice was served. I guess this was a sort of rite of passage in itself. I took karmic law into my own hands, and now I get to live with the consequences. I have no doubt that Garbanzo, at least, fully appreciates what I did. After all, what greater measure of love can there be than the willingness to commit murder?

*

"[F]alse spirituality can be spoken of in every case in which, for example, the psychic is mistaken for the spiritual."
—Rene Guénon, *The Reign of Quantity*

While Garbanzo made a full recovery, soon after this incident I began suffering some of the most serious symptoms I have ever undergone, in a life beset with physical ailments. I had had chronic digestive problems from my early twenties, but during this period the symptoms took on a new intensity. I was diagnosed with hookworm, a fact which struck me as curious, since I was working on a script about vampires at the time. The medication I was prescribed was so powerful it did even more harm to my internal system than the parasites had, and for a period I was unable to digest anything besides pea soup and crackers. Besides stomach pains, heat, and gas, I suffered a kind of internal constriction that went all the way up my chest and throat and made it difficult to swallow. It felt as though a poisonous snake were wrapped around the central strip inside my chest, and besides the sheer physical discomfort, it created in me a black despair that bordered on panic.

While I quickly connected this parasitical invasion to my interest in vampires, what didn't occur to me until much later—in fact until I was recapitulating the events for this present work—are the parallels between my own distress and what I had done to those dogs. From what I read online, there were certainly similarities: strychnine poisoning often causes strangulation due to spasm of the muscles involved in respiration. The other thing that didn't occur to me until I was going over this chapter for publication is something that's even more starkly apparent now I have seen it. The act described above meets all the requirements of *a ritual animal sacrifice*. Until now, I had never seen it as such; if someone had asked me if I'd ever performed such a ritual, I would probably have denied it—so apparently it's possible to perform ritual sacrifice and not even be fully aware of doing so. I don't know if I ever thought about Crowley at the time of conducting the ritual, but the idea of slaying an animal in order to release the energy of its dying, and to use that energy for some "magickal" end, is an idea that *can only have first entered my awareness via Crowley's* 1991 work, *Magick: In Theory and Practice*.

I was drawn to Crowley out of intense curiosity at the age of twenty. My interest in him increased as a result of reading several texts over the next four or five years (*Moonchild, Magick, Liber AL, Portable Darkness,*

Book 4, Book of Thoth, Magick without Tears). What he wrote impressed me with its lucidity, depth, authority, and seeming wisdom and insight. I responded to his "voice," you could say, resonating with it and finding affinity there. In fact, when, at twenty-four, I disinherited a personal fortune and traveled to Morocco to live on the streets, my aim was to leave everything behind and reduce myself to nothing, to see what would rise from the ashes of my previous existence. The handful of possessions I carried with me as the bare bones of that new existence included *Portable Darkness: An Aleister Crowley Reader*, and *Liber AL*. Later, I came across *The Book of Thoth* in a tiny library in Tangier, by sheer chance, and I must have read it perhaps a dozen times over the next year or two (with *Liber AL*, it was by then the only book I owned).

I was convinced at the time that the book had been placed there (by "the Secret Chiefs") expressly for me to find it. As a direct result, I ended up learning to read Tarot and, once I had bought a Crowley deck in Gibraltar, that became my first ever means of income. My first Tarot reading was on a Spanish street in La Linea called Calle Real—meaning both Royal and Real Street. Clearly this was a formative time in my life, and Crowley's influence was central to that formation. Perhaps, via the "magick" power of mirror neurons, I had tuned into Crowley's brain state and, finding I liked the frequency, continued to tune in. Over roughly the next fifteen years, at an only partially conscious level, I developed a kind of trans-temporal, nonspatial connection to Crowley, a psychic link. As I adopted my "walk" to match his "talk," is it any wonder I ended up committing an act of ritual sacrifice without even realizing it? That's the power of a strange attractor. How many others besides myself have fallen into this same sorcerous pattern? C. S. Lewis wrote in *The Screwtape Letters*:

> As the great sinners grow fewer, and the majority lose all individuality, the great sinners become far more effective agents for us. Every dictator or even demagogue—almost every film star or crooner—can now draw tens of thousands of the human sheep with him. They give themselves (what there is of them) to him; in him, to us. There may come a time when we shall have no need to bother about individual temptation at all, except for the few. Catch the bellwether, and his whole flock comes after him. (2002, pp. 193–194)

I think it's beyond reasonable doubt that Crowley and his work was, and is, a key element in a larger cultural/occult set of beliefs, beliefs that inspired *me*, at least, into some very destructive behaviors. Despite *knowing* that Crowley/Thelema was a "Luciferian Lighthouse," I *still* steered my ship by it and wound up crashing into the rocks, as partially described in this account. Crowley's influence didn't inspire me to abuse children; but it apparently *did* inspire me to feed my own trauma-based drive for power over others, and to commit some highly unpleasant acts. I hope I am not flinching from sharing the evidence of this.

CHAPTER XXVII

Circles of denial: checking in with the experts

"What is being reported by these patients is a variously integrated mix of kabbalistic teachings ... ceremonial magick, sex magick, brainwashing techniques, a peculiar brand of theosophy that emphasizes blood and death rites in the core rituals of its system of worship, and an organizational and secrecy structure patterned much along the lines of secret societies ... An extensive reading and integration of many occult source documents over the course of considerable time is required in order to reconstruct the basic tenets and practices with which nearly every SCS [satanic cult survivor] seems readily familiar."
—George B. Greaves, "Alternate Hypotheses Regarding Claims of Satanic Cult Activity"

While I was working on this exploration, I had email exchanges with a couple of Crowley researchers. I emailed Hugh Urban citing the quote that appears in Chapter 25 back at him, with this question: *How far*

beyond do you think Crowley went in his deliberate acts of transgression?
Urban replied with the following:

> For his time, at least, I would say quite far indeed. In some ways,
> his acts of transgression were more extreme and antinomian than
> Hindu Tantric acts of transgression typically are (since the latter
> don't include acts such as sodomy, etc). His drug use was of course
> infamous, and on at least one occasion he consumed human excre-
> ment. On the other hand, however, I don't know of any reports of
> him performing human sacrifice, which is perhaps the most extreme
> rite in left hand forms of Tantra.

I replied: "I am still seeking a Crowley scholar willing to look into the
evidence that Crowley sexually abused children, possibly infants. Those
I have asked or read so far seem inclined to avoid the question entirely,
which of course is the norm around child sexual abuse." I included a link
to my piece on Crowley and Alfred Kinsey (from the first part of this book),
as well as a passage referring to Crowley's boast of rape. Urban did not
respond, so three weeks later I sent a follow-up email asking if he had deliberately ignored my last … He replied the next day with these three lines:
"The connections you're exploring are intriguing. I'm not really working
on Crowley at the moment, so I would suggest you contact others who are
more active in that area now—Marco Pasi is the first that comes to mind,
and then maybe Gordan Djurdjevic. Good luck."

Sometime before this, in January 2016, before I began work on this
section of the book, I emailed the author Peter Levenda (who has
written and spoken about Crowley on countless occasions) to ask if he
was aware of any evidence of Crowley's involvement in child sexual
abuse. Levenda's response was superficially thoughtful but, I thought,
rather dismissive. It included these lines (quoted with Levenda's permission): "I know members of the OTO (and have known many since
the 1970s) and one could not accuse any of them of pedophilia or using
children for sexual rituals. If there was even the whiff of that, you can
be sure I would have followed it up."

In response, I sent him the passage from the 1920 journal. He did not
reply so I left it at that. Then in late June, while working on this chapter,
I sent him a reminder. There followed over a period of two days a rapid-
fire exchange of emails, the net result of which was that I temporarily

abandoned this work. The total of our exchange came in at around 10,000 words, so I'm not going to reproduce it here (the entire exchange can be found at my website[1]). On the surface what transpired was a prickly debate between two researchers who do not agree, with one researcher, Levenda, trying to steer another away from some "erroneous" assumptions, and the other, me, resisting that effort and becoming increasingly argumentative. And in fact, I had written to Levenda to get him on the record as an example of a Crowley scholar who was resistant to my "thesis" (that Crowley was complicit with child sexual abuse). What I got was a lot more than I bargained for.

Levenda's second response included the following:

> Scholarly examination of the evidence has to take into account the actual evidence first, and if scholars cannot find evidence of sexual abuse of children it is probably because it is not there to be found .... We have an enormous record of AC's sexual rituals, almost tedious in their attention to explicit detail. In that case, why would we expect that he would suddenly become coy and neglect to detail for us his sexual conquest of minors? ... What is the Kabbalistic correspondence for sexual acts with children? What is the Golden Dawn context? There isn't any .... All of his workings—at Cefalù, in North Africa, etc.—were based on GD rituals. *Liber AL* itself is written using GD imagery, for instance. You can't understand AC without understanding the GD, as I have written and proven already. His magical diaries are replete with references that only make sense to someone deeply familiar with GD terminology.

Levenda dismissed my citing the *Liber AL* prescriptions of child sacrifice by writing: "Those verses (and the whole of AL) have been subjected to all sorts of deconstruction and explication, and you would have to show me that you were aware of those arguments and could refute them." He offered his own experience as evidence, claiming to have spent extensive time among "occultists, Thelemites, satanists, witches, neo-Nazis, magicians, and even Republicans," to have "witnessed all sorts of mayhem, from sexual promiscuity to drug abuse to threats of violence, etc.," and "never seen any hint of pedophilia in any of the groups I have known, nor in connection with any individual person I have known."[2]

The day after composing this chapter, I received an email from the Crowley scholar whom both Urban and Levenda recommended I contact, Marco Pasi. In a very different response to Levenda's, Pasi's email was as follows:

> The question you ask is very interesting indeed. I am not aware of any scholarly (actually even non-scholarly) research on the subject. And I agree there are probably interesting things to say about it. I have read your online piece. In relation to Crowley, the key period for the topic is surely the Cefalù period (1920–1923). I don't remember ever seeing any evidence that Crowley personally had sexual contact with children, but it seems like children from his community in Cefalù were allowed to watch the performance of sexual magical rituals (between consenting adults). This was done not out of simple carelessness, but with the idea that freely watching adults having sexual intercourse would prevent the formation of sexual repressive complexes in those children. Even if this did not involve coercion (from what I remember children were allowed to watch if they were around but were not forced to do so), I guess this behavior would already fall into what you define as "beliefs and activities with larger social engineering goals that include the deliberate sexual traumatization of children in a ritualistic fashion". But a difference should probably be made between involving children directly and physically in sexual activities and letting them watch sexual activities of others, even if both behaviours lead to some form of traumatization. To be honest, I never went very deep into the matter, so I would have to go back to the sources and check, and also think a bit further about it. I hope this helps.

*

> "This attitude is, of course, characteristic of that vast class of moral cowards, whose only remedy for evil is to remove the occasion; whether it is a glass of cognac, a piqué blue blouse or a dollar left lying about. They feel themselves helpless. Sin must follow temptation. Righteousness is only possible in the absence of an alternative. We of Thelema pursue a policy exactly contrary. We resist temptations through the moral strength and the enlightening experience which comes of making a series of

systematic experiments with divers iniquities. A few trials soon
teach us that wrongdoing does not pay."

—Crowley, *Confessions*, p. 866

The exchange with Levenda left me feeling psychologically "handled."
I was left wondering if I'd been the target of a sophisticated attempt
to neutralize all my efforts to get to the truth about Crowley and the
occult. Whether or not Levenda, with his Jesuit training, was intentionally trying to derail me in my investigations, or whether he was simply
trying to help me see some of the flaws in my arguments, the effect was
the same. I was stopped in my tracks. Rightly or not, I felt I had been
subjected to what Raimond Gaita calls "illegitimate persuasion."

So far, none of Crowley's defenders (including those who claim not
to be, like Levenda) have explained why they believe someone bidding
for spiritual power through social and moral transgression would draw
the line at *anything at all*, or why they insist that, when *Liber AL* says
"take strange drugs" it means it literally (just as Crowley followed it
literally), but when it says "sacrifice cattle little and big, after a child," or
"the best blood is that of a child," it is using occult code known only to
the few, and that anyone who has done the proper reading would know
this. Anyone stupid enough to take these passages literally, according
to Levenda, Duquette, and a legion of Crowley apologists, can't blame
Crowley or Thelemic doctrine, only themselves for not having done the
proper reading.

While I don't wish to argue that a written text should be held responsible for the actions people commit upon reading it, to argue that a prescription for child sacrifice is not a prescription for child sacrifice—no
matter how it *looks*—indicates the sort of doublethink and pretzeled
logic that uncouples occult beliefs from any sort of accountability *at all*.
When the so-called "circumstantial" evidence is this overwhelming,
isn't the onus of proof on those who, like Levenda, insist there's nothing to see here? Isn't it up to them to show exactly *why* this evidence
doesn't *count as evidence*, and not simply dismiss our concerns with a
condescending remark about how we haven't done the proper reading
or attended enough O.T.O. meetings?

Regarding Levenda's insistence that there are no direct—or even
coded—references to "pedophilia" in occult tracts, this may be missing
the point, but if such are desired, they certainly exist. Crowley's most
recent biographer Kaczynski mentions how two children are listed as a

central part of Crowley's Gnostic Mass; he places "children" in inverted commas, however, as if to deflect any fears the reader might have that this instruction would ever be taken literally. The only reason I can think that it wouldn't be taken literally is that it would be illegal to do so, which is also a good reason to insist that it is meant "metaphorically." The onus is then on Kaczynski, Levenda, or whoever, to explain why this is so—or how they can be sure that it is.

There is at least one person who claimed to have been sexually abused as a child by Crowley, though tellingly, his allegations were less complaint than boast. This was the English occultist Alex Sanders, the founder of Alexandrian Wicca. (Sanders also introduced Sharon Tate to witchcraft when he was hired as a consultant for Tate's first film in 1967, *The Eye of the Devil*. The film is about ritual sacrifice.) Sanders's "well known bi-sexuality [sic]," is even attributed to his early encounter with Crowley. In 1978, in an interview with Jack Pleasant, Sanders claimed to have been introduced to Crowley by his grandmother, Mary Biddy, when he was only ten. Sanders was initiated as a witch, he claimed, at aged seven, by Biddy, "whom he had chanced on standing naked in the kitchen in a circle drawn on the floor." At ten, Biddy took him to London to meet Crowley.

> "She left me with Crowley for the night and he carried out some of his sex magic with me," said Alex. "It wasn't a very nice experience. To me, as a young boy, he was just a horrible, smelly, old man. Before I left he tattooed his 'mark of the beast' on my hand. It's still there. It hardly turned me off sex though. At one time when I was still in London with my second wife, Maxine, I also had two mistresses and nine male lovers." (Pleasant, 2004)

Sanders also referred to this meeting, in more sanguine terms, when he was asked by Stewart Farrar how he had come by a ring that once belonged to the famous nineteenth-century French occultist Eliphas Levi. Sanders said it had been given to him by a magician his grandmother had introduced him to at the age of ten, called "Mr. Alexander." Sanders later realized it had been Crowley.[3]

*

While I was completing the first draft of this book, in February 2017, I came across an article called "Beast Wing 666: Ritual Abuse UK" at the website of Nathaniel Harris. Harris is, or was, an occult writer and illustrator who published several books in the Chaos magic field (as well as illustrating one by Phil Hines). Some of this work was published by the well-known independent UK occult publisher Mandrake Press. As Harris reports, "It turned out that several people I knew … had all been involved in the cult of convicted ritualistic paedophile [and Thelemite] Colin Batley." Harris lists several individuals "who have been successfully prosecuted in the UK for ritualistic child abuse and are all known to have been involved in a wide paedophile ring"; he claims that he has met nearly every single one of them. "I also know of many more people who are just as guilty and currently still active in the U.K. … It is my unhappy experience that occultism in the UK not only harbours paedophiles, but is thoroughly infected with them." Harris claims "There are a number of prominent occultists in the UK who were involved in the same 'cult network' as Colin Batley and are guilty of ritual child abuse. Nothing is being done about them by the police or by hardly anyone on the 'occult scene.'" He warns that, as the truth comes to light,

> Outsiders may well come to assume that all occultists are either paedophiles or involved in the cover up—since so few occultists seem to care regarding the warnings and disclosures from survivors and their advocates. This will not be the fault of corrupt therapists or sensationalist newspapers. It seems it is easier to convince most occultists that masturbating off over sigils is all it takes to do "real magic" than it is to point out that the scene's leaders and teachers might be self-aggrandizing abusive sociopaths with delusions of grandeur. (Harris, 2017)

Batley's group (to which Harris believes his parents also belonged) "were connected to a wider cult, whose members were never identified or charged by the police [and] included many who are not only recognized for supposed contributions to occultism, but are also trusted and respected members of the 'community.'"

> It took a decade before police took allegations against Colin Batley seriously, during which time he and his cult remained free to abuse. Even after three of his child victims had grown to adulthood and came forward independently it still took another three years before anything was done. I am reliably informed (by

someone directly involved with the investigation) that the officers who successfully prosecuted him had to go against orders from "higher up," and were passed up for promotion. Doing the right thing, it seems, proved bad for their careers. Although the police seem to have assumed the cult has been closed down and is no longer a danger there were many active abusers among its members who continue to pose a serious threat to children—especially the vulnerable and disaffected. Although police at the time could not identify the members of the wider cult surrounding Batley it has been confirmed through disclosures from various sources that he was a member of the Illuminates of Thanateros. (ibid.)

The Illuminates of Thanateros was founded by Peter J. Carroll, one of the fathers of Chaos Magic. Not surprisingly, Mandrake Press has disassociated itself from Harris at the author bio at their site, accusing him of insanity:

Nathaniel Harris is currently unwell. He is suffering some form of mental illness, one symptom which [sic] is misdirected rage against former friends and associates. He has been making unpleasant, unsubstantiated accusations on various Internet forums. Under no circumstances should any of these accusations be given credence. He is receiving professional help and we wish him well for the future …. (*Mandrake of Oxford*, 2017)

Mandrake Press was founded in 1929 and Aleister Crowley was the chairman in 1930 (Mandrake published some of his works, as well as those of D. H. Lawrence). Since writing this chapter, I have spoken to Harris at length. He showed no signs of mental imbalance and I found his testimony entirely credible.[4]

CHAPTER XXVIII

Over to Satan's Side: Espionage, Black Mass, and Blackmail

"Then again the master shall speak as he will soft words, and with music and what else he will bring forth the Victim. Also he shall slay a young child upon the altar, and the blood shall cover the altar with perfume as of roses. Then shall the master appear as He should appear—in His glory."

—Aleister Crowley, *Liber LXVI, Liber Stellæ Rubeæ*

While I was corresponding with Peter Levenda, at a certain point, in exasperation, I mentioned that my own family history seemed to veer improbably close to Crowley on numerous occasions, to the extent that my grandfather "may even have met Crowley." Levenda replied,

And what if he had? It's possible that my maternal grandfather met Crowley, too, but it's not something I can prove so there is relatively little value in even discussing it. So what? ... You say you are referring to your own "personal history and knowledge" but I am quite certain that personal history did not include being abused by Crowley. Why don't you stick to your own personal story without making claims you can't support?

THE VICE OF KINGS

Levenda is safe in his certainty I was not abused by Crowley, since Crowley died twenty years before I was born. But what if I *was* abused by someone who, at the time or later, was a match for Crowley in some way? When I tried to get to the bottom of my brother's life and death, it included both the possibility that he was a victim of abuse and that he was a perpetrator of it—with myself as his most likely earliest (or only) victim. In many ways, thinking it over now, my attempt to bust open my brother's cover story was like a practice run for taking on Crowley; and yet the reverse is also true, by taking on Crowley, I am really coming full circle, back to my brother's case—which is also my own—from a new angle. It is as if I am hoping to somehow trick the truth into revealing itself—or to trick my own psychic defense system into *letting me see it*.

If you had asked me ten years ago if I thought there might be any links between Aleister Crowley and my family, I would likely have dismissed the idea as fantasy. Yet fairly early on in my research, it started to seem as though every other lead I followed (starting from my grandfather's known associates) led to Crowley sooner or later, generally sooner. More striking still, my discovery of these many links seemed to correspond with, in fact be a direct result of, Crowley's closeness, at just about every turn, to the historically-identifiable circles involved in the hidden sexual abuse of young children in the UK, during the twentieth century. In other words, the connecting tissue between Crowley and my family appears to be characterized by the sexual deviations of powerful individuals, including child predation and worse.

If Crowley associated with individuals who were indisputably involved in the most appalling crimes we have names for, including the torture and murder of children, is it rash to ask if he might have taken part in those dark rituals? By this time (the 1940s), his reputation as "The Beast 666" would have preceded him wherever he went. Is there any reason to think he failed to live up to it? The fact Crowley worked as a double agent for British and German intelligence during World War II has generally not been incorporated into an understanding of his magickal mission and modus operandi, despite the clear overlaps between the worlds of intelligence agencies and occultism in the lore of ritual abuse. Richard Spence suggests that Crowley was "recruited (probably by Max Knight) to run some sort of 'occult training school for selected agents.' … Another possibility is … a counterintelligence ploy to attract, compromise, and recruit subversive elements.

That, too, suggests Knight's guiding hand. *Occult rites, especially sexual ones, produced excellent opportunities for blackmail"* (Spence, 2008, p. 241, emphasis added).

The main source on this is Kim Philby, a high-ranking British intelligence agent who was revealed in 1963 as a member of the "Cambridge Five" group of Soviet-British double-agents (it included Guy Burgess and Anthony Blunt). In a 1942 report given to his Soviet handlers and based on an MI6 investigation, Philby lists a number of nightclubs (most or all probably located in London) "frequented by RAF officers who are under the influence of drugs, alcohol, sexual orgies or Black Mass [and] are induced to part with information. An important side-line is blackmailing officers" (West & Tsarev, 1999, p. 317). (Philby also mentions, without explanation: "Another method is to introduce dubious doctors to healthy clients at THE DORCHESTER, GROSVENOR HOUSE, etc." (ibid.)) The authors of this work (*The Crown Jewels: The British Secrets at the Heart of the KGB Archives*) are skeptical of Philby's claims almost sixty years later, rather ironically perhaps, considering what has come to light in the past few years about the criminal subculture of British high society. "In retrospect," they write, "it seems highly unlikely that such misbehavior could be going on at Leeds Castle, the splendid home in Kent of Olive, Lady Bailey, not least because a fairly regular weekend guest there was Sir Stewart Menzies"—the Chief of MI6. They do allow, however, that "As regards authenticity, the people identified in Philby's notes and the charts really existed [and] similarly, the nightclubs mentioned also operated during the war, so there is an element of verisimilitude to a rather bizarre tale that links the notorious occultist Aleister Crowley to, of all people, the Soviet ambassador Ivan Maisky" (ibid., p. 316). As it happens, Ivan Maisky lived in London during World War I, and was close friends with George Bernard Shaw, H. G. Wells, and Beatrice and Sidney Webb.

Evan Morgan or Lord Tredegar was another friend of Crowley's from British Intelligence, a little known branch called MI8, the Radio Security Service. Tredegar hosted parties at his house in Newport, and frequent guests included Aldous Huxley, H. G. Wells, G. K. Chesterton, and Augustus John.

> Evan was an expert in the occult and even built himself a "magik room"—the spelling was deliberate—at Tredegar House. Crowley visited him many times, and declared the room the best equipped

> he had ever seen. Crowley, known throughout Europe as "the Great
> Beast," took part in many weird and perhaps terrifying rituals at
> Tredegar Park and christened Evan "adept of adepts." Sometimes
> those rituals frightened even Crowley. (Carradice, 2011)

There is little information about Evan Tredegar (a biography of him
was due out in 2013 but has been tied up in litigation), but one excellent source is Robin Bryans's *The Dust Has Never Settled*. Robin Bryans
was little known in his life (he died in 2005), though in 1990 he did
receive some attention when he stated publicly that Lord Mountbatten,
Anthony Blunt, and others were involved in an old-boy network sexually abusing minors in country houses and castles throughout Great
Britain and Ireland, including the infamous Kincora Boys' Home.
Of Bryans's eight memoirs, four were written under the name Bryans
and were of a similar thrust, based on Bryans's inside knowledge of the
British political aristocracy. In *Mask of Treachery*, a study of the Soviet
Cambridge spy ring, John Costello wrote of Bryans: "Bizarre though
some of [his] theories may be, those that could be checked mesh with
established record" (1988, p. 467).

Despite such endorsements, all four of Bryans's works are not merely
out of print but unavailable online (perhaps suggesting a coordinated
effort to take them out of circulation). Fortunately I have a PDF copy of
The Dust Has Never Settled. The book is almost impenetrable: a seemingly
endless series of names and places (and occasional dates) that shifts
mid-paragraph, sometimes mid-sentence, back to some (possibly) previously described person or event, often using only first names. There
is no apparent structure to the work and no narrative cohesion, and
the book seems almost to be written in code. Perhaps this is partially
because Bryans can't state things plainly without risking being sued,
but also I suspect because he is describing a very unfamiliar world from
the inside. It is a world in which circles of government, intelligence,
literature, occultism, homosexuality, drugs, rape, and murder intersect
and overlap so seamlessly as to be all-but indistinguishable.

At one point Bryans comments, in passing, "Incest and child sex abuse
disgust me yet neither activity could be dissociated from people I had
the misfortune to have dealings with" (1992, p. 289). Yet Bryans seems
to have no misgivings about his close—possibly sexual—friendship
with Evan Tredegar, whom he casually implicates not merely in Black
Mass rituals and sadomasochism but also murder. He names Tom

Driberg, Max Knight, and Aleister Crowley as participants within the same shadowy vice-world, describing Tredegar as "a great master of the black mass" (ibid., p. 84) and Crowley as his "fellow high-priest" (ibid., p. 129).

"Human blood [as well as semen] was essential for any version of the black mass as I had learnt when some of Crowley's devotees celebrated, and as a boy of sixteen I had seen how Evan Tredegar brightened up more than house parties, and indulged in doings from which women, such as Lady Cunard, were banned" (ibid., p. 115). Bryans notes that his lover Guy Burgess's "... main task seems to have been the procurement of young blond boys for sexual gratification of both Archdeacon Sharp and Captain Macnamara. They took a large party of English schoolboys to the Nuremberg Rally, and others to the Olympic Games in Berlin. The fact-finding missions of the Anglo-German fellowship were related ... as wild homosexual orgies." After Macnamara died in the war, "Archdeacon Sharp turned more and more to the black masses, practiced in the same way as before by [Macnamara's] friend Evan Tredegar" (ibid., p. 119).

> Many people besides me have pointed out that boys' bodies are temples of the Holy Ghost, but on consecrated ground they bugger those temples, sometimes drugging the boys before sex as part of the black mass .... The Sussex police knew as I did that some of the drug traffic in and out of the country was run by people who had been introduced to drugs via the black mass. Aleister Crowley wrote the banned *Diary of a Drug-Fiend*, and Driberg added that, "It was alleged that he lured well-known women to these orgies, drugged them until they participated, and then had them photographed for blackmailing purposes." (ibid., pp. 481–483)

Bryans becomes especially cryptic when insinuating that ritual murder was also part of the black mass orgy program: "Nor were there inquests on a number of suspicious deaths involved with Evan Tredegar and Aleister Crowley ... The police asked if we had seen much of Aleister Crowley's black mass people around Ovingdean because more than usual black chicken feathers and blood had been seen, and the unsolved murder of [a schoolboy] was still on police record" (1992, pp. 584–585). Earlier Bryans asks the same question that began this exploration: "But was Crowley serious or joking when he boasted to reporters that he only sacrificed the best bred children at his black masses? The Sussex police liked neither the Hymn of Pan being chanted in a frenzy by Crowley's devotees in Brighton's municipal cemetery at Bear Road nor events over the hill at Ovingdean where a boy had been murdered" (1992, p. 114). Based on everything else that Bryans all-but-outright states in his book, his question about Crowley's "joke" seems largely academic.

CHAPTER XXIX

A worn-out toy: Poupée's death, God-identification, Garbanzo's passing

"My secret comes out in my most innocent poems, essays, pictures, etc. and frightens people, they know not why .... It is therefore capable of all, is wholly divine as it is fiercely fleshly or darkly devilish."
—Aleister Crowley, *Magickal Diaries*, August 17, 1920 (five days after "the assault")

In Crowley's heavily sanitized version of his time at the abbey in his *Confessions*, he describes Thelemic child-rearing practices in a few lines:

In the abbey, our plan was to watch the children to discover in what direction they wanted to develop, having given them the greatest possible variety of facts from which to choose .... Extending this principle to the world at large, my plan would be to classify children in infancy according to the subtle indications afforded by their gestures and reactions to various stimuli .... His lessons should be a relief; the satisfaction of a real appetite. (1989, p. 854)

"Subtle indications," "gestures," "reactions to various stimuli," "the satisfaction of a real appetite": It would be a stretch to argue that Crowley is using coded language here, but on the other hand, this is just the sort of thing we would expect to find if we were looking for coded language. Even an innocuous term like "lessons" has to be read in the context of a "school" set up by a man who believes he is the living incarnation of Satan, whose professed task is to free humanity from all sexual and moral repression by committing every last act of transgression.

In chapter 5 of *Confessions*, Crowley describes how, as a teenager, in the midst of a struggle to follow his father's influence and become the perfect Christian, he "simply went over to Satan's side; and to this hour I cannot tell why."

> I was anxious to distinguish myself by committing sin. Here again my attitude was extraordinarily subtle. It never occurred to me to steal or in any other way to infringe the decalogue. Such conduct would have been petty and contemptible. I wanted a supreme spiritual sin; and I had not the smallest idea how to set about it. There was a good deal of morbid curiosity among the saints about "the sin against the Holy Ghost" which "could never be forgiven." Nobody knew what it was …. I must find out what that sin was and do it very thoroughly. (ibid., p. 67)

There's nothing to suggest Crowley ever abandoned this goal—on the contrary. So how exactly did Crowley go about his mission to sin against the Holy Ghost? Was it through trial and error? Presumably, one gauge would be his own resistance (self-restriction) at the thought of committing certain acts; in other words, whatever was most appalling and painful for him to do, he would be tempted to do it. There may be a universal element to this. Since we are most totally vulnerable as children, the most intensely distressing and destructive ("sinful") experience we can have is to be sought out in the realm of childhood. For Dostoyevsky, the one unforgivable sin was the corruption of innocence, the sin against children. As George Steiner writes:

> Dostoyevsky regarded the torment of children, and especially their sexual degradation, as a symbol of evil in pure and irreparable action. He saw in it the incarnation—some critics would call it the

"concrete" universal—of unforgivable sin. To torture or violate a child is to desecrate in man the image of God where that image is most luminous. But even more dreadfully, it is to put in doubt the possibility of God, or, rigorously stated, the possibility that God retains some affinity to His creation. (1996, p. 203)

*

> "I've turned repulsion into passion, fear into love, disgust to worship; but here beside me lies a worn-out toy."
> —Aleister Crowley, *Magickal Diaries*, August 12, 1920

In his 1920 journal, July 28, Crowley writes the following:

> Suppose we ask the Idea of Physical Fatherhood one question? Would you rather lose your son when he is twenty, and bound your life's hope to him; or when he's ten, and keeps you wild with pride, anxiety, and the like; or when he's five, and you have just begun to take him seriously, build on him, adjust your future to his career … ; or at his birth, when … your child's life but a bubble-dream as yet; or while his being is no more than promise? … Father-Will, wouldst thou not rather face thy fate at the first, fall Roman on thy sword, and cheat the torturer Hope-Deceived? (1972, p. 238)

Translation: isn't it better to have one's child die in infancy, before one has been able to invest too much hope and desire in their lives, than later? There can be no doubt that Crowley was desperately worried about the well-being of Poupée. The child was (allegedly) sickly from birth, and he expresses his concern on various occasions:

> We are desperate about Poupée. I never liked that "diminution" symbol, and she is literally wasting away. She can't digest any food …. I have been howling like a mad creature nearly all day. I want my epitaph to be "Half a woman made with half a god." It is not My Will to save my baby's life. What is "mine"? Not to save all the babies in the world, as I should do if I started to save one. My Will is to be the Logos of the Aeon; I am Thelema. Do what thou wilt shall be the whole of the Law. Beyond that, I am more helpless than the veriest quack magician. (ibid., p. 110)

After this, Crowley consults the *I Ching* about Poupée's health, and all the indications are of a concerned father doing everything he can to help his infant daughter survive. Does it really seem likely he would submit her to sexual molestation rituals? Then again, does it seem likely that someone so concerned for the welfare of his child would keep her in such a sex, drug, and dementia-fueled environment? The answer depends on our understanding what Crowley considered harmful to his child's spirit (which is not necessarily the same as what threatens her physical well-being).

In *Confessions*, Crowley writes: "There is nothing in the universe which is not indissolubly one with every other thing; and the greatest man is he who makes no difference between any one thing and any other thing. He becomes the 'chief of all' as stated in *The Book of the Law*" (p. 829). The period (between 1920 and 1923) during which Crowley performed sex magick rituals involving, to one degree or another, small children was also the period during which—Kenneth Grant claimed, as did Crowley himself—Crowley attained some sort of enlightenment. There can be no doubt that the death of Poupée had a profound effect on Crowley; there can also be little doubt that the circumstances surrounding the infant during this period contributed to her early death. What is unknown is how much of this was consciously manipulated or exploited by Crowley.

A magician is given power over a child, one he believes could be the incarnation of a god, a cosmic being or "star" that cannot be harmed by any earthly interference. He believes it is only his false sense of ego that allows him to experience the child as separate from his own consciousness. He has sworn to serve Horus/Aiwaz/Satan at any personal cost to himself, and vowed never to let personal affection for others interfere with his True Will. He is committed to performing every known act of violation and discovering the ultimate sin; he views total sexual freedom as the foundation of his new religion. He participates in the ritual sexual "initiation" of the child, *to whatever degree*, and reports it in his journal, including tortured child screams that gave pleasure to his woman's ears. He undergoes a kind of breakdown, suffering the hideous agony and remorse which is the only way to destroy his "illusory" sense of separation, forcing himself into a state of unified consciousness that is somehow entangled with the terrible process of a child's suffering and death, and with his experiencing the child's agony *as his own*.

"All forms of violence are quests for identity," wrote Marshall McLuhan. What could be more potentially violent than the quest to identify with a God? To achieve oneness with all things is to seek the destruction of all that separates one thing from another, which is to seek the destruction of *all forms*.

*

> "[V]eil not your vices in virtuous words: these vices are my service; ye do well, & I will reward you here and hereafter."
> —*Liber AL*, II: 52

There is a famous account, reproduced in most of the Crowley biographies, of how Crowley received a visit from the German head of the O.T.O., Theodor Reuss, in 1912. Reuss accused Crowley of having improperly revealed the "innermost secret of the O.T.O." Crowley denied any such knowledge, whereupon Reuss (in the now standard account) went and took a copy of *The Book of Lies* from Crowley's bookshelf and opened it at chapter 36, "The Star Sapphire," a ritual Crowley allegedly wrote in a trance state five years earlier, in 1907. The ritual begins with a reference to the Adept being "armed with his Magick Rood" and "provided with his mystic rose." As this account has been passed down and endlessly repeated, Crowley realized that he had unwittingly been referring to the penis and the vagina and hence to the sex act as the basis of the ritual, in other words, the idea of sex magick, *per se*, was *the* big secret. By proving he had been able to discern this secret wisdom by his own intuitive capacities, Crowley was deemed worthy of the highest initiatory degree of the O.T.O. Crowley described the revelation as "one of the greatest shocks of my life." Even allowing that Crowley was raised in Victorian times, this whole anecdote, complete in its minted form, seems *somehow lacking*.

By chance, while listening to Peter Levenda being interviewed by Whitley Strieber about Levenda's 2016 book (*The Lovecraft Code*), I discovered that the Latin portions of the Star Sapphire ritual, according to Levenda's own analysis, refer to *mother-son and father-daughter incest*. An online search turned up surprisingly little on the subject. Crowley refers to incest in *Magick*: "The twins of Set-Isis, harlot and beast, are busy with that sodomitic and incestuous lust which is the traditional formula for producing demi-gods, as in the cases of Mary and the Dove;

244 THE VICE OF KINGS

Leda and the Swan, etc." (1991, p. 338). Crowley was someone who took his myths literally, as blueprints for action, and he may not have been alone in this, considering the psyche-plundering procedures of MKULTRA and the attempt to create psychic spies, super soldiers, and creative geniuses ("demigods"), via the traumatization of infants, and how the child's parents have allegedly often been recruited into the brutalization process.

In his *Confessions*, Crowley describes "the fundamental principles of early education" based on his "experience with these two boys" (the ones he called Dionysus and Hermes): "I had to break up the Oedipus complex," he writes. "I had to destroy the false and fatal link between mother and son" (ibid., p. 861). One of Crowley's hagiographers, Thomas Churton, confirms this sentiment: "Saving Man from 'Mother' was as big a priority for Crowley as saving boys and girls from wedlock's chains" (Churton, 2012, p. 129).[1] The idea that mother-son bonds are frequently unhealthy, and at the root of the vast majority of adult male pathologies, is one I would agree with. But breaking a mother-son bond prematurely, and/or in a forceful or violent manner, is arguably even more harmful to the infant psyche than letting it continue too long. It is also allegedly one of the primary methods of ritual abuse and trauma-based mind control (see Hoffman, 2016). If Crowley's primary educational goal was to "destroy the false and fatal link between mother and son," it's reasonable to ask what *means* he considered legitimate for achieving this. Would they include father-daughter incest, as prescribed by the forbidden and most secret Star Sapphire ritual?[2] Is *this* the great central secret of the O.T.O. which Crowley divined?

The other item that showed up while searching online for more on this subject was, perhaps not surprisingly, in *The Gates of the Necronomicon*, written by Levenda's alter-ego, Simon.[3] Levenda/Simon quotes Mircea Eliade quoting Paracelsus: "He who would enter the Kingdom of God must first enter with his body into his mother and there die." This return to the womb (Eliade writes) is "sometimes presented as a form of incest with the mother." Simon continues, "Although veiled, this impulse survives even today among the relatively modern (early twentieth century) rituals of Thelema, for example in the rite known as *Liber XXXVI, The Star Sapphire*. In this ritual, Latin incantations allude to a unity between Mother and Son and between Daughter and Father." Simon then parallels the dangerous gate of occultism to the *vagina dentata*. "A dentate or otherwise dangerous vagina could only belong to a tabooed female, and the queen of tabooed females is the Mother, to be followed by the Sister and other women with whom sex would be considered incest or forbidden (such as very young, premenstrual girls)" (p. 52).

This is *the same Simon-Peter*, remember, who, in his correspondence with me, denied *all evidence* of any magickal basis for child abuse.

*

> "It is a mistake to suppose that the victim is injured. On the contrary, this is the most blessed and merciful of all deaths, for the elemental spirit is directly built up into Godhead—the exact goal of its efforts through countless incarnations. On the other hand, the practice of torturing animals to death in order to obtain the elemental as a slave is indefensible, utterly black magic of the very worst kind, involving as it does a metaphysical basis of dualism. There is, however, no objection to dualism or black magic when they are properly understood. See the account of the Master Therion's Great Magical Retirement by Lake Pasquaney, where he "crucified a toad in the Basilisk abode."
> —Aleister Crowley, *Confessions*, p. 95.

Negative identity equals seeing only things to oppose oneself against. It is the hammer that sees everything as a nail. To a large extent, that is my unconscious/conscious purpose in writing about Crowley: to hit that nail on the head and be done with it, forever. To find something *big* to oppose and so assert my own tenuous sense of identity. I am opposed to the sexual abuse, torture, and murder of children. Perhaps even more than that, I am almost violently opposed to the deliberate distortion of the truth by which unpalatable realities (such as child abuse) are dressed up in poetic, romantic, or humorous garb, and are rationalized with "magickal" or philosophic arguments and made to seem something other than what they are. Yet what does such opposition achieve, besides more written explorations? Does it lead to understanding, or only to condemnation?

Child sexual abuse and torture is a reality with consequences. Crowley was complicit with this reality, but then, so are we all. There are degrees and degrees, however. Writing about Crowley's complicity with child abuse feels urgent to me. If anything in this world is important, it is exposing this reality, and this distortion. I am sure there will be readers who feel opposed to my act of poisoning two dogs in retribution for attacking my cat. I can't disagree with them, yet nor do I regret that act or consider it inherently wrong. I am ambivalent, partly proud, partly ashamed, and hence neither. Had I acted differently, perhaps Garbanzo wouldn't have survived his wounds (or would have been attacked again) and we would have been deprived of ten good years together. What a small price to pay for those years! On the other hand, my ritualistic dog-slaying may have been entirely gratuitous, an unconscious acting out of traumatic imprints. It may have been a way for me not to be consumed by powerlessness and rage at failing to protect my cat from the irrational forces of nature/nurture, making it a wanton act of destruction. Perhaps the dogs were standing in for my parents? Whatever the case, I paid for the act almost immediately via the severe pain and distress of hookworm, suggesting I was in some way *harming myself* via the ritual.

If I am so ambivalent about my own actions, if I am forced to own up to the impossibility of knowing the rightness or wrongness of them, how can I hope to judge another man's? Behind every veil is a mirror that reflects back at us the truth. And since a veil is there to conceal, what reflects back at us is always one part divine, one part animal. There is no revelation without the beast.

Writing this work has been like walking a tightrope over an abyss with no safety net. I am hoping throughout that the correlation between the two narratives will become clear in the process of juxtaposing them. I am still not sure it has, but here's one way in which it might. In September of 2014, Garbanzo was diagnosed with *cor pulmonale*, an enlarged heart due to chronic asthma. He was given six months to live. I went for a second opinion and the next vet not only confirmed the first diagnosis but told me that the X-rays revealed a large mass in his stomach that could also prove fatal! Despite this double death sentence, Garbanzo lived another twenty-one months before finally passing, in May of 2016, ending his ninth and final life. Significantly, Garbanzo changed over the years in ways that human beings change—or at least in the way I have experienced change as a human being. He seemed more and more comfortable with being a cat, just as I've become more comfortable being human (rather than identifying as an alien, a god, or a fallen angel). He took to purring more frequently and he became increasingly receptive to affection. In the last few months of our time together, he sometimes slept under the covers, stretched out like a tiny human, his head resting on my armpit, his arm across my chest. Did I become more like a cat while he became more like a human? Did we meet and merge somewhere in the middle?

By his final morning, Garbanzo couldn't move without extreme pain. It was so bad that at one point he bit my thumb down to the bone (on my right hand; the wound got infected). When I spoke to the vet, she said it was almost certainly a blood clot in his back leg paralyzing him and that there was nothing to do for him anymore. I'd had almost two years to prepare for this but it still came as a shock. I spoke to several different vet assistants, trying to find someone who would come to the house so Garbanzo could die at home, in peace, but none of them would do it. In the end, I took him in a taxi to his regular vet's, inside his traveling case, for one final journey. There wasn't much to think about anymore. If Garbanzo was unable to move without crippling pain, life would be a hellish experience for both of us. Even so, making a decision to end his life seemed unthinkable. At the vet's, numb, dazed, crying, I looked at Garbanzo and saw his expression was clear and firm. It was the same steely look in his eyes he so often had, and it communicated the simple fact: *It's time.* He was conscious to the end. He knew what was happening and he wasn't afraid. He was ready, so I was ready too.

Having already given him a mild tranquilizer, and after several failed attempts to find a vein, the vet injected the poison into his stomach. She left us alone together and I rested my head on the table, gazed into his eyes, and watched the light fading from them. I had told him everything I needed to. Nothing was left unsaid. His death was peaceful yet devastating, like witnessing my own. This was the nature of existence. After Garbanzo was gone, in my grieving, I felt the gaping hole in my life where his body had once been. The love I felt for him was not diminished by his death but *magnified.* I experienced that love as a single force: myself, Garbanzo, the continuum between us. It was all love, all one. It was what I was, what *we all are.*

To experience this "ultimate oneness" at the highest level—that of an imagined "enlightened state" of "Ipsissimus," say—is to experience the erasure of any separation or distinction between self and other, to exist as part of a conscious continuum with all creation. Perhaps this was even the closest I came to experiencing this, when Garbanzo died and I recognized the hole he had left as being the whole of *my own soul,* made of pure, everlasting love. I believe, I choose to believe, that was the truth which Garbanzo came into my life to share with me. But also that it was a truth he could only show me by dying.

I don't want to draw a parallel between the natural death of my cat and Crowley's sex and drug ritualizing with, or in close proximity to, his dying daughter. But I do wonder if that was an event Crowley may have used to try to access a "unified" (or profoundly dissociated) state of consciousness. And as I push my way through this jungle with nothing but a pen, I can only follow the two narratives where they need to go, and acknowledge the points at which they *appear* to run parallel, and at which they may begin to intersect.

CHAPTER XXX

Spectral justice: the unconscious confession of the taboo-breaker

"The practical goal of dissociation is to 'make things invisible.'"
—Richard Mangen, "Psychological Testing and Ritual Abuse"

Six months before Garbanzo died, in November 2015, a couple of weeks after I began writing "Occult Yorkshire," I had a dream. In the dream, I am on a train with an older man sitting opposite me and we are playing a game that is some sort of exercise. An Asian woman sits across the aisle from us. She asks me to imagine I am at the scene of the JFK assassination. After a moment, I tell her I cannot play this game because I wasn't there at the time. The woman begins to describe a different scenario to me. Although it seems at first as if she is inventing it, I gradually realize she is recounting an event from my past.

She describes a child in a car with a woman, the child's caregiver, and a man, a stranger. I am that child, and the woman is perhaps my mother. The Asian lady tells me the child was raped by the man while the woman was present. Even as I am realizing that this was an event in my past, I realize also that the man sitting next to me on the train is *the man who raped me*. I stare into his eyes and feel an almost overwhelming upsurge of emotions: rage, anguish, *relief*. I shift from this dream into an in-between space where I am screaming in anguish. I am hoping the

249

dream-scream will cause me to scream out loud, in my body, and wake my wife. I wake a second time and my wife is sleeping beside me.

The man in the dream was in his fifties or sixties, mostly bald but with a thin layer of grey hair, sunken eyes, and a thick, fleshy face with mottled skin. In retrospect, he bore some resemblance to an older Crowley, though this didn't strike me at the time (the man was also swarthy, perhaps not fully Caucasian). I understood that the dream was a direct result of digging into my past, both directly and indirectly, writing *Seen and Not Seen* and its follow-up, "Occult Yorkshire." I didn't know if the event described by the Asian woman—which I recognized in the dream as real, without actually remembering it clearly—happened or not. I knew that the feelings triggered *within* the dream were real enough.

The dream describes a process by which I am becoming conscious of a traumatic rape in my past without actually remembering it. It begins with a woman telling a story *as if* it is fictional, and it is only my willingness to recognize the true meaning of the story that allows me to realize its reality. This suggests a process occurring in my own consciousness of allowing myself to *see* something incrementally, in a way that allows for healing and integration to occur, without re-traumatizing myself in the process.

Since that time, I have had several more dreams that suggest the same, including two dreams in which I experienced the sensations, and the terror, of being raped as an infant. In neither dream was there any visual or aural content; it was purely sensational and emotional, pure *affect*. I experienced myself as being tiny of form, in complete darkness, and being physically manipulated by unknown human hands. I felt myself being flipped over, and then experienced the first—I would say almost preliminary—sensations of being anally penetrated. At this point, the terror was so great that I entered into a different state of consciousness, sometime after which I woke. I have not accessed any kind of "formal" memories, however. If these experiences constitute some kind of true event, then the memory is confined to the body. My mind, as such, has no access to it.

*

> "The traumatic events we deny return to us cumulatively."
> —Greg Mogenson, *A Most Accursed Religion*

On June 21, 2016, forty days (and nights) after Garbanzo died, I dreamt of being in a forest with Garbanzo. We are in communication for a time, then Crowley appears. There is a different version of *The Book of the Law* and I am deconstructing it, including some Hemingway-esque phrase like "Going, she was gone," that has something to do with God. I ask Crowley, how is this possible with Garbanzo? (How is it possible for a God to live in a cat? I don't use this phrase but that's the gist of it.) Crowley answers that we are all made up of more than just our own DNA, that our DNA includes everything we're not. The deepest, oldest part of us is an aspect of the Earth which is eighty billion years old. (Officially, the Earth is 5 billion years old at most.) This part presumes to be our God, he says, or puts itself forward as our God, because it is the oldest organic part of us. I understand from this that I connect to that God-part of me through the most primal part of my life, which is Garbanzo. This is then the aspect that presents itself to my awareness *as God*; it is coming not *from* but *through* Garbanzo—*the beast*—to me.

Garbanzo is there throughout but I can't see him. I go deeper into the forest to make myself seen to him. If I lie down on the hard ground, naked, he will come to where I am and rest underneath me, briefly.

I understand something about Crowley, the man. Everything he did was magick, everything was a ceremony. He was constantly battling to try to create the circumstances he wanted and to avoid those he didn't, using magick, making his life a never-ending struggle. The specific example I am given is when he was in an underdeveloped country in Asia, and there was a woman who was trying to get custody of his children. Crowley kept on doing spells to keep the children in his care, the woman was learning some sort of expertise that would give her the power to take the children from him, and Crowley was resorting to everything he knew, magickally, to stave off this fate.

Crowley is trapped inside his own belief system. He is completely convinced this is the only way to address the situation, but from my per-spective he doesn't even *know* if his magick is working, because there are other variables he isn't seeing. If he just let go, the situation might turn out the same. There is no real proof the magick is working besides his convic-tion that it is, and he is trapped by that conviction. There is something in his doctrine, or in *The Book of the Law*, about having to act constantly to try to control the forces of one's life. I want to say to him that a much better principle to live by would be "Nothing works but surrender." I am reluctant to use the phrase however, because I got it from John de Ruiter, who is not that much more trustworthy to me than Crowley.

*

In 2014, I wrote this email to Sebastian's closest childhood friend:

> Assumptions are dangerous but lack of them can also be—if your house is filling up with smoke, best to assume there's a fire somewhere ... Around this issue of—was there or wasn't there (sexual abuse) or did he or didn't he (participate), and so on, one thing that causes so many people to back away from it, besides the obvious, is that remaining in a state of not-knowing is so very difficult, even about small things, never mind life-affecting ones. My wife asked me what I thought of the idea of Sebastian having sex with children last night; after a briefly defensive response, I told her that I was 90% sure of it, based on all the evidence (some of which being my own behavior and interests). It seems to me he was in that world too long not to have gone deep into it, perhaps not all the way but far enough; the question is—what would have stopped him? Certainly not moral issues and hard to imagine lack of interest or desire. He scoffed at the sex trafficking trade publicly as "a myth," and to me insisted that forcing oneself on infants would do them no harm.
>
> So what is one—am I—to think in the end? That not to accept the extreme likelihood of his involvement in these circles is illogical and probably based more in denial (programming, loyalty to Sebastian, and to keep the secret protected) than reasoning. Still and all, this doesn't = knowledge, so the question is rather—what am I willing to do to find out (if it's even possible)? How important is it to know? And why?
>
> I think it has to do with reclaiming a part of me that's been rendered impotent, that's been shut away, silenced—if I am to say, yes he did these things, then that has to end with "to me"—which requires some regaining/reclaiming of memory/experience; only then would the unknowing end, and acceptance be possible.

I have been over and over the clues my brother left, both in what I know about him from my childhood, the things he said to me, and the things he admitted to in his own memoir and elsewhere. At the end of that process, I have no doubt that he suffered some form of early sexual abuse. The question of whether he went on to perpetrate abuses of his own is less clear. There seems no doubt he did things *to me*—I even remember some of them, though nothing overtly sexual. But the evidence for acts he might have committed later in life, as part of his dandy-Luciferian philosophy of nihilism and self-worship, is mostly circumstantial, the sort of evidence which Levenda calls "spectral"—at least when it pertains to Crowley.

In both cases, the question that burned the fiercest was the same: Knowing what I knew about my brother—about Crowley—about what he was capable of, what he admitted to, and the reasons behind it, what *could I reasonably deduce* he had committed in secret? As with Crowley, I did find some evidence (however tenuous) that my brother might have sexually interfered with someone besides myself as a child. On November 4, 2007, two months after *Dandy in the Underworld* was released, someone identifying himself as Kyle Cowper commented the following at Sebastian's blog (I have included the typing errors):

> As a boy close to Sebastian, i remember him and my father being close but i also remember sebastian touching me as a child. It traumatises me every day and the only reason im typing this is cause im drunk. I wouldnt admitt it otherwise as id be utterly humiliated. This man is an animal who slagged his wife off after she died to show class. And refused to speak to my sister when she confronted him to defend his actions what a joke! (S. Horsley, 2007)

The comment was followed by another on the same day, from "James Duff." It said simply "Child abuser u did me too!" Perhaps the oddest thing about these comments is that they were left up, unanswered, and remain there to this day (March 5, 2018). But what do they prove? Anyone can make accusations, and for any number of reasons, and all it really proves is that someone was angry with my brother (and that they apparently cared a lot about his first wife, who, like most people in my brother's memoir, got the short shrift of it). At the same time, the first post has enough veracity to it—the circumstances described, the claim of drunkenness, the typos, the expressed fear of humiliation—to make it impossible to dismiss.

When I told my brother about the incident with the cat in Guatemala, his face expressed distress and he made a comment about how much he hated cruelty to animals. Though he was never an animal lover, and though I don't recall ever seeing him expressing any particular interest in an animal, I think his pain was genuine. On the other hand, he also told me quite emphatically that forcing one's penis into a baby's mouth would not harm it. (I wish I could remember the context for this bizarre statement—it left me speechless—though presumably it was during a conversation about the effects of sexual abuse.)

After my brother died, when I was finding out as much as I could about him online, I came upon a disturbing YouTube video in which he was interviewed for the UK TV show *This Morning*, in 2008, about the government "crackdown" on prostitution in relation to the sex trafficking industry. Sebastian's response, after regurgitating an irrelevant string of scripted witticisms, was to categorically deny the existence of sex trafficking. "That's a myth," he cried, "it's one of these great myths, this trafficking thing. It's like a witch hunt. It's like paedophilic—[interrupted] It's a myth! It's part of the rescue industry, for the politicians, and the social workers, and the people who read *The Guardian*!" (*This Morning*, 2008).

I found the video excruciating to watch. It wasn't just how pathetically divorced from social reality my brother's denials were. I had frequently been on the receiving end of that same blind, insensate stonewalling, and watching the video was like reliving countless experiences of having my voice drowned out by his denials. That girls are trafficked against their will into the sex industry was apparently an unacceptable (or inadmissible) reality to my brother. Why? Perhaps it was because the notion of prostitutes as "the most honest creatures on God's earth" was central to his philosophy, and to his dandy lifestyle. He believed these girls were his "friends," and the idea they might be victims of exploitation not only stripped them of their sovereignty and dignity—it made *him* the victimizer. So then, why deny the reality of sex trafficking, rather than making a clear distinction between women who *chose* the occupation and girls who did not? Apparently my brother was heavily invested in denying even the *idea* that some prostitutes might not be doing it entirely by choice.

Sebastian took pride in having had sex with over a thousand prostitutes. ("Quantity is not quality, but even so, it's difficult not to be impressed, isn't it?" he quips at the start of the show, ignoring the interviewer's questions.) But according to his close friend Robert Pereno, in the later phase of his life, my brother's excessive use of heroin had rendered him largely impotent, suggesting that he was no longer having sex with anyone but himself. It's easy for me to imagine how hard it would have been for him, when so much of his social identity and self-image revolved around his "cock"—his brazen sexual arrogance and peacock strutting. Did he give up on sexual conquests entirely? Or did he seek out ever more provocative (and forbidden) acts to stimulate and inspire him? In the same interview, he repeats twice (at the start and the end) how much he relishes breaking laws. "The best things in life are forbidden," he says. "Laws are only good fun because they're great things to break." And then again: "I like laws. It gives me something to break. There's no picture without a satisfactory frame." Like Crowley, my brother's self-image—his sense of identity—was determined by a willingness—an imperative—to break taboos.

What is it about the allure of breaking taboos? Both Crowley and my brother were compelled to shock; and the best—really the only—way to shock people is to break taboos, both trivial and profound. Breaking taboos is a way to assert one's individuality and superiority, yet for this to work, it's essential—to some degree—that people *know* what one is doing, otherwise there will be no frisson or tension. There is no picture without a satisfactory frame, and it's no good to flaunt social conventions if no one sees you doing it. There is an inherent double-bind in this, because, if persisted in for long enough, taboo-breaking eventually veers into law-breaking, which potentially entails consequences more severe than mere moral outrage, or even social condemnation. At this point, the taboo-breaker—the philosophical criminal of whom Dostoyevsky's Raskolnikov is perhaps the starkest literary example—must become both crafty and coy in his methods. Since he seeks the satisfaction of boasting about his crimes without the inconvenience of being prosecuted or persecuted for them, it is here that the joke, the *bon mot*, the philosophical platitude becomes an invaluable tool in the transgressor's arsenal. His art then becomes the art of framing himself for crimes he claims do not exist.

When my brother went on national TV and denied the reality of sex trafficking (a historically proven fact), it was equivalent to insisting that all prostitutes are such by choice. This is similar to child molesters denying that children are the victims of their predations, but rather "hustlers … sending signals." It is a way to justify one's behavior by denying the humanity of one's victims, blotting out their inner experience with the force of one's own desire. Because my brother wanted to have sex with prostitutes (now "sex workers"), then obviously they wanted to have sex with him. Because Vidal or O'Carroll lusted after children or adolescents, they saw a green light regardless of what was actually being signaled. It takes a modicum of innocence to recognize innocence. Without it, the boundary between abuser and victim is erased, and the latter is absorbed—in psyche if not in body—into the former.

Yet innocence is what every soul longs to return to—perhaps the worst most of all. Beneath the transgressor's desire to brag of his crimes, is there an even deeper, less conscious need to confess? Is the taboo-breaker, as he seeks to "individuate" from the mass through his rebellion, unconsciously courting condemnation *by* it? By the same token, is he, like Raskolnikov, seeking the only possible means to receive forgiveness *from* it, to be restored his own humanity? If this was my brother's unconscious goal, it remained unfulfilled at the time of his death, and certainly, it wasn't completed *by* it. Now I am in the role of his posthumous "accuser" (and that of Crowley). Is it possible I am responding to clues and cues they left behind, in a shared attempt to finally put these demons to rest?

CHAPTER XXXI

Abuse culture and the law of the strong

"Compassion is the vice of kings: stamp down the wretched and the weak: this is the law of the strong: this is our law and the joy of the world."

—Aleister Crowley, *Liber AL vel Legis*, II:21

One major factor in the maintenance of the illusion of the world as a more or less civilized or benign space (the belief that the kinds of things reported in this book simply *do not happen*) is our unconscious assumption that the people in positions of authority are *reliable narrators* who can be trusted to provide an accurate account of reality. We implicitly, unthinkingly, trust those who have assumed power in our society, just as we tend to distrust those without power—the poor, the old, the sick, the homeless, the drug-addicted, the mentally unstable. To a large extent, social authority is the authority to determine *what is true or false*, to dominate the narrative. Yet, somewhat paradoxically, those who are able to define what is true—truthfully or not—are for this very reason able to attain power in society. The lawmakers are also the spell-casters.

Whatever the true nature of the universe, human society is not inherently just. People who abuse their social power are not automatically stripped of it. On the contrary, the primary aim and result of the abuse of power seems to be to ensure that power continues to be given to those who would abuse it. Those who are guilty of abusing power create the criteria for deciding what constitutes abuse of power, what makes a narrator reliable and a narrative believable. In such a cultural context, many (though not all) claims about how the powerful abuse their power seem *inherently unreliable,* hence unbelievable, to us. Victims of power abuse are traumatized by their experiences, often to the extent of being visibly damaged individuals (drug addicts, the mentally unstable, socially maladroit, and low status); because of this, they are seen to be telling exaggerated or unfounded stories.

While much of this work is speculative, it's also based on and inspired by quite visceral, non-intellectualized, lived insights into my own personal history and background. It may be a mistake to try to extend those insights outward to society at large; or it may just be an inevitable part of the attempt to make sense out of my experience by finding the larger context for it. Either way, much of the evidence and the recent flurry of exposés in the UK would *seem* to confirm the links between organized crime, law enforcement, intelligence agencies, the entertainment industry, high-ranking politicians, peerages, the sexual abuse of children, child pornography and worse, all concealed, somewhat thinly, behind a massive institutionalized cover-up. There really *is* a difference between looking into conspiracy theories and staring at conspiracy *facts,* however, for me at least. One oft-touted criticism of a conspiratorial reading of history is "People just can't keep a secret that long!" I think the truth is the opposite. I think we have been keeping secrets for so long we have got it down to a science. And few behaviors are more naturally conducive to secrecy than sexual ones.

How many of the individuals (men and women, but mostly men) who can be identified as "players" at varying levels within the grand game of social engineering either betray a tendency for child molestation or have been victims of it—or both? If we can believe the accounts at all, it's a truly alarming number. Can we hypothesize from this that "situational" child molestation (taken to sometimes unimaginable extremes) is the unconscious (and in some cases conscious) drive behind the many, myriad master plans of the elite? Perhaps not, but it's at least consistent with what we know about human individuals, which is that the sex drive is one of the strongest motivating factors there is for human beings. It's also consistent with the way the sexual element of criminal and conspiratorial networks, such as the Krays or

Jimmy Savile, while well-concealed, eventually turns out to be the most remarkable thing about them. My suspicion is that there's a narrowing of sexual (and therefore all other) interests as an individual ascends the social hierarchy and has his or her sexual neuroses inflamed and indulged, into a fine diamond point of pathology. To know what a man or woman is made of, look into his or her sexual drives; it is the drives that are the most carefully hidden that run the deepest.

This is my own particular bias, and the evidence I have cited for it is that sexual deviancy and social status seem to be inextricably intertwined in our present society, and to increase in tandem. The indication is that, even as worldly success augments and distorts libido, a distorted libido enhances worldly success. If there is any truth at all to this, I think it has to do with how the drive for worldly power is sourced in *formative infant experiences of powerlessness*, particularly those relating to abuse, usually sexual in nature. The more severely abused a person is (provided other social and psychological elements are also in place), the fiercer becomes their drive to achieve power and influence in the world. At the same time, there is an equally powerful, unconscious need to *reenact* early experiences of abuse, only now from the opposite end (that of abuser), as a way to feel powerful and offload psychic toxins of the past *onto others*.

Such a social system of abuse, while maintained by human beings, clearly isn't set up to benefit humans, not even those who *appear* to be in control of it. But if the system's nature is somehow *in*human and *anti*-human, our chances of understanding it are slim at best. It would lie beyond any human definitions of good and evil, malign or benign. We call a cancer malign because of what it does to our bodies, yet on its own terms it is merely growing and flourishing. So it may be with this world. Its apparent insanity and destructiveness may be entirely inseparable from its inherent nature as "the world." Organized malevolence may simply be the inevitable consequence of a divinely bestowed free will.

*

"[N]o member of the modern liberal intelligentsia can stare at a social problem for very long. He feels the need to retreat into impersonal abstractions, into structures or alleged structures over which the victim has no control. And out of this need to

> avoid the rawness of reality he spins utopian schemes of social
> engineering."
>
> —Theodore Dalrymple, *Our Culture, What's Left of It*

When I was growing up, Mary Whitehouse was a despised name in our household—a Christian conservative tight-ass whining about "family values" which seemed inseparable from fear and hatred of homosexuals and other kinds of "moral deviants." The National Front was seen as even more beyond the pale, a bunch of moronic, neo-Nazi skinheads. But when looking at the history of the Paedophile Information Exchange, I discovered that Mary Whitehouse and the National Front were two of the fiercest voices speaking out against the group (Pace, 2014b)! Whitehouse's nemesis at the time was Sir Hugh Greene, Graham Greene's brother and the director general of the BBC from 1960 to 1969; Whitehouse—a Christian—once referred to Greene as "the devil incarnate." "If you were to ask me to name the one man who more than anybody else had been responsible for the moral collapse in this country," she said, "I would name Greene" (*Irish Times*, 2001). It will perhaps come as no surprise to learn that, in the early days of his career, Greene did something suspiciously resembling intelligence work as head of the BBC Department for Germany in the late 1930s, "studying the National Socialists' propaganda" (Potschka, 2012). Nor, perhaps, that Greene was director general of the BBC in 1968, when Jimmy Savile first came aboard—this despite the fact that

> the BBC allowed MI5 to investigate the backgrounds and political
> affiliations of thousands of its employees, including newsreaders,
> reporters and continuity announcers. [T]he BBC's hitherto secret
> links with the Security Service [which reached a peak in the late
> 1970s and early 1980s] show that at one stage it was responsible for
> vetting 6,300 different BBC posts—almost a third of the total work-
> force. (Hastings, 2006)

As this point, the reader may be tempted to say, "BBC, MI5, what's the difference?" Yet the fact remains, somehow Savile slipped through this net. Suggesting—like so much else around his activities—that he was part of it.

Regarding Mrs. Whitehouse, I mention this subject because it is certainly one of the richest ironies of the current work that I have found myself taking a similar position to a woman I once considered—forty years ago—as the most contemptible of human beings. Nor was I alone in thinking so, only imitating a general feeling among progressive liberals. As her obituary had it, "The determination with which Mrs. Whitehouse pressed home her attack earned her vilification from all quarters of the permissive society. Students bellowed obscenities, intellectuals affected a lofty disdain, satirists pilloried her, lunatics sent death threats, and for four years the BBC (always her prime target) refused to allow her to appear on its programmes" (*The Telegraph*, 2001). Whitehouse's moral indignation appears to have been far more justified than I ever suspected, however. In a 1986 debate, she "chilled the Cambridge Union with *the horrors perpetrated upon children*," after which "the House voted 331 to 151 that censorship was a lesser evil than pornography" (ibid., emphasis added). It is a temptation, on learning all this, to correct my unfair judgment of Whitehouse by swinging to the other extreme and painting her as a misunderstood heroine of British abuse culture. This would probably be an error, however, especially since Whitehouse, for all her moral vigilance, singled out *Jim'll Fix It* for special praise, adding: "I don't know anything about Jimmy's lifestyle and, in any case, it's no business of mine."[1] Epic fail.

The Nazis allegedly had the Fabians on their hit-list: from which we can deduce that a shared enemy does not necessarily make a trustworthy ally. The *hubris* of social engineering transcends ideology, and begins with any attempt to control and direct others, whether towards mind expansion/socio-sexual liberation/spiritual "realization" or *away* from it, into ignorance and repression, moral "piety" and suffocating restriction. The end never justifies the means, when there is no way to separate end from means.

As I hope this work at least somewhat demonstrates, the agendas of social engineering are only ostensibly implemented by the ruling class as a means to benefit greater humanity. Their actual effect is to create an increasing gulf between the ruling class and those it rules over, even as, somewhat paradoxically, the insidious, toxic, and profoundly *inauthentic* values of our rulers trickle down into society, until the vice of kings has every last man, woman, and child in its grip. Since the cryptocracy adheres to its own private mores and values, these programs aren't limited to political policies or confined to any specific groups. They cross-pollinate over generations, cultures, creeds, and philosophies. It may even be that keeping us "hopping" is the primary purpose of every manufactured ideology: to prevent us from ever planting both feet squarely on the ground and figuring out what is really happening. The tensions of a divided loyalty in the psyche, between "good" and "evil," "right" and "wrong," liberalism and fascism, collectivism and individualism (mother and father), keep us marching in lockstep, into barracks or battlefield, to the never-ending beat of "Left, right, left, right!" (And since every tempo needs variation, today we have Alt-Left and Alt-Right.)

*

> "[O]f all the manifestations of sexual psychology, normal and abnormal, they ['erotic symbolisms,' i.e., sexual deviations] are the most specifically human. More than any others they involve the potently plastic force of the imagination. They bring us the individual man, *not only apart from his fellows, but in opposition, himself creating his own paradise. They constitute the supreme triumph of idealism."*
> —Havelock Ellis, *Studies in the Psychology of Sex v5: Human Sexuality* (emphasis added)

Researching and attempting to map the scope of social engineering *can* be overwhelming at the best of times, but perhaps never more so than when we begin to see that the "villains" are quite unlike our conventional expectations of how villains should look and behave. After all, they designed the template for understanding villainy. Like body snatchers or secret agents, the social engineers may walk among us, but they are not *us*.

Many people have heard about the old boy networks, and about how only those who belong to the "club" (Oxford, Cambridge, Yale, Harvard) get to advance within the extended club of society, in the various fields of government, military, intelligence, science, law, medicine, mass media, entertainment, and so on. But how far does this old boy network extend? For those who don't belong to it, there may be no way to ever know. Perhaps the exciting, sensationalized narratives of some conspiracy theorists are a way for the real situation to filter into our conscious awareness, the real situation being that we live in a world overrun by intelligence operatives and their informants, operatives who exist in a very different world to the rest of us, a "parallel universe." This is the broad brushstroke of the paranoid worldview. I make no bones about sharing it in essence, if not in the specifics. My primary objection to this kind of conspiratorial worldview is that it leaves out the essential element of *our own complicity* with the programs of social control—and, whether or not such complicity has been engendered in us by some sort of organized malevolence, this does not make us any less complicit.

In the UK in recent years (following the revelations about Savile), a series of high-ranking members of society have been "outed," one by one, as child sexual abusers. Many of them were dead and gone by the time their crimes were revealed, though a few were still living. Even a former prime minister, Edward Heath, was not exempt from posthumous charges: the allegations included "the rape of a male child sex worker aged 11 and sexual assault against four other children and two adults" and apparently "would have met the legal threshold for police to interview Heath under criminal caution had he still been alive" (Dodd & Morris, 2017). How is it possible such offenders were given the highest peerages of British society, OBEs, lordships, and the like? How is it that, despite their (sometimes widely-rumored) involvement in such activities, they were nominated for titles and ascended the social ranks as easily as they did? Famous OBEs implicated in the alleged sexual abuse of children include Jimmy Savile (DJ, TV presenter); Benjamin Britten (composer); Cyril Smith (MP); Jess Conrad (pop singer); Cliff Richard (pop singer); Rolf Harris (children's entertainer); Jimmy Tarbuck (comedian); John Peel (DJ); and Robert Boothby (politician). Of course, there are people implicated in alleged child abuse who *don't* have OBEs (hello Freddy Starr), so it's reasonable to suppose the reverse is also true (i.e., that some people with OBEs do not sexually abuse children). The culture of abuse obviously extends well beyond the political realm, anyway: the music industry has long been known as a haven for sexual predators (Murphy, 2015); Hollywood has been called a hunting ground for child molesters by actors Corey Feldman and Elijah Wood, among others, and (partially) exposed by the recent, little-seen documentary, *An Open Secret*; the Pentagon has been a massive consumer of child pornography; and in 2015 FBI Assistant Director Joseph Campbell informed the BBC of "an epidemic of child sex trafficking and pedophilia sweeping America." And yet major media outlets almost totally ignored the story (Handrahan, 2016). The day I was updating this chapter—March 11, 2018—the "Telford sex scandal" broke; it is being called "Britain's biggest ever child abuse scandal," spanning several decades and more than 1,000 child victims (Adams, 2018).

It would be difficult to claim that the many revelations in the UK have resulted either in changes in government and legal policy or in a more aware, alert, and vigilant public. The most likely result of all this "exposure"—perhaps even the desired one —is that the public are increasingly unable to separate in their minds the idea of great men or cultural icons from that of child-diddling predators. The net result of this is the further "democratization" of society, ever downward, to the lowest common denominator of shared venality. The vice of kings becomes the moral relativity of the intelligentsia, which becomes the much coveted freedom to do what thou wilt (without fear of consequences) for the common people—who invariably get the dregs of the barrel and so suffer the worst toxic contamination. Now we the people have the right to the freedom to choose our identities according to whim, free not only from conventional morality or social responsibility but—the final frontier—from our own gender biology, which becomes just another tool for oppression of the white, straight, cisgender, privileged patriarchy. We are free to evolve and express "not only apart from [our] fellows, but in opposition" to them, as the means to create our own (presumably private) paradises. It is unification through atomization: since we are equally special, we can all ignore one another and retreat into endless gazing at our own internally generated, culturally engineered self-images. Narcissus reigns supreme.

If the abuse of free will is original sin, what happens when a virtual infinitude of choices is elevated to the highest social goal? Evil becomes our good, and we are given free rein in Hell—for what else is free will to do with itself but take the paradise it caused us to lose by storm? Havelock Ellis's utopian prophecy is fulfilled, in accord with Crowley's "word of sin is restriction" and human perversion becomes "the supreme triumph of idealism."

The question of why, exactly, the proverbial road to Hell is paved with good intentions is both central to this study and, considering how much it reflects our social reality, something that has been strangely *under-*examined. How did this become an axiom for our existence? What is it about human intentions that they so often bring about the opposite results? In a conversation I had with Theodore Dalrymple while finishing up this manuscript, Dalrymple addressed this uneasy correlation between Hell and (apparent) human benevolence by pointing out that,

"There are people who desire providential roles for themselves, because a providential role, as a very important role in society, answers your problems as to what you do with your life and what life is for." The desire to do good, he noted, is generally mixed up with the desire to *feel good about oneself*, and this mixing of motives may be at the root of how and why progressive politics in the UK and elsewhere have ended up creating so much misery for so many. The central question in my conversation with Dalrymple was essentially this: At what point do incompetence and malevolence overlap and become indistinguishable? Dalrymple's response was succinct and sobering:

> I suppose there comes a point when good intentions actually turn into malevolence, or at any rate, people who started off with good intentions become malevolent because they're not prepared to change their mind about the results of their activities. And actually, their pride is more important for them than actually doing good .... It's when you let your pride and your desire to feel good about yourself overwhelm the evidence that what you're doing is actually harmful, that you become malevolent.

That methods which *appear* to be aimed at one result can bring about the exact opposite result is something we are all familiar with, even if we tend to attribute it exclusively to *unconscious* behavior. The principles of reverse psychology go back as far as the Garden of Eden. Could it even be a natural configuration of such a self-perpetuating social misery machine—something to do with psychological laws applied to crowds—that the beliefs, values, principles, and policies that gain traction are ones that *aspire* to the exact opposite end to the one eventually achieved? As Freud said a century or more ago: If you want to divine a man's intentions, don't waste time listening to what he says; look at the *results* of his actions. Sociopolitically speaking, it might even be reduced to as simple a principle as: If you want to create a demand for—or at least an acceptance of—increasingly intrusive levels of social engineering, simply spread values that espouse (unearned) freedom and hence generate chaos. Paranoid? Certainly. But the jury is still out as to whether, when trying to get to the bottom of the strange paradoxes of government policy, social progress, and cultural engineering, this sort of paranoia is a sign of a legitimately or an illegitimately disturbed mind.

It would of course be a mistake—illegitimately paranoid—to assume that bad ideas introduced into society are invariably done so consciously and deliberately (i.e., with the same end in mind which they eventually achieve). Yet it would be equally rash to assume the opposite, that no one ever deliberately and successfully introduced erroneous ideas, principles, or policies, in a Machiavellian fashion, knowing they would backfire, to bring about specific results. Many of the progressively "bad ideas," described in this book, about how to implement—or at least lay the groundwork for—a fair, egalitarian, and sexually liberated society via rational, scientific means, can (in Britain at least) be tracked back to the society whose emblem was a wolf in sheep's clothing and who took its name from a Roman emperor (Fabius) whose innovation in military strategy entailed painstakingly slow, incremental progress over long periods of time. When I asked Dalrymple if he was familiar with the Fabians (knowing the answer in advance), he replied, "Of course. Everyone in Britain is familiar with the Fabians—whether he knows it or not. He has been *Fabian-ized*."

What I have attempted to do with this work is to map the general onto the particular, the macro to the micro, and demonstrate that we are looking, not at two separate terrains, but at a single territory. I believe that doing so reveals a sort of positive feedback loop in which individuals possessed by socially conditioned "complexes" (unconscious behavioral traits) adopt, develop, and pursue ideological principles and social goals, shaping the society that shaped them and that will go on to shape new generations of ever-more enculturated (and ever less cultured!) individuals, chasing after ever-more distant and amorphous utopian dreams of human perfection. I am unsure, at this stage, whether discovering these "levers" of social engineering is leading to the validation of a grand conspiracy theory of history or, conversely, to making such a view quaint, simple-minded, and redundant, even as a much larger, deeper, and more ancient pattern of human behavior reveals itself. I suspect it is really both at once, a "conspiracy theory" that will neither please nor validate anyone, least of all the arch-conspirators or their aspiring opponents (both of whom seem motivated by the desire for a providential role in society). A conspiracy in which we are all deeply embedded and complicit is, at base, no conspiracy at all, just The Way Things Are. But there is a long and dark tunnel to traverse before we can reasonably end on so "light" a note.

CHAPTER XXXII

Blood Treason

"But I say unto you, That ye resist not evil: but whosoever shall smite thee on thy right cheek, turn to him the other also."
— Matthew, 5:39

In the last week of rewriting this book, in early March of 2018, I had a dream. In the dream there is a circle or "ring." My brother watches from both inside and outside it. It is a place of confrontation or combat, inside which what is evil or primal—bestial—within us must confront the same in another. Like monsters battling for supremacy, two forces meet and collide, in a battle to the death, or at least to the end.

My brother taunts, gloats, or warns me that this is what I have failed to face up to, the need to be primal, to confront what is basest using that which is basest within myself—or perhaps to integrate what is basest within myself by facing it outside of myself? The dream is a nightmare. It has the quality of despair, despair at seeing how wrong I have been in the same moment in which I must face the consequences of my error, and realize my inadequacy in confronting my brother's darkness. Perhaps it is he I go head to head with in the ring. Either way, my very goodness, because uncompleted or untested by evil, has become weakness.

If studying the world—the deep, dark politics of exploitation and abuse behind it—is a way to get free of the world, then every nightmare is a means of awakening. The moment it becomes too awful to bear is the moment we are ready to come back to reality. If we can't ever remove ourselves entirely from the world, perhaps, by the grace of God, we can remove the tattoo of the world from our own souls? In this sense, I wrote this book so I could finally close it. If the world I have begun to see—and described here to the best of my ability—is truly a reflection of my own distortions, it can only be because the teeth of the world match the wound in my soul. Is it then like a kind of collective stigmata, by which the psychic contents of the past are repressed and projected outward, creating a shadow that haunts my every attempt to move forward? Perhaps what is required is a true and lasting Father-God-affect to replace the trauma-stamp of abuse, "the Mark of the Beast" that all-but obliterated the image of Heaven within me? To see the world as the substance of our own shadow is to turn away from it and face the light. But then it is the same light we were always suffused with, only that we were too preoccupied with our shadows to notice its gentle and warming sensation.

The process of seeing the world as-it-is naturally gives rise to disbelief. This in turn gives over to horror and revulsion. But the world we are seeing is the world that—to some degree at least—we belong to. We are not just *in* this world but *of* it, because it has left its affective imprint on our psyches. The scope of manipulation and control within society has inevitably led me to conclude that nothing good comes out of Babylon. This has left me in a very tight spot in which anyone in a position of power or influence must, by such "elective affinity" (on behalf of both the world and themselves), be complicit with a culture of abuse. The belief that there are no great cultural figures who are not complicit with the abusive underlayer of culture—because if they weren't they wouldn't have been granted influence within it—is a convenient one for me because I have always aspired (due to my cultural conditioning) to become a great cultural figure. Holding to this belief means I can tell myself that my failure is really a mark of success, or at least personal integrity! Unfortunately, like all absolutes, it is unlivable because it denies the infinite variety of existence and reduces it to a closed system of control. That this is the goal of social engineers—and that it has been successful beyond most people's capacity to imagine—I have no doubt. But this is a far cry from believing that it has been *entirely* successful.[1]

Writing a book is like casting a spell. It entails setting forces in motion with no guarantee they can be made to heel when the time comes to rein them in. (The play on the word "heel" is deliberate.) These occult forces, once summoned, have to be addressed. Any book may present a seemingly insoluble problem to its author: By the time it is near finishing, it is no longer the same book as when it began. By the time the unconscious arrives, whatever my conscious motives were for inviting it, they no longer match the results. They have been banished—*routed*—by the awareness that came from writing the book.

This book started innocently enough as a hunt for the truth about my past. Over time, it morphed into a sort of strangled cry for justice, as if truth itself was not enough and something had to be *done* about it. What this came down to, for me, was the vain attempt to *force* the truth to submit to a sentence; to wrestle it down into a linear, coherent narrative, one in which crimes are solved, victims acknowledged, and criminals identified, exposed, and punished. In other words, nothing remotely like life—not even much like a real criminal investigation outside of pulp fiction.

God knows I have tried to turn my life—or Whitley Strieber's or Jimmy Savile's or Aleister Crowley's—into pulp fiction. But somehow I just haven't been able to do it. My brother pulped himself for fame and glory, just as he nailed his myth to canvas and celluloid via his "crucial fiction." He successfully framed his Dorian Gray self-portrait inside a starched, tailor-made suit and top hat named "Taboo." But the result (now his name and memory live on behind a papier-mâché masque of red velvet death) is a plague on both our houses (*su casa es mi casa*). Or so I experience it, at least.

*

"The ancient tradition that the world will be consumed in fire at the end of six thousand years is true, as I have heard from Hell. For the cherub with his flaming sword is hereby commanded to leave his guard at the tree of life; and when he does, the whole creation will be consumed and appear infinite and holy, whereas it now appears finite and corrupt. This will come to pass by an improvement of sensual enjoyment. But first the notion that man has a body distinct from his soul is to be expunged."
—William Blake, *The Marriage of Heaven and Hell*

Once upon a time, I thought the above quote referred to polymorphous perversity and orgasms unlimited. I realize now that it has nothing to do with a beefed-up sex life, but rather with the restoration of original *affect*, that of a soul perfectly aligned with—landed in—the body. This is the return to the Garden of Earthly Delight that we existed in before our bodies and souls were torn asunder by a serpentine intrusion. More sex, more intense sex, or more and more varieties and "kinks" of sex, is not—as Ellis, Crowley, Mead, and Kinsey (and my brother), would have us believe—the means to increased sensual enjoyment. On the contrary, since sensual enjoyment is a state of being and not a mode of action, it is more likely to come about via a *de*-emphasis on sex, at least as a means of personal fulfillment and gratification rather than an *inherent* aspect of our natures. When Paradise is lost, attempting to force our way back in by seeking the intensification of sensation to counteract our numbness can only widen the gulf. Any man who ever tried to cajole or pressure a woman into his bed knows this—or at least used to.

To resist not evil, to turn the other cheek when struck, means not to react to the blows life deals us, neither to contract nor harbor resentment but to remain open—to not take the *affective imprint*. As children, we have no choice about being imprinted or contracting when we are faced with an abusive environment, because contraction is necessary for our psychic survival. But as adults—even ones who were imprinted deeply as children—we do have that choice. In some sense—at least until we have been fully restored our true natures—it may be the only meaningful choice there is.

Crowley once defined evil as "meaningless but malignant, in so far as it craves to become real" (1989, p. 623). The ego likewise is that which strives to exist precisely because it lacks true reality. To paraphrase Roger Lewis on my brother, unless it is experiencing extreme sensations, the ego doesn't feel like it exists. As it is with ego, so with evil: Its existence *depends* on our resistance to it. In Lacanian terms, the ego is the child's internalized image of the surface of the body, so it makes sense that the ego affirms its illusory existence via *sensation*, whether by masturbation, stimming, cutting, nose-picking, or voluntary crucifixion (or heroin addiction, which combines self-harming with blissful dissolution). By contrast, psychological peace is only to be found in existence itself; the body at harmony with its environment can experience no real separation from it and so it ceases to exist as an idea (or an image, unless it be in God's eye). Original traumatic affect—the contraction of awareness against the experience of separation (such as birth, or perhaps even conception)—is original sin.

So then am I doing penance for my brother's, father's, grandfather's originary sins by writing this book? Is that why it has become so punishing for me, so hard to finish, like a prison sentence waiting on the final full stop—or why at certain points I have almost felt the need to apologize for it? When and how is my rehabilitation to come? The family legacy I inherited is a crime scene to an ongoing conspiracy. The only place I have there is that of the whistleblower, the lowest and most despised station of all, a traitor not just to my class but to my blood—*a dirty rat*. *Blood Treason*—now *there's* a suitably pulpy title! Except this is no Philip Marlowe yarn—not even a Ross MacDonald family gothic—and I don't get to be the tarnished knight-detective with no private life outside his profession, mining family secrets for a living and always finding gold in the dirt. It just ain't like that. In MacDonald's *The Drowning Pool*, there is an exchange between the P.I. Lew Archer and his client: "You asked for the straight story," she says. "It doesn't make me look nice." "No one's straight story ever does," says Lew.

What you have read is as straight as I could bear to make it, and somewhere between these crooked lines is a veiled confession. To be true to our own souls is to betray our blood—at least the parts that can't be separated from poison. This typeset imprint is a copy of the world as I see it, but also as I project it. It maps the affect that drove me to write it as closely and faithfully as my own mental defenses allowed me to. An infant's cry—if such this is—is never really coherent; but then, it doesn't need to be. Words can't carry such a truth, they can only be carried by it, like furniture inside a hurricane. The mind-forged manacles that have encumbered me for my whole life can't be unfastened by application of mind. Too many generations have passed for that, and the manacles have shaped the mind that once forged them, remolding it after their own image. But does it matter, when the words are the least of it? Maybe it doesn't even matter if the infant's cry is heard. So at least I can tell myself, as it bounces off the wall of the world, that this is all just the echo of unbearable affect.

The truth of affect

"When events defy the imagination's capacity to differentiate
between them, they assault the soul as a unified, monotheistic,
omnipotent presence."

—Greg Mogenson, *A Most Accursed Religion*

The prevalence of child sexual abuse in our society is a bitter pill to
swallow. The idea that it could be organized, systemic and intentional
(part of a hidden "policy") is a whole bottle of bitterness. Correlation does not equal causation; just because we can map an interest in
promoting the idea of child sexuality, or in prematurely sexualizing
children through various forms of interference, or, most disturbingly of
all, in using the psychological trauma (stress) of sexual abuse to "crack"
psyches open and thereby shape culture at large, none of this proves
that widespread child sexual abuse is a direct result of these interests or
agendas. But I trust even the most skeptical reader will allow for *some*
relation between the two.

The Jewish religion practices child abuse ritually in a socially sanctioned act called "circumcision"—the slicing off of a newborn male
baby's foreskin, followed in Orthodox Judaism by *metzitzah b'peh*, which
is when the rabbi sucks the blood from the baby's penis. Horrifying as

this ritual seems to many non-Jews (and, I am sure, to many Jews), it slips under the radar of collective outrage because it is hard to address it as a *moral* question without giving rise to counterarguments about anti-Semitism and the like. If the question of the *effects* of such a ritual on the infant psyche—the *affect*—were instead addressed, it might be a very different debate. Female circumcision is seen in the West more or less universally as barbarism, and there is very little wiggle room to question the *wounding* nature of male circumcision, at least without simply denying the sentience of newborn babies. Yet, essentially, this is what we do. Since overwhelming trauma creates a wall of amnesia to unbearable affect, it gives rise to a form of consciousness cut off from our sensational being. To the mind-self that's created, it is literally as if the traumatic event never happened.

I imagine that one reason for resisting the findings in this present work will be the sheer difficulty of accepting just how prevalent child sexual abuse is in our world. I have avoided citing some of the statistics about this (e.g., Lloyd deMause), because statistics are always questionable at best, and in this case they are so shocking as to be unbelievable to many people. Even for myself, after many years immersed in this material, I find a strange disconnect between what I am aware of and what I am able to believe. Each time I allow some distance from what I have written, I find myself doubting my own conclusions. It is only when I return to them and revisit the evidence that my doubts again dissolve. But even all this evidence would be insufficient, without the confirmations of more direct experience.

Since beginning this investigation in 2013, I have been running a thrift store in a small Canadian town (pop: 6,000). This has involved lots of mostly superficial interactions with ordinary people, particularly, though not exclusively, poor (often homeless) and old people. Through no efforts of my own, I have discovered just how many of our customers either know of someone who has suffered childhood sexual abuse or are themselves victims of it. Bear in mind that this is not occurring within the context of group therapy but that of a used goods store, which makes it fair to suppose I am only hearing about a small percentage of the actual cases. Even so, it appears to be everywhere. In Canada, this is literally true, because the extent of sexual and physical abuse of Native American children forced to attend residential schools was found, in some areas, to be *100 percent* (Milloy, 2011).

If fish don't recognize water because it is all they know, what of fish who swim in poisoned water? Poisoned fish have no choice but to assume that poison is simply the nature of water and keep swimming. If sexual abuse comes to seem like the nature of existence, it follows that it is not abuse at all, simply existence. The extent to which the fishes' faculties are impaired by a reliance on poisoned water might mean that, essentially, we have *no idea* about the extent of abusive behavior in our culture. Partly, this would be a survival mechanism and a necessary defense, because, if we were to see how toxic our culture has become while having no other option but to depend on it, we might give in to total despair or go insane. It's possible that many people are doing just this.

Trauma creates an imprint on the body and psyche too intense and overwhelming to process mentally (consciously), too profound to speak or think about, or even have choate feelings about. And so it remains as affect, as pure bodily impression. Such an unbearable sensation (or series of sensations) never goes away, however, because the effect of unbearable affect is to render us too numb to feel it, or much of any-thing. This permanent numbness—our lives of quiet desperation—is in itself a distant source of torment that drives us to seek relief, to find some way to make the affect *conscious*. We seek out environments, situ-ations, and relationships that *simulate* the original traumatic experience and give us something to react to *in the present*, thereby breaking the spell of amnesia/anesthesia by *reexperiencing the past affect in present terms, via thoughts and feelings*.

The tragedy of denied affect is that it ends up as the death of empa-thy. This is why "compassion is the vice of kings." The denial of our own traumatic affect entails denying the sentience not only of our own bodies but that of other bodies also, most specifically *the bodies of children*. These children then become serial sacrifices on the altar of a culture of self-idolatry whose most concrete and triumphant expression is self-mutilation and self-destruction. They are the silent—because voiceless—consequences of superego-centered "liberation" that denies the reality of consequences, because it denies the truth of affect.

Because thoughts and feelings, by their very nature, cannot encom-pass affect (much less account for it), we find ourselves moving from one intolerable set of circumstances (a job, a relationship, a living situ-ation) to another, feeling as if we are caught in a Groundhog Day of frustrated intentions and desires. Our trauma has become our God, and in His traumatic guise He is a wrathful, jealous God, the mere thought of approaching Whom fills us with terror.

Yet this same terror—the unbearable affect of original "sin"—may also be the beginning of wisdom.

NOTES

Introduction: glamor vice

1. From *Seen and Not Seen*: "A year after his release, in 1983, Jimmy Boyle and his wife Sarah (Boyle's psychiatrist in prison, and daughter of the aristocrat and British film censor, John Trevelyan) opened The Gateway Exchange, a rehabilitation center in Edinburgh for alcoholics and drug addicts that encouraged creative expression. My brother and his then-girlfriend (later wife), Evlynn Smith, also came aboard the project. 'Within a month of its launch,' Sebastian wrote in *Dandy in the Under-world*, 'the Gateway was full of murderers, junkies, lunatics and sexual deviants—I was well camouflaged.' He describes himself as Boyle's 'servant': 'When [Boyle] gave commands there was nothing to do but obey. For me, he took the place an absent parent .... What I loved about Jimmy was that he allowed me to express forbidden impulses, secret wishes and fantasies. He seduced me because he did not have the conflicts that I had'" (J. Horsley, 2015, p. 233).

Chapter I

1. https://en.wikipedia.org/wiki/List_of_Sheriffs_of_Kingston_upon_Hull
2. "What sort of satanic pact he made we may not know even when he publishes his memoirs (and what a read those should be), but Lord Mandelson has acquired the sort of immortality generally confined to Greek mythology and science fiction" (*The Independent*, 2009).
3. https://en.wikipedia.org/wiki/Rupert_Alec-Smith
4. *A Russian Journey*. Alec's fellow missionaries included Donald Soper, later Lord Soper, a Christian Socialist (CS is closely tied to Fabianism) who got his doctorate at the London School of Economics, and mathematician Ebenezer Cunningham.

Chapter II

1. "As Shaw, Webb, Olivier and Wallas became the Fabian Society's dominant 'Big Four,' it becomes clear that the Society was a private organisation run by elements in the employ of media outlets representing liberal capitalist interests. Indeed, the Society's financial backers included John Passmore Edwards, an associate of textile manufacturer and leader of the Liberal 'Manchester School,' Richard Cobden himself. It follows that both Karl Marx and the Fabian Society were bankrolled by industrial interests with links to the left-wing Manchester School and the media world" (Cassivellaunus, 2013).
2. The Nehru jacket was popular in the late 1960s and early 1970s, its popularity spurred by growing awareness of foreign cultures, by the minimalism of the Mod lifestyle and, in particular, by the Beatles and subsequently the Monkees.
3. "From inception, Labour candidates standing for parliament included a fair number of Fabian Society members and the Society has retained a large proportion—about 50 per cent—among Labour candidates since the 1940s. In 1945, 393 Labour candidates were elected to Parliament, out of whom 229 were Fabian Society members. In 1997, 418 Labour candidates were elected, out of whom 200 were Fabian Society members. By the time we come to the Labour Party leadership, the proportion of Fabians comes close to 100 per cent" (Cassivellaunus, 2013).
4. "In 1939 [Hulton] helped set up the bogus news agency Britanova and, in 1941, used the *Picture Post* as a front for another intelligence creation,

the Arab News Agency (ANA). Both news agencies were resurrected after the war by IRD. Tom Clarke, who was Deputy Director of News in the Ministry of Information, went on to become Hulton's representative in Latin America and head of another front news agency. Also on the Committee was Christopher Mayhew, at the time working for ANA's controlling body, the Special Operations Executive. 'Teddy Hulton ... has a mania,' Mayhew wrote at the time, for 'getting key people together and starting a new nation-wide political movement'" (Dorril & Ramsay, 1990, p. 7).

5. "Chairman of Booker Brothers, and Alec Horsley, Chairman of Northern Dairies, were the Round Table's main British backers" (Potts, 2002, p. 178).

6. (Martin, pp. 335, 338). "His widely publicized attacks on the gold standard ... eventually persuaded the British people and certain Treasury officials as well, that the use of gold as a basis for monetary value was the chief cause of unemployment in England and the only begetter of the Great Depression .... This was a delicate way of suggesting that a government's spending need not be limited to the amount of its income, actual or anticipated. By inference, cheap money could always be borrowed to meet any threatened day-to-day deficits—leaving the long-range Government deficit a mere item of Treasury bookkeeping" (ibid., pp. 328–329).

7. "During the desperate winter of 1940, as the threat of German invasion hung over England, the British government mounted a massive, secret campaign of propaganda to weaken the isolationist sentiment in America and manipulate the country into entering the war on England's behalf. Under the command of the now legendary INTREPID, the British planted propaganda in American newspapers, covertly influenced radio stations and wire services, and plotted against American corporations doing business with the Third Reich. They also pushed President Roosevelt to create a similar covert intelligence agency in the US, and played a role in the selection of William Donovan as its head. Now for the first time, with great research and reporting, Jennet Conant reveals that the beloved author Roald Dahl was a member of Churchill's infamous dirty tricks squad, and tells the full story of how he was recruited to spy on the Americans during World War II." Copy for *The Irregulars: Roald Dahl and the British Spy Ring in Wartime Washington*, by Jennet Conant, 2008. New York: Simon & Schuster.

8. This led to the creation of institutions like the British Economic Association (later Royal Economic Society) and LSE. Economic theories

were seen as a "scientific" backing for their Socialist ideology, just as Marx had used them earlier. Educational institutions teaching Fabian economics was a means to "create whole generations of professional economists—a new ruling class—who, working as civil servants and other government officials, would implement Fabian policies (M. Cole, p. 88)." According to this same source, there was an Economic and Social Research Council (ESRC) founded in 1965 under the government of former Fabian Society chairman Harold Wilson. The chief executive of the ESRC was a Fabian called Michael (later Lord) Young, who allegedly "was responsible for the creation of over sixty like-minded organizations." The ESRC was originally known as Social Science Research Council (SSRC), and evidently a branch of the US organization of the same name.

Chapter III

1. "Richard von Krafft-Ebbing first coined the term *paedophilia erotica* in his 1886 work, *Psychopathia Sexualis*, although he regarded it as being extremely rare. Of the hundreds of case histories that he discussed in his work, only one actually dealt with a case of pedophilia. Other early sexual pioneers including Havelock Ellis and Magnus Hirschfeld touched on pedophilia briefly but the term did not appear much in the clinical literature prior to 1950" (Providentia, 2008).
2. The English version, which Nabokov himself translated, replaces "tiny tots of every imaginable sex, who practice every Graeco-Roman sin, constantly and everywhere, from the Anglo-Saxon industrial centers to the Ukraine" with "tiny tots mating like mad" (Nabokov, 1966, p. 203).

Chapter IV

1. My mother did volunteer work for this hospital (in Hampstead) in the later years of her life. I visited her there sometimes.
2. It has been proposed, originally in the Druidic journal Aisling that Gerald Gardner's New Forest coven was the pagan section of the Order of Woodcraft Chivalry; this order performed rituals in the New Forest in the early 1920s and its pagan section honored a moon goddess and a horned god, and believed in ritual nakedness. One of Ronald Hutton's informants reports that Gardner was familiar with this order at least by the 1950s. A major difficulty with identifying this group

with the New Forest coven is that it does not appear to have met in the New Forest between 1934 and 1945. Gardner records a working by the coven in the New Forest in 1940 against the projected Nazi invasion (Hutton, 2001, p. 216).

Chapter V

1. The closest I got was the Orkney SRA scandal, which did include a Quaker group, but which seems to have been pretty much unanimously dismissed as a case of "mass hysteria" (Gall, 2011). I also found a recent (2012) case of a Quaker sexually abusing a pupil in Hessle, where my granddad lived till his death in 1993. It appears to have been an isolated incident (Watson, 2013).
2. In 1514 it was granted by Henry VIII to the Duke of Norfolk as a reward for services against the Scots. Later it came into the possession of the Stanhope family.
3. Savile "was first introduced to the Royal Family, he reveals, by Lord Mountbatten. In 1966, Jimmy became the first civilian to be awarded a Royal Marines' green beret. Mountbatten was commandant general at the time and realised that Savile could be a useful contact" (Edge, 2008). See also Davies, 2014 [Not the Davies in Refs].

Chapter VI

1. Ibid., this series of quotes from "The Girl Factory," pp. 218–222.
2. Lamont, 1986, p. 131.

Chapter VII

1. Eden was in the second year of his premiership when the United States refused to support the Anglo-French military response to the Suez Crisis. Across party lines critics regarded this as a historic setback for British foreign policy, signaling the end of British predominance in the Middle East. Many historians believe that Eden made a series of blunders, most of all by not realizing how opposed the US was to military action, and that Eden completely dominated the British decision-making process in the Suez crisis. While Eden is generally ranked among the least successful British prime ministers of the twentieth century, two broadly sympathetic biographies (in 1986 and 2003) have partially redressed the

balance of opinion. Jonathan Pearson argues that Eden was more reluctant and less bellicose than most historians have judged. D. R. Thorpe
considered the Suez Crisis a truly tragic end to Eden's premiership, one
that came to assume a disproportionate importance in any assessment
of his career.

Chapter VIII

1. "Harrisson found Madge's letter because it was printed on the same
page as Harrisson's first and only published poem (called 'Coconut
Moon: A Philosophy of Cannibalism in the New Hebrides') in the *New
Statesman and Nation*" (*Visual Culture and Mass Observation*, 2015).
2. Harrisson was attached to Z Special Unit (also known as Z Force), part
of the Services Reconnaissance Department (SRD), a branch of the combined Allied Intelligence Bureau in the South West Pacific theatre. See
Osborne, 2017.

Chapter IX

1. See Sensory Committee (1945). The Common Wealth was founded in July
1942, during World War II, by the alliance of two left wing groups, the
1941 Committee and the neo-Christian Forward March movement, led
by Acland (as well as independents and former Liberals, who believed
that the Liberal party had no direction). Disagreeing with the electoral
pact established with other parties in the wartime coalition, key figures
in the 1941 Committee began sponsoring independent candidates. After
the electoral success of Tom Driberg with their support in 1942, there
was a move to form the 1941 Committee into a political party through a
merger with Acland's Forward March. Many members disliked the idea
of being a political party rather than a social movement, so the word
"Party" was never formally part of Common Wealth's name.
2. See Horsley, *Prisoner of Infinity*, Aeon Books, 2018.

Chapter X

1. https://en.wikipedia.org/wiki/Project_MKUltra
2. According to author Jim Keith (1997, p. 48), Sargant also worked for the
Tavistock Institute. Sargant writes about Tavistock's methods in *Battle
for the Mind*.

Chapter XI

1. "He could not have thought it admirable to be a vampire, but since he thought it necessary to maintain the prodigious levels of energy he needed for his anti-war work, he was prepared to be one" (Monk, 1996, p. 476). There is also a quote from Russell himself, which I found on the cover of another biography, but have been unable to locate.
2. "Certainly, as Bertrand Russell noted (and his statement hangs emblazoned in Mahatma Gandhi's home in Ahmedabad), 'It is doubtful that the method of Mahatma Gandhi would have succeeded except that he was appealing to the conscience of a Christianized people'" (Marbaniang, 2010).

Chapter XII

1. Marks & Spencer founder Israel Sieff gave a public speech in 1934 in which he said: "Let us go slowly for a while, until we can see how our plan works out in America." According to Martin, "*[T]he plan to which he referred was the New Deal.* Why on earth ... should a British national living in London refer to the New Deal as 'our plan'? Unintentionally, Sieff had revealed a relationship between Fabian Socialist planners in England and in the United States" (Martin, p. 302).

Chapter XIII

1. For the dozens of separate hospital reports of Savile's fifty years of sexual abuse, see Department of Health, 2014.
2. "In June 1924 the Chief Medical Officer of the Board of Education, Sir George Newman, appointed a committee to consider the problems presented by the 'mentally defective' child. A year later the committee was asked to include 'adult defectives' in its inquiry, so the report was presented, in January 1929, both to Newman and to the Chairman of the Board of Control. The chair of the committee was Arthur Henry Wood. Born in Reading in December 1870, he was educated at Cranbrook Grammar School and New College Oxford. The 1901 census describes him as an examiner for the Board of Education and he went on to become Assistant Secretary to the Board. He served as secretary for the Consultative Committee's 1909 report Attendance, Compulsory or Otherwise, at Continuation Schools .... Also on the committee was the eugenicist Cyril Burt" (Gillard, 2013).

3. John Bowlby told Milton Senn in 1977: "The London Child Guidance Clinic was set up in a part of Islington called Canonbury. That clinic, I think, was founded in 1929. It trained educational psychologists, social workers and child psychiatrists. Each year three fellowships in child psychiatry were advertised—they were half-time fellowships for one year—and in 1936 I was successful in being appointed to one of them. I used to spend every morning at Canonbury and a bit of the afternoon usually as well, and then I went on and did analysis later in the day. *I should say that I always had a few hundred pounds of private money—very important—*which meant to say that I was not pressed for bread and butter. *I was at the time also much influenced by two close friends who were academic economists,* one of whom is my brother-in-law and one of whom was a very close personal friend with whom I shared a flat, and they represented a strong academic interest .... Both were very able people, both have gone a long way though unfortunately, one, Evan Durbin, died in a very tragic accident in 1948. They were first-class people which was very important, really, because I was espousing a very novel and peculiar outlook as an analytically oriented child psychiatrist as we might call it. That was what I was aspiring to be. The whole field was still very controversial and needed a lot of academic justification. Well, to cut a long story short—first of all I had had a good scientific training at Cambridge, and secondly, *my academic friends were very powerful debaters and any position which I took up I had to justify up to the hilt by argument and evidence.* This was an invaluable discipline I think" (Senn, 2007).
4. FABIAN SOCIETY, 77th Annual Report, 1 JULY 1959 TO 30 JUNE 1960, Eve Saville is listed among "HONORARY SECRETARIES OF REGIONAL AND AREA COMMITTEES OF LOCAL FABIAN SOCIETIES" (Fabian Society, 1960).

Chapter XIV

1. Founded by William Tuke, it was originally run by and for Quakers but gradually became open to everyone. It inspired other progressive facilities such as the American Brattleboro Retreat, Hartford Retreat and Friends Hospital.
2. The project was abandoned after Angela Willans, a trustee who was the *Woman's Own* agony aunt, saw a draft and branded it monstrous. The Albany Trust said: "Albany Trust wishes to make it clear it entirely

dissociates itself from any organisation promoting the sexual abuse of children. Albany's counselling services continue to provide much-needed support for individuals from all backgrounds, across the spectrum of sexuality" (Pace, 2014b).

Chapter XVI

1. The death penalty had already been suspended, and Labour supported bills to decriminalize abortion and homosexuality, relax censorship and make divorce easier. Jenkins also embarked on what the *Telegraph* called "… the most radical programme of penal reform since the Second World War. His Criminal Justice Act of 1967 said very little about the victims of crime, but plenty about the perpetrators." It introduced the parole system of early release for offenders serving three years or more, and the system of suspended sentences. "The legalization of homosexuality has not been the end of the chapter, but merely the beginning, with an aggressive 'gay rights' lobby demanding more and more concessions. The policy of early release of prisoners has had a catastrophic effect on the safety of the general public: 14 per cent of violent criminals freed early are convicted of fresh violence within two years of their release. As *The Sunday Telegraph*'s Alasdair Palmer states: 'Scores of men, women and children have been assaulted, raped and murdered as a result of the policy of releasing dangerous criminals before their sentences are completed'—a policy initiated and endorsed by Jenkins." Debatable rhetoric aside, it does tie in to my grandfather's interest in and sympathy for violent offenders.
2. For a partial list of pro-pedophile organizations and publications from an easily searchable database of 174 known pedophiles and pro-pedophile advocates, see: https://sites.google.com/site/kaztiggrfiles/paedo-mags

Chapter XVII

1. The only time the Groucho Club has been in the mainstream news since this story failed to break was a 2016 *Daily Mail* piece about "open drug use taking place on the premises."
2. See also *PinkIndustry*, 2011.
3. From *Demos Quarterly* Issue 11/1997, "The New Age: a religion for the future?" By Paul Heelas: "Finally, at the world affirming pole, spirituality

is seen as a straight forward means to external success. The emphasis is on power, on tapping what lies within to obtain results in what amounts to—anthropologically speaking—magical fashion. The radical world rejecter sees capitalistic modernity as irredeemably flawed, while the radical world affirmer supposes it can be made to work even better. Inner spirituality informs very different new worlds from that of an intrinsically spiritual realm to living as a spiritually informed person, enjoying inner growth alongside external life, and maximising what capitalism has to offer."

Chapter XX

1. The following is a poem by Crowley, called "A Ballad of Passive Pederasty": "Boys tempt my lips to wanton use / And show their tongues, and smile awry / And wonder why I should refuse / To feel their buttocks on the sly / And kiss their genitals, and cry / 'Ah! Ganymede, grant me one night!' / This is the one sweet mystery: / A strong man's love is my delight! / To feel him clamber on me, laid / Prone on the couch of lust and shame / To feel him force me like a maid / And his great sword within me flame / His breath as hot and quick as fame / To kiss him and to clasp him tight / This is my joy without a name / A strong man's love is my delight / To feel again his love grow grand / Touched by the langour of my kiss / To suck the hot blood from my gland / Mingled with fierce spunk that doth hiss / And boils in sudden spurted bliss / Ah! God! the long-drawn lusty fight! / Grant me eternity of this! / A strong man's love is my delight!"

2. All of which is discussed in depth in my previous work, *Prisoner of Infinity*.

3. She also worked in the tsunami ravaged Maldives and "advised UNICEF on the best ways to assist the Maldivians to overcome the effects of the trauma [and] protect children from abuse and exploitation in the aftermath of the disaster." She has worked in Indonesia, Canada, the Philippines, and Malaysia to promote the protection of children. She "has led calls for a Royal Commission to examine the nature and extent of organised pedophilia[mixed UK/US spellings], child pornography and child prostitution in Australia." She was awarded the Vice Chancellor's Medal for Excellence in Research for her PhD thesis on the prevention of child sexual abuse, Young Australian of the Year for community service and Young Victorian of the Year for community service (CAPS, 2018).

Chapter XXI

1. There are other, less first-hand testimonies to go on. On page 413 of *Dr. Kinsey and the Institute for Sex Research* (Yale University Press, 1972), for example, Wardell Baxter Pomeroy writes that "The great Beast and his followers were against any kind of religion, in any form, except their own. They held group orgies as part of their ritual, and included in them the small children the women had brought with them." This charge is not backed by any citations, however.

2. "She was, of course, instantly flung into the street, but she continued her operations for bettering herself …. I owned up, tremulous and tearful, that I had been in the tobacconist's. He would have doubted a merely innocent alibi. The girl was, of course, discredited, and nothing more was heard of the matter. And I had had her on my mother's very bed! That is the state of affairs which is caused by puritanism. First we have a charming girl driven to attempt blackmail, next a boy forced to the most unmanly duplicity in order to exercise his natural rights with impunity, and incidentally to wrong a woman for whom he had nothing but the friendliest feelings. As long as sexual relations are complicated by religious, social and financial considerations, so long will they cause all kinds of cowardly, dishonourable and disgusting behaviour. When war conditions imposed artificial restraint on the sister appetite of hunger, decent citizens began to develop all kinds of loathsome trickery. Men and women will never behave worthily as long as current morality interferes with the legitimate satisfaction of physiological needs. Nature always avenges herself on those who insult her" (Crowley, 1989, pp. 79–80).

Chapter XXII

1. Ibid., p. 562.
2. As for there being any relation between Theodore Kaczynski, the Unabomber, and Richard Kaczynski, author of *Frater Perdurabo*, I am assured by Richard K that there is none.

Chapter XXV

1. *Book of the Law*, III:45, II:78.
2. The words on Savile's tombstone, until it was torn down.
3. *Book of the Law*, I:18.

Chapter XXVII

1. "Discussing Crowley, Occultism, and Ritual Child Abuse with Peter Levenda," July 2, 2016. https://auticulture.wordpress.com/2016/07/02/crowley-ritual-abuse-levenda/
2. As ex-occultist Nathaniel Harris once put it to me: either Peter Levenda is a truly terrible researcher, or he is lying. In either case, Levenda is unlikely to admit to it.
3. This interview appears in *What Witches Do*, 2012, by Stewart Farrar, David & Charles, Kindle edition.
4. To say that occultism overlaps with ritual child abuse is not the same as saying that all occultists practice pedophilia. Ideological frameworks (whether Islam, Christianity, occultism, or the much less clearly defined ideological framework of the "intelligentsia") shouldn't be made equivalent to specific behaviors. But they can be viewed as fertile ground from which types of behavior emerge. Catholicism can easily be viewed as the ground in which the Spanish Inquisition took root, without in any way suggesting that all Catholics are witch-burners. In exactly the same way, Western occultism, and specifically for my present purposes Thelema, seems to provide a compelling context—an ideological rationale—within which unconscious urges that might lead to the ritual abuse of children can and do flourish. Students of the occult such as Levenda are either foolish or dishonest (or both) if they choose to ignore evidence of an overlap between occult ideology and child sexual abuse, and opt instead to dismiss it as a "witch hunt."

Chapter XXIX

1. Crowley's primary aim was to free himself of all social conditioning and become "his very own self" (Ipsissimus). At the deepest level (at least pre-biological), this would mean clearing the imprints left on his infant psyche by his mother and father, but especially his mother. (In *Confessions*, Crowley notes that he "dreamed repeatedly that his mother was dead"–1989, p. 53.) Crowley's potentially pathological drive to get free of his mother appears to have overlapped with—if not been the source of—his occult drive to become Magus of the Aeon whose Word is Law. This interpretation is borne out by the fact that it was Crowley's mother who first gave him the name of Beast—when she caught him masturbating in his room. And Crowley's lifelong bid

to discover and commit the unforgiveable sin forms a precise match with a rebellious son's determination to do everything in his power to go against his mother's Christian sense of moral decency. If Crowley was seeking to break free of that which most defined him, and hence imprisoned him, as a personality, the "logical" place to start would be with his mother.

2. Crowley's view on women (when not worshipping them for their harlotry) is well known. In *Confessions*, he writes that they are "beneath contempt," that intellectually they "did not exist," and that "it was highly convenient that one's sexual relations should be with an animal with no consciousness beyond sex" (ibid., p. 143). Instead, he favored sodomy, than which was "no better way to avoid the contaminations of women." He wrote that "all great men of antiquity were sodomites," and that it was "an aristocratic virtue which our middle class had better imitate if they wish to be smart" (2008, p. xxix). He referred to pederasty at Oxford (specifically Balliol) as "the great tradition of statesmanship" (1989, p. 113). He admitted to suffering from "congenital masochism," as a result of which "[H]e liked to imagine himself in agony; in particular, he liked to identify himself with the Beast" (ibid., p. 44). This is quite the checklist, and it paints a stark picture of Crowley's psyche. His fear and hatred of his mother—and of women in general—appear to have created a culture of congenital masochism, blasphemy, and transgression, Satanism and identification with the Beast, sexual perversion, sodomy and pederasty, all mixed up with inflated aspirations towards aristocracy and genius. What I wish to suggest is that Crowley's infancy-sourced maternal hatred, pushed down into unconsciousness, developed into an aristocratic superego driven to transcend every last Christian constraint of morality—and of humanness—through willed acts of transgression. And that this entailed a philosophy of forcefully severing the mother-child bonds of his own and other children, by whatever means *necessary*. More controversially, it raises the possibility that his desperate quest to extricate himself from the tentacles of his mother's psyche might lead to acts of ritual violation.

3. While Peter Levenda has denied being the actual author (Simon Cabana) of *The Necronomicon* and its sequels, there is a host of evidence, including Levenda's name on a copyright application for one of the books, and a recorded interview with "Simon" in which he used a voice distorter; when the speed is altered the voice is recognizable as Levenda's (J. Horsley, 2017). Levenda's continued denials meanwhile

are unconvincing and ineffective, and I don't know of anyone who believes them, or who much cares either way. Perhaps because he wishes to maintain the illusion of being an impartial scholar of occultism, however, rather than an occultist *per se*, Levenda continues to stick to his shaggy Simon story.

Chapter XXXI

1. "Like the one about the girl Jimmy said he was going to marry and they got engaged with a huge cuddly toy just a few days before she died' (extraordinarily sinister in light not just of knowledge of Savile's abuse of children, but also his fascination with dead bodies)" (Pace, 2014a).

Chapter XXXII

1. To give a current example, I recently discovered the writer Theodore Dalrymple while preparing this MS for publication (hence the generous sprinkling of quotes from his work). Dalrymple (whose real name is Anthony Daniels) is a British author and speaker who worked for fifteen years as a prison psychiatrist and has written for the *City Journal* for two decades. He is also a senior fellow of the Manhattan Institute for Policy Research, a nonprofit American think tank focused on domestic policy and urban affairs, cocreated by ex-CIA director Bill Casey. Within the context of cultural conspiracy dot-joining that makes up much of this book, this raises a blazing red flag to the investigatory bull in me. Is it paranoia or is it logic—or the logic of paranoia—that says a think tank started by an ex-CIA director can only serve social engineering agendas and that anyone who is made a senior fellow of such an organization must be complicit, or at least compatible, with its goals? Yet Dalrymple—who reminds me in some ways of my father—has been open to correspondence and we have just done a podcast together (March 2018). Clearly he is *simpatico*. Accordingly, my perspective on these matters has somewhat softened.

REFERENCES

Acland, A. (1981). *A Devon Family: The Story of the Aclands*. London: Phillimore, p. 153.

Baker, P. (2009). *The Devil is a Gentleman: The Life and Times of Dennis Wheatley*. Sawtry, UK: Dedalus.

Berlin, I. (1969). *Four Essays on Liberty*. Oxford: Oxford University Press.

Bryans, R. (1992). *The Dust Has Never Settled*. London: Honeyford Press.

Bullough, V. L. (1996). *Science in the Bedroom: A History of Sexual Research*. New York: Basic Books.

Burke, J. (1957). The beast with two backs. *Real Action for Men*, 1(3). New York: Four Star Publications.

Carradice, P. (2011). *Snapshots of Welsh History: Without the Boring Bits*. New York: Simon & Schuster.

Cheit, R. E. (2014). *The Witch-Hunt Narrative: Politics, Psychology, and the Sexual Abuse of Children*. New York: Oxford University Press.

Childs, D. J. (2013). *The Birth of New Criticism: Conflict and Conciliation in the Early Work of William Empson, I. A. Richards, Robert Graves, and Laura Riding*. Kingston, Canada: McGill-Queen's University Press.

Churton, T. (2012). *Aleister Crowley: The Biography—Spiritual Revolutionary, Romantic Explorer, Occult Master and Spy*. London: Watkins.

Cole, R. T. (2015). *Liber L. Vel Bogus: The Real Confession of Aleister Crowley*. Chicago: New Aeon.

Costello, J. (1988). *Mask of Treachery*. London: William Collins Sons.

Crowley, A. (1972). *The Magickal Record of the Beast 666*. London: Duckworth.

Crowley, A. (1975). *The Commentaries of AL: Being the Equinox Volume V, No. 1, Issue 1*. Newburyport, MA: S. Weiser.

Crowley, A. (1989). *The Confessions of Aleister Crowley*. London: Penguin.

Crowley, A. (1991). *Magick: In Theory and Practice*. New York: Castle Books.

Crowley, A. (2008). *The World's Tragedy*. Austin, TX: 100th Monkey Press.

Dalrymple, T. (2005). *Our Culture, What's Left of It*. Chicago, IL: Ivan R. Dee.

Davies, H. A. (2010). *The Use of Psychoanalytic Concepts in Therapy with Families*. London: Karnac.

Dawkins, R. (2008). *The God Delusion*. Boston, MA: Houghton Mifflin Harcourt.

Dorril, S. (2002). *MI6: Inside the Covert World of Her Majesty's Secret Intelligence Service*. London: Touchstone, p. 456.

Dorril, S., & Ramsay, R. (1990). In a common cause: the anti-communist crusade in Britain 1945–60. *Lobster*, 19, May 1990: 4–23.

Duquette, L. M. (2003). *The Magick of Aleister Crowley: A Handbook of the Rituals of Thelema*. Newburyport, MA: S. Weiser.

Edgell, D. (1992). *The Order of Woodcraft Chivalry, 1916–1949, as a New Age Alternative to the Boy Scouts*. Lewiston, NY: E. Mellen Press.

Edwards, B. L. (2007). *C.S. Lewis: Fantasist, Mythmaker, and Poet*. Westport, CT: Greenwood Publishing Group.

Empson, J. (2012). *Hetta and William: A Memoir of a Bohemian Marriage*. Bloomington, IN: AuthorHouse.

Faithfull, M. (2000). *An Autobiography*. New York: Cooper Square Press.

Faithfull, M. (2007). *Memories, Dreams, Reflections*. New York: HarperCollins.

Field, J. (2000). Alternative Living, Alternative Learning: the Grith Fyrd Movement in England in the 1930s. In: A. Cooke & A. MacSween (Eds.), *The Rise and Fall of Adult Education Institutions and Social Movements*. Oxford: Peter Lang.

Gatto, J. T. (2006). *Underground History of American Education*. New York: Oxford Village.

Goldman, J. (2015). *The Central Intelligence Agency: An Encyclopedia of Covert Ops, Intelligence Gathering, and Spies [2 volumes]*. Santa Barbara, CA: ABC-CLIO.

Grey, A. (2011). *Quest for Justice: Towards Homosexual Emancipation*. London: Random House.

Grotstein, J. (2003). Early Bion. In: R. M. Lipgar & M. Pines (Eds.), *Building on Bion: Roots: Origins and Context of Bion's Contributions to Theory and Practice* (pp. 9–28). London: Jessica Kingsley.

Haffenden, J. (2006). *William Empson, Volume II: Against the Christians*. Oxford: Oxford University Press.

Hamnett, N. (1932). *Laughing Torso*. Whitefish, MT: Kessinger, 2004.

Hinton, J. (2013). *The Mass Observers: A History, 1937–1949*. Oxford: Oxford University Press.

Hitchens, C. (2011). *Hitch-22: A Memoir*. Toronto, Canada: McClelland & Stewart.

Hoffman, W. (2016). *White Witch in a Black Robe*. London: Karnac.

Horsley, J. (2015). *Seen and Not Seen: Confessions of a Movie Autist*. Winchester, UK: Zero Books.

Horsley, S. (2007). *Dandy in the Underworld*. London: Hodder & Stoughton.

Hutton, R. (2001). *The Triumph of the Moon: A History of Modern Pagan Witchcraft*. Oxford: Oxford University Press.

Huxley, A. (2001). *Complete Essays: 1936–1938*. Chicago, IL: Ivan R. Dee.

Jones, J. H. (2004). *Alfred C. Kinsey: A Life*. New York: W. W. Norton.

Kaczynski, R. (2012). *Perdurabo, Revised and Expanded Edition: The Life of Aleister Crowley*. Berkeley, CA: North Atlantic Books.

Karlinsky, S. (2001). *Dear Bunny, Dear Volodya: The Nabokov-Wilson Letters, 1940–1971*. Berkeley, CA: University of California Press.

Katchen, M. H., & Sakheim, D. K. (1992). Satanic beliefs and practices. In: D. K. Sakheim & S. E. Devine (Eds.), *Out of Darkness: Exploring Satanism & Ritual Abuse* (pp. 21–43). New York: Lexington.

Keith, J. (1997). *Mind Control, World Control*. Kempton, IL: Adventures Unlimited Press.

Lamont, S. (1986). *Religion Inc: The Church of Scientology*. Los Angeles, CA: Harrap.

Leary, T. (1990). *Flashbacks: A Personal and Cultural History of an Era: an Autobiography*. New York: Putnam.

Leitch, V. B. (2009). *American Literary Criticism Since the 1930s*. Hove, UK: Routledge.

Simon (Levenda, P.). (2010). *The Gates of the Necronomicon*, by Simon. HarperCollins e-books.

Lewis, C. S. (2002). *The Screwtape Letters*. London: HarperCollins.

Makaryk, I. R. (1993). *Encyclopedia of Contemporary Literary Theory: Approaches, Scholars, Terms*. Toronto, Canada: University of Toronto Press.

Martin, R. L. (1966). *Fabian Freeway*. Chicago, IL: Heritage Foundation.

Milloy, J. S. (2011). *A National Crime: The Canadian Government and the Residential School System*. Winnipeg, Canada: University of Manitoba Press.

Monk, R. (1996). *Bertrand Russell: The Spirit of Solitude, 1872–1921, Volume 1*. New York: Simon & Schuster.

Morton, W. A. (1999). Cocaine and psychiatric symptoms. *Primary Care Companion to the Journal of Clinical Psychiatry*, Aug 1999: 109–113.

Nabokov, V. (1966). *Speak, Memory*. New York: G. P. Putnam's Sons.

Norman, P. (2012). *Mick Jagger*. Toronto, Canada: Doubleday Canada.

Ounsworth, T. (1987). *Joy and Woe*. Beverley, UK: Hutton Press.

Palmer, R. (1993). Child abuse sex ring found. *The Sunday Times*, August 1, p. 12.

Partridge, B. (1960). *A History of Orgies*. New York: Bonanza.

Pasi, M. (2014). *Aleister Crowley and the Temptation of Politics*. Bristol, UK: Acumen.

Pomeroy, W. B. (1972). *Dr. Kinsey and the Institute for Sex Research*. New Haven, CT: Yale University Press.

Potts, A. (2002). *Zilliacus: A Life for Peace and Socialism*. London: Merlin.

Reisman, J. (2010). *Sexual Sabotage: How One Mad Scientist Unleashed a Plague of Corruption and Contagion on America*. Medford, OR: WND Books.

Russell, B. (1931). *The Scientific Outlook*. Hove, UK: Routledge, 2009.

Russell, B. (1932). *Education and the Social Order*. New York: Routledge, 2013.

Salter, M. (2013). *Organized Sexual Abuse*. New York: Routledge.

Scott, S. (2001). *The Politics and Experience of Ritual Abuse: Beyond Disbelief*. Buckingham, UK: Open University Press.

Shaw, G. B. (1949). *Sixteen Self-Sketches*. London: Constable.

Spence, R. B. (2008). *Secret Agent 666: Aleister Crowley, British Intelligence and the Occult*. Port Townsend, WA: Feral House.

Steiner, G. (1996). *Tolstoy or Dostoevsky: An Essay in the Old Criticism*. New Haven, CT: Yale University Press.

Stewart, H. (2012). *The Happy Manifesto*. London: Happy.

Streathfield, D. (2008). *Brainwash: The Secret History of Mind Control*. London: Macmillan.

Thomas, G. (1989). *Journey Into Madness: The True Story of Secret CIA Mind Control and Medical Abuse*. New York: Bantam.

Torres, N. (2003). Gregariousness and the mind: Wilfred Trotter and Wilfred Bion. In: R. M. Lipgar & M. Pines (Eds.), *Building on Bion: Roots: Origins and Context of Bion's Contributions to Theory and Practice* (pp. 85–117). London: Jessica Kingsley.

Urban, H. B. (2006). *Magia Sexualis: Sex, Magic, and Liberation in Modern Western Esotericism*. Oakland, CA: University of California Press.

Webb, B. (1948). *Our Partnership*. B. Drake & M. Cole (Eds.). London: Longmans, Green.

Webb, S. (1889). The basis of Socialism: Historic. In: G. B. Shaw (Ed.), *Fabian Essays in Socialism*. London: Fabian Society.

West, N., & Tsarev, O. (1999). *The Crown Jewels: The British Secrets at the Heart of the KGB Archives*. New Haven, CT: Yale University Press.

Wheen, F. (1992). *Driberg: His Life and Indiscretions*. London: Pan.

Wilson, C. (2005). *Aleister Crowley: The Nature of the Beast*. London: Aeon.

Websites

All sites last accessed February 25, 2018

Abra, A. J. (2009). On with the Dance: Nation, Culture, and Popular Dancing in Britain, 1918–1945. Dissertation for University of Michigan. https://deepblue.lib.umich.edu/bitstream/handle/2027.42/63821/aabra_1.pdf?sequence=1

Adams, C. (2018). 1,000 children may have been victims in Britain's biggest ever child abuse scandal. *The Telegraph*, 11 March 2018. https://www.telegraph.co.uk/news/2018/03/11/1000-children-may-have-victims-britains-biggest-ever-child-abuse/

Adams, G. (2013). Apologists for paedophiles. *Daily Mail*, 14 December 2013. www.dailymail.co.uk/news/article-2523526/How-Labour-Deputy-Harriet-Harman-shadow-minister-husband-Health-Secretary-Patricia-Hewitt-linked-group-lobbying-right-sex-children.html

Atwill, J. (2015). Gregory Bateson and the Counter-Culture. *Postflaviana*, 19 May 2015. https://postflaviana.org/gregory-bateson-and-the-counter-culture/

Baker, P. C. (2016). Bad Intelligence. *The Nation*, 16 June 2016. https://www.thenation.com/article/bad-intelligence/

Bateman, T. (2014). Paedophile Peter Righton advised Home Office on policy. *BBC Radio 4*, 18 August 2014. www.bbc.com/news/uk-28793654

BBC News (2011a). Kidwelly sex cult members face long jail sentences. *BBC News*, 9 March 2011. www.bbc.com/news/uk-wales-12690580

BBC News (2011b). Kidwelly sex cult leader Colin Batley may never be free. *BBC News*, 11 March 2011. www.bbc.com/news/uk-wales-12703785

BBC News (2014a). Stephen Fry: Drug use different from sexual abuse cases. *BBC News*, 2 Oct 2014. www.bbc.com/news/entertainment-arts-29454296

BBC News (2014b). Jimmy Savile and Peter Jaconelli sex abuse: Police admit chances were missed. *BBC News*, 18 December 2014. www.bbc.com/news/uk-england-york-north-yorkshire-30514237

Berlin, F. S. (2014). Pedophilia and DSM-5: The Importance of Clearly Defining the Nature of a Pedophilic Disorder. *The Journal of the American Academy of Psychiatry and the Law Online*, 42(4): 404–407. http://jaapl.org/content/42/4/404.full

Bernstein, C. (1977). The CIA and The Media. *Rolling Stone*, 20 Oct 1977. http://carlbernstein.com/magazine_cia_and_media.php

Bits of Books (2015). May 1975: Albany Trust & National Association of Youth Clubs Joint Training "Psychosexual Problems of Young People." *Bits of Books*, 17 May 2015. https://bitsofbooksblog.wordpress.

com/2015/05/17/may-1975-albany-trust-national-association-of-youth-clubs-joint-training-psychosexual-problems-of-young-people/

Boffey, D. (2014). Revealed: how Jimmy Savile abused up to 1,000 victims on BBC premises. Jimmy Savile. *The Guardian*, 18 January 2014. www.theguardian.com/media/2014/jan/18/jimmy-savile-abused-1000-victims-bbc

Braziers Park (2016). Norman Glaister and the Sensory Process Before the Founding of Brazier's Park. www.braziers.org.uk/Research%20pdfs/24/Norman_Glaister_and_sensory.pdf

Braziers Park (2017). John Norman Glaister (1883–1961). www.braziers.org.uk/research-and-publications/john-norman-glaister/

Brinkmann, S. (2005). Sordid Science: The Sex Research of Alfred C. Kinsey (The Catholic Standard & Times–Part 3 of 7). www.drjudithreisman.com/archives/2005/08/sordid_science_4.html

Burrell, I. (2010). Girls' club that's a refuge for boys who refuse to grow up. *The Independent*, 1 March 2010. http://www.independent.co.uk/news/media/tv-radio/girls-club-thats-a-refuge-for-boys-who-refuse-to-grow-up-1913488.html

Califia, P. (2003). The Age of Consent: The Great Kiddy-Porn Panic of '77. *Ipce* (International Pedophile and Child Emancipation). www.ipce.info/ipceweb/Library/califa_aoc_frame.htm

Capel, M. (1998). Learn Pedophilia at Cornell University. *Hidden Mysteries*. www.hiddenmysteries.org/news/america/usa/090700a.html

Cassivellaunus (2013). The Fabian Society: the masters of subversion unmasked. *Free Britain Now*, 31 March 2013. http://www.freebritainnow.org/0/fabiansociety.htm

CAPS (2018). About Dr. Reina Michaelson. *Child Abuse Prevention* site. https://childabuseprevention.com.au/reina-michaelson/

Catalyst (2008). New/transition paradigm higher educational institutions. Scoping Study–Schumacher College, September 2008. https://catalyst-course.files.wordpress.com/2011/03/institutions.pdf

Chapman, C. (2005). "If you don't take a job as a prostitute, we can stop your benefits." *The Telegraph*, 30 January 2005. http://www.telegraph.co.uk/news/worldnews/europe/germany/1482371/If-you-dont-take-a-job-as-a-prostitute-we-can-stop-your-benefits.html

Child Abuse Wiki (2012). Ritual Abuse. http://childabusewiki.org/index.php?title=Ritual_Abuse

Christian, J. (2006). Fabian Influence on Council Developments in New Zealand. Archived at author's own site: https://auticulture.com/wp-content/uploads/Fabian-Influence-on-World-Affairs-2.pdf

Clark, N. (2003). Roy Jenkins made Britain a far less civilised country. *The Telegraph*, 9 January 2003. www.telegraph.co.uk/comment/

personal-view/3586178/Roy-Jenkins-made-Britain-a-far-less-civilised-country.html

Clements, T. (2011). The Art of Camping by Matthew de Abaitua: Review. *The Telegraph*, 25 July 2011. www.telegraph.co.uk/culture/books/bookreviews/8652595/The-Art-of-Camping-by-Matthew-de-Abaitua-review.html

Davies, D. (2014). The man who groomed Britain: How Jimmy Savile's crimes and his cover-ups fooled a nation. *Daily Mail*, 12 July 2014. www.dailymail.co.uk/home/event/article-2687779/Jimmy-Savile-book-reviewed-Craig-Brown-The-man-groomed-Britain.html

deMause, L. (2005). The Childhood Origins of the Holocaust (speech). Psychohistory.com. http://psychohistory.com/articles/the-childhood-origins-of-the-holocaust/

Department of Health (2014). NHS and Department of Health investigations into Jimmy Savile. Department of Health, 26 June 2014. www.gov.uk/government/collections/nhs-and-department-of-health-investigations-into-jimmy-savile

Dobbs, Z. (1962). *Keynes at Harvard: Economic Deception as a Political Credo*. New York: Probe. Online resource: http://keynesatharvard.org/index.html

Dodd, V., & Morris, S. (2017). Ted Heath would have been questioned over abuse claims, police say. *The Guardian*, 5 October 2017. https://www.theguardian.com/politics/2017/oct/05/ted-heath-would-have-been-questioned-over-seven-abuse-claims-police-say

Drokhole (2013). British Guy Takes Mescaline, Polite and Measured Reflection Ensues. *Disinfo*, 28 August 2013. http://disinfo.com/2013/08/british-guy-takes-mescaline-polite-and-measured-reflection-ensues-2/

Dunt, I. (2007). Stephen Fry opens up about school sexual assault. *Pink News*, 28 March 2007. www.pinknews.co.uk/2007/03/28/stephen-fry-opens-up-about-school-sexual-assault/

Edge, S. (2008). How Jim really did fix it. *Daily Express*, 8 May 2008. www.express.co.uk/expressyourself/43798/How-Jim-really-did-fix-it

Elgot, J. (2016). Stephen Fry criticised for telling "self-pitying" abuse victims to grow up. *The Guardian*, 12 April 2016. www.theguardian.com/culture/2016/apr/12/stephen-fry-fury-comments-abuse-victims-self-pity-charity-mind

Ellis, H. (1898). Mescal: A New Artificial Paradise. *The Contemporary Review*, January 1898. www.mescaline.com/artificialparadise/index.html

ESATDT (2012). Understanding the Difference Between Preferential and Situational Child Sexual Abusers. *Evil Sits at the Dinner Table*, 6 August 2012. https://ordinaryevil.wordpress.com/2012/08/06/understanding-the-difference-between-preferential-jerry-sandusky-and-situational-most-incest-cases-child-sexual-abusers/

Fabian Society (1960). Fabian Society, 77th Annual Report, 1 July 1959 to 30 June 1960. www.archive.org/stream/fabiantract1959a60fabiuoft/fabiantract1959a60fabiuoft_djvu.txt

Fairweather, E. (2014). Jimmy Savile sex abuse: "Islington is still covering up." *The Daily Telegraph*, 6 April 2014. www.telegraph.co.uk/news/uknews/crime/jimmy-savile/10746412/Jimmy-Savile-sex-abuse-Islington-is-still-covering-up.html

Field, J. (2012). Learning liberation: young men and the pedagogy of primitivism. The Learning Professor, 20 July 2012. https://thelearning-professor.wordpress.com/2012/07/20/learning-liberation-young-men-and-the-pedagogy-of-primitivism/

Fleischhauer, J., & Hollersenup, W. (2010). The Sexual Revolution and Children: How the Left Took Things Too Far. *Der Spiegel*, 2 July 2010. www.spiegel.de/international/zeitgeist/the-sexual-revolution-and-children-how-the-left-took-things-too-far-a-702679.html

Free Republic (2002). The Sexual Child (Corse [sic] at Cornell U). *Free Republic*, 9 October 2002. www.freerepublic.com/focus/news/766040/posts

Fry, S. (2011). Oh, Sir Jimmy Savile. *Twitter*, 29 October 2011. https://twitter.com/stephenfry/status/130396311320137728

Gall, C. (2011). Orkney child sex abuse scandal: 20 years since ordeal that horrified a nation. *Daily Record*, 4 April 2011. www.dailyrecord.co.uk/news/real-life/orkney-child-sex-abuse-scandal-1099361

Gillard, D. (2013). The Wood Report (1929): Report of the Mental Deficiency Committee, a Joint Committee of the Board of Education and Board of Control. *Education in England*, 13 July 2013. www.educationengland.org.uk/documents/wood/index.html

Gilligan, A. (2015). Paedophilia is natural and normal for males: How some university academics make the case for paedophiles at summer conferences. *The Telegraph*, 5 July 2014. http://www.telegraph.co.uk/comment/10948796/Paedophilia-is-natural-and-normal-for-males.html

Gordon, B. (2014). Does Stephen Fry ever think before he opens his mouth? *The Telegraph*, 15 July 2014. www.telegraph.co.uk/women/womens-life/10966212/Does-Stephen-Fry-ever-think-before-he-opens-his-mouth.html

Groucho Club (2014). The Official History. www.thegrouchoclub.com/club/history/

Handrahan, L. (2016). Child Rape Crisis in America. *Medium.com*, 9 June 2016. https://medium.com/@LoriHandrahan2/child-rape-crisis-in-america-afcf60c0d3c1

Hardcastle, E. (2014). Stephen Fry's "lurid" speech was too much even for some of the liberal minded guests at dinner event. *Daily*

Mail, 2 May 2014. www.dailymail.co.uk/debate/article-2618339/ EPHRAIM-HARDCASTLE-Stephen-Frys-lurid-speech-liberal-minded-guests-dinner-event.html

Harris, N. (2017). Beast Wing 666—Ritual Abuse in the UK. 20 January 2017. https://nathanieljharris.wordpress.com/2017/01/20/beast-wing-666-ritual-abuse-in-the-uk/

Haskins, C. (2004). Nicholas Horsley (Obit). *The Guardian*, 23 January 2004. www.theguardian.com/news/2004/jan/23/guardianobituaries.food

Hastings, C. (2006). Revealed: how the BBC used MI5 to vet thousands of staff. *The Telegraph*, 2 July 2006. https://www.telegraph.co.uk/news/uknews/1522875/Revealed-how-the-BBC-used-MI5-to-vet-thousands-of-staff.html

Hine, P. (1991). Breeding Devils in Chaos: Homosexuality & the Occult. www.philhine.org.uk/writings/flsh_breeding.html

Horsley, J. (2006). I gave up my £500,000 inheritance. *The Guardian*, 26 February 2006. www.theguardian.com/lifeandstyle/2006/feb/25/familyandrelationships1

Horsley, J. (2017). Further Ruminations on the 2nd Matrix of Conspiratainment & Occultism (Inc. Peter Levenda-Simon Cabana Update). *Auticulture*, 22 November 2017. https://auticulture.wordpress.com/2017/11/22/levenda-simon-update/

Horsley, S. (2004). Trip of a lifetime. *The Observer*, 20 June 2004. www.theguardian.com/theobserver/2004/jun/20/features.magazine67

Horsley, S. (2007). Why are there no prostitutes at Number 7 Meard Street? (comments). *Sebastian Horsley Blog*, 23 March 2007. http://sebastianhorsley.typepad.com/sebastian_horsley/2007/03/post.html

Hunt, T. (2009). Close-up on a Noble Savage. 18 January 2009. www.theguardian.com/books/2009/jan/18/edward-carpenter-sheila-rowbotham

Independent (1995). Blair's brains trust. *The Independent*, 12 December 1995. www.independent.co.uk/news/blairs-brains-trust-1525441.html

Irish Examiner (2016). Baftas 2016: Stephen Fry shocks with reference to paedophilia. *Irish Examiner*, 14 February 2016. www.irishexaminer.com/breakingnews/entertainment/baftas-2016-stephen-fry-shocks-with-reference-to-paedophilia-720613.html

Irish Times (2001). Self-appointed campaigner against "tide of filth" in Britain. *Irish Times*, 1 December 2001. https://www.irishtimes.com/news/self-appointed-campaigner-against-tide-of-filth-in-britain-1.340060

Irvin, J. R. (2015). The Secret History of Magic Mushrooms: Overview. *Gnostic Media*, 2015. http://www.gnosticmedia.com/SecretHistoryMagicMushroomsProject

Kent, S. (2012). Religious Justifications for Child Sexual Abuse in Cults. *International Journal of Cultic Studies*, 3: 49–74. www.icsahome.com/articles/religious-justifications-for-child-sexual-abuse-in-cults-kent-ijcs-2012

Kerr, P. (1987). "Cocaine Psychosis" Taking Its Toll. *New York Times News Service*, 19 March 1987. http://articles.chicagotribune.com/1987-03-19/news/8701210845_1_cocaine-crack-addicts

Koenig, P. R. (1999/2011). History of the Solar Lodge of the O.T.O. Charles Manson and the Occult. *Parareligion*. http://parareligion.ch/sunrise/manson.htm

Lattice, T. (2011). Groucho Club's website forum hit by child pornography scandal. *Pressflow*, 1 October 2011. www.pressreleasepoint.com/groucho-club%E2%80%99s-website-forum-hit-child-pornography-scandal

Laville, S., & Halliday, J. (2015). Jimmy Savile given free rein to sexually abuse 60 people, report finds. *The Guardian*, 26 February 2015. www.theguardian.com/uk-news/2015/feb/26/jimmy-savile-given-free-rein-to-sexually-abuse-60-people-report-finds

Lewis, J., & Duffin, C. (2012). Jimmy Savile gave job to chief porter who had keys to the wards. *The Daily Telegraph*, 4 November 2012: www.telegraph.co.uk/news/uknews/crime/jimmy-savile/9653901/Jimmy-Savile-gave-job-to-chief-porter-who-had-keys-to-the-wards.html

Lewis, R. (2007). Disliking Sebastian Horsley. *The Telegraph*, 27 September 2007. https://www.telegraph.co.uk/culture/books/non_fictionreviews/3668168/Disliking-Sebastian-Horsley.html

Libcon (2012). 1926: British general strike. http://libcom.org/history/1926-british-general-strike

Long, V. (2011). Often there Is a Good Deal to Be Done, but Socially Rather Than Medically: The Psychiatric Social Worker as Social Therapist, 1945–70. *Medical History*, April 2011, 55: 223–239. www.ncbi.nlm.nih.gov/pmc/articles/PMC3066687/#fn11

Mandrake of Oxford (2017). Nathaniel J. Harris. http://mandrake.uk.net/nathaniel-j-harris/

Marbaniang, D. (2010). The War of Kalinga and Modern Religious Conscience. Posts on Scripture and Theology, November 27 2010. https://marbaniang.wordpress.com/2010/11/27/the-war-of-kalinga-and-modern-religious-conscience/

Marquand, D. (2003). Lord Jenkins of Hillhead. *The Guardian*, 6 January 2003. www.theguardian.com/news/2003/jan/06/guardianobituaries.obituaries

McElwee, M., & Tyrine, A. (2002). Statism by Stealth; New Labour, new collectivism. Centre for Policy Studies. https://andrewtyrie-admin.conservativewebsites.org.uk/sites/www.andrewtyrie.com/files/statism_by_stealth_new_labour_new_collectivism.pdf

Mendick, R., & Fairweather, E. (2014). Margaret Hodge "sorry" as council she led told to investigate Savile abuse allegations. *The Daily Telegraph*, 6 April 2014. www.telegraph.co.uk/news/uknews/crime/jimmy-savile/10747257/Margaret-Hodge-sorry-as-council-she-led-told-to-investigate-Savile-abuse-allegations.html

Metcalf, S. (2005). Lolita at 50: Is Nabokov's masterpiece still shocking? *Slate*, 19 December 2005. www.slate.com/articles/arts/books/2005/12/lolita_at_50.html

Murphy, M. (2015). On Jackie Fuchs' rape and "the bystander effect." 15 July 2015. http://www.feministcurrent.com/2015/07/15/on-jackie-fuchs-rape-and-the-bystander-effect/

Neville, S. (2014). Former Northern Foods chairman Lord Haskins slams his firm's new owner for bullying suppliers. *The Independent*, 17 December 2014. www.independent.co.uk/news/business/news/former-northern-foods-chairman-lord-haskins-slams-his-firm-s-new-owner-for-bullying-suppliers-9932271.html

Nikolopoulos, S. (2014). Allen Ginsberg, Timothy Leary, and the CIA. https://stephanienikolopoulos.com/2014/07/31/allen-ginsberg-timothy-leary-and-the-cia/

Nobel Media (2007). Lord Boyd Orr—Biographical. Nobelprize.org., 23 January 2017. www.nobelprize.org/nobel_prizes/peace/laureates/1949/orr-bio.html

Northern Voices (2012). History of the Blacklist & the MI5 Connection. *Northern Voices*, 21 March 2012. http://northernvoicesmag.blogspot.ca/2012/03/history-of-blacklist-mi5-connection.html

O'Carroll, T. (1980). *Paedophilia: The Radical Case*. London: Peter Owen. www.ipce.info/host/radicase/radical_new_cleaned1.pdf

O'Carroll, T. (2013). Why children may want to keep a secret. *Heretic TOC*, 29 May 2013. https://tomocarroll.wordpress.com/2013/05/

Osborne, J. W. (2017). Tom Harrisson: An Anthropologist's War in Borneo. *Warfare History Network*, 28 March 2017. http://warfarehistorynetwork.com/daily/wwii/tom-harrisson-an-anthropologists-war-in-borneo/

Pace, I. (2014a). Mary Whitehouse's Favourite TV Programme—Jim'll Fix It. *Desiring Progress*, 7 July 7, 2014. https://ianpace.wordpress.com/2014/07/07/mary-whitehouses-favourite-tv-programme-jimll-fix-it/

Pace, I. (2014b). Antony Grey and the Sexual Law Reform Society 2. *Desiring Progress*, 29 September 2014. https://ianpace.wordpress.com/2014/09/29/antony-grey-and-the-sexual-law-reform-society-2/

Pace, I. (2014c). Gore Vidal–paedophile, literary lover of child rape. *Desiring Progress*, 11 August 2014. https://ianpace.wordpress.com/2014/08/11/gore-vidal-paedophile-literary-lover-of-child-rape/

Payne, S., & Fairweather, E. (1994). Silence that cloaked child sex conspiracy. *Evening Standard*, 27 May 1994. https://spotlightonabuse.wordpress.com/2013/03/07/silence-that-cloaked-child-sex-conspiracy-27-5-94/

Philanthropy Impact (2010). Leading youth champion and former ACF chairman Sir Harold Haywood dies. *Philanthropy Impact*, 24 June 2010. www.philanthropy-impact.org/news/leading-youth-champion-and-former-acf-chairman-sir-harold-haywood-dies

PinkIndustry (2011). The Mezzanine. https://pinkindustry.wordpress.com/demos-think-tanks/

Pleasant, J. (2004). Recalling Alex Sanders. *Peacockangel Incense*. https://web.archive.org/web/20040805161832/http://www.peacockangel.net/index.htm

Potschka, C. (2012). Transnational Relations Between the BBC and the WDR (1960–1969): The Central Roles of Hugh Greene and Klaus von Bismarck. *View Journal*, 1(2). http://viewjournal.eu/europe-on-and-behind-the-screens/transnational-relations-between-the-bbc-and-the-wdr-1960–1969/

PowerBase (2008). Better Regulation Task Force. *PowerBase: Public Interest Investigations*. http://powerbase.info/index.php/Better_Regulation_Task_Force

Price, D. H. (1998). Gregory Bateson and the OSS: World War II and Bateson's Assessment of Applied Anthropology. *Human Organization*, Winter, 57(4). http://homepages.stmartin.edu/fac_staff/dprice/Price-Bateson-OSS-HO1998.pdf

Providentia (2008). What Is A Pedophile? Providentia, 9 November 2008. http://drvitelli.typepad.com/providentia/2008/11/what-is-a-pedophile.html

Rankin, J. (2015). Remembers only: group buy Groucho Club and its legacy of celebrity tales. *The Guardian*, 19 June 2015. www.theguardian.com/uk-news/2015/jun/19/investors-buy-groucho-club-legacy-celebrity-tales

Reference for Business (2010). Northern Foods PLC—Company Profile. www.referenceforbusiness.com/history2/89/Northern-Foods-PLC.html

Reid, R. (2015). Selling used underwear online for £35: Welcome to the world of student sex work. *Telegraph*, 27 March 2015. www.telegraph.co.uk/women/sex/11499381/Student-sex-work-the-secret-industry-in-Britains-universities.html

Roberts, A. (2017). Mental Health History Timeline. Studymore.org. http://studymore.org.uk/mhhtim

Rockhill, G. (2017). The CIA Reads French Theory: On the Intellectual Labor of Dismantling the Cultural Left. *The Philosophical Salon*, 28 February 2017.

http://thephilosophicalsalon.com/the-cia-reads-french-theory-on-the-intellectual-labor-of-dismantling-the-cultural-left/

Senn, M. (2007). John Bowlby Interview with Milton Senn, M.D. *Beyond the Couch: The Online Journal of the American Association for Psychoanalysis in Clinical Social Work*, 2, December 2007. https://web.archive.org/web/20150317000309/http://www.beyondthecouch.org/1207/bowlby_int.htm

Sensory Committee (1945). "Why Sensory?" March 1945, proposal to Common Wealth. http://www.braziers.org.uk/pdfs/why_sensory.pdf

Simkin, J. (2014). Common Wealth Party. *Spartacus Educational*. http://spartacus-educational.com/Pcommonwealth.htm

Spotlight on Abuse (2013). Was Islington at the centre of a vast paedophile network? *Spotlight on Abuse*, 19 March 2013. https://spotlightonabuse.wordpress.com/2013/03/19/was-islington-at-the-centre-of-a-vast-paedophile-network/

Stevens, S. (2011). Mick Jagger—London School of Economics. *My Life in the Day*, 24 February 2011. http://rockphiles.typepad.com/a_life_in_the_day/2011/02/mick-jagger-london-school-of-economics.html

Strieber, W. (2003). The Boy in the Box. *Unknown Country*, 14 March 2003. www.unknowncountry.com/journal/boy-box

Swaine, J. (2013). Gore Vidal terrified paedophilia claims would be make public, family says. *The Telegraph*, 11 November 2013. www.telegraph.co.uk/news/worldnews/northamerica/usa/10441697/Gore-Vidal-terrified-paedophilia-claims-would-be-make-public-family-says.html

The Better Regulation Task Force (2003). Report. Archived at author's site. https://auticulture.files.wordpress.com/2017/02/champions_of_better_regulation.pdf

The Bulletin (1969). Six-year old boy held captive in packing crate. *The Bulletin*, 29 July 1969 (p. 7). https://news.google.com/newspapers?id=uwFYAAAAIBAJ&sjid=IPcDAAAAIBAJ&dq=anthony-saul-gibbons&pg=3970%2C4937233

The Commonwealth Fund (2014). Foundation History. www.commonwealthfund.org/about-us/foundation-history

The Dish (2013). Fascist Fashion. *The Dish*, 28 February 2013. http://dish.andrewsullivan.com/2013/02/28/fascist-fashion/

The Economist (2004). Lord of the raiders. *The Economist*, 4 November 2004. www.economist.com/node/3353060

The Guardian (1999). Hand over fist. *The Guardian*, 23 January 1999. www.theguardian.com/theguardian/1999/jan/23/weekend7.weekend3

The Guardian (2015). John Lydon says he was "banned from BBC" over Jimmy Savile comments. *The Guardian*, 24 September 2015. https://

www.theguardian.com/music/2015/sep/24/john-lydon-says-he-was-banned-from-bbc-over-jimmy-savile-comments

The Independent (2009). How to be Peter Mandelson. *The Independent*, 28 September 2009. http://www.independent.co.uk/news/people/profiles/how-to-be-peter-mandelson-1794679.html

The Needle (2013). Conservative Homosexual Group (CHE) Was Always A Front For Paedophilia. *The Needle*, 5 April 2013. https://theneedleblog.wordpress.com/2013/04/05/conservative-homosexual-group-che-was-always-a-front-for-paedophilia/

The Needle (2014). Blair Paedophile Minister? Ask Peter Mandelson. *The Needle*, 28 April 2014. https://theneedleblog.wordpress.com/2014/04/28/blair-paedophile-minister-ask-peter-mandelson/

The Telegraph (2001). Mary Whitehouse obit. *The Telegraph*, 24 November 2001. https://www.telegraph.co.uk/news/obituaries/culture-obituaries/tv-radio-obituaries/6605110/Mary-Whitehouse.html

The Wonders of Sicily (2015). Aleister Crowley and the Abbey of Thelema in Cefalù. www.wondersofsicily.com/cefalu-aleister-crowley-abbey-thelema.htm

This Morning (2008). Uploaded by solongdearie on 28 Novemberr 2008. www.youtube.com/watch?v=8UjiiVFqP8k

Twigg, J. (1981). The Vegetarian Movement in England, 1847–1981: A Study in the Structure of Its Ideology. London School of Economics. www.ivu.org/history/thesis/education.html

U.S. National Library of Medicine (2006). Early Psychiatric Hospitals & Asylums. *U.S. National Library of Medicine*, 21 September 2006. www.nlm.nih.gov/hmd/diseases/early.html

UK Data Base (2015). All about: Kincora boys home cover-up. *UK Data Base*, July 2015. https://theukdatabase.com/uk-child-abusers-named-and-shamed/childhood-abuses/uk-childrens-homes-crisis/kincora-boys-home/

Visual Culture and Mass Observation (2015). Mass Observation. https://web.archive.org/web/20131023014900/http://archiveadventure.wordpress.com/mass-observation-a-history/

Ward, J. (2012). Illegal camerawork at The Groucho Club. The Slog, 6 September 2012. https://hat4uk.wordpress.com/2012/09/06/illegal-camerawork-at-the-groucho-club/

Watson, L. (2013). Former teacher at £28,000-a-year school jailed for sexually abusing boy, 14, while coaching him at rugby. *Daily Mail*, 4 January 2013. www.dailymail.co.uk/news/article-2257186/Keith-Ruby-Former-teacher-28-000-year-school-jailed-sexually-abusing-boy-14.html

Wells, J. (2005). Interview with Kathleen Sullivan (Part One). *Rigorous Intuition*, 25 February 2005. http://rigorousintuition.blogspot.ca/2005/02/interview-with-kathleen-sullivan-part.html

Wiggin, E. (2016). Of Pedophilia and Child Molestation. *Medium.com*, 18 January 2016. https://medium.com/pedophiles-about-pedophilia/of-pedophilia-and-child-molestation-50fb042a46d

Wikispooks (2016). Centre for European Reform. www.wikispooks.com/wiki/Centre_for_European_Reform

Winter, R. (2018). Gregory Bateson: The Master of Double-Bind Black Propaganda. *The New Nationalist*, 14 February 2018. http://www.newnationalist.net/2018/02/14/gregory-bateson-the-master-of-double-bind-black-propaganda/

Wood, T. (2015). Paedophile linchpin Peter Righton "carried out sadistic murder." *Exaro*, 26 February 2016. https://web.archive.org/web/20160513081306/http://www.exaronews.com/articles/5501/paedophile-linchpin-peter-righton-carried-out-sadistic-murder

World Heritage Encyclopedia. *Fabianism*. http://self.gutenberg.org/articles/eng/Fabianism

Zwartz, B. (2006). "Cult" fights claims of child sacrifice. *The Age*, 22 November 2006. www.theage.com.au/news/national/cult-fights-claims-of-child-sacrifice/2006/11/21/1163871404937.html

INDEX

child pornography
  Groucho Club forum, 131
  O'Carroll involvement in
    distributing, 120–123
child sexual abuse, 273. *See* organized
    ritual abuse; pedophilia;
    sexual abuse; sexual pleasure
    in child
  abusers, 154
  abusive behavior in culture,
    273–275
  child pornography, 120–123
  circumcision, 273–274
  condemnation of abstract child
    molestation, 157
  denial, 157
  evidence for, 174
  forms of, 155
  hospital reports of, 93, 283
  involvement in, 174, 287
  in Islington care home system,
    101–102, 107
  Kinsey, A., 112–113
  Kinsey's experiments, 114
  military-based child abuse, 171
  moral outrage, 157–158
  OBEs implicated in alleged, 263
  and occultism, 210
  organized, 100–101, 155
  Paedophile Action for Liberation, 121
  paedophilia erotica, 22, 280
  pederasty at Oxford, 289
  pedophile gothic, 24
  in prevention of, 286
  reactions to, 156–157
  research on children, 113
  Rex King, 113
  ritual child abuse, 210, 232, 288
  ritualistic sexual abuse and murder
    of children, 163–164
  Savile, J., 261, 290
  Sexual Child, The, 24
  sexual exploitation of children, 25
  situational child molestation, 258
  tragedy of denied affect, 275
  traumatized children, 152

Child Sexual Abuse Prevention
    Program, 172
Christian Socialist (CS), 278
CIA, 41, 71, 75, 77, 89, 111, 128, 215
  CCF, 74
  involvement in domestic US affairs,
    188–189
  MKULTRA, 45, 67–70, 99, 112, 114,
    188–189, 213, 244
  Operation Mockingbird, 70, 188
  OSS, 111
  techniques of subversion and
    conquest, 112
circumcision, 273–274
CND. *See* Campaign for Nuclear
    Disarmament
Cocaine, 50, 182, 194, 207
  effects, 201–206
  psychosis, 206
Cole, R. T., 181
  on *The Book of the Law*, 181–182
Coming of Age in Samoa, 111
Common Wealth, 28, 61, 282. *See also*
    Order of Woodcraft Chivalry
  Fund, 94
  human dichotomy, 30
  interest in optimizing social
    organization, 62
  Our Struggle, 31
  Sensory Committee, 30, 31–32
Communist Party Soviet Union
    (C. P. SU), 69–70
compartmentalization, 79
condemnation of abstract child
    molestation, 157
Congress for Cultural Freedom
    (CCF), 74
  Encounter, 74
  meeting, 75
Conservative Group for Homosexual
    Equality (CGHE), 18
conspiracy phenomenon, 63–64
Council on Foreign Relations, the
    (CFR), 69, 88
C. P. SU. *See* Communist Party Soviet
    Union

ABOUT THE AUTHOR

Jasun Horsley is the author of several books, including *Paper Tiger* and *Dark Oasis*. *The Vice of Kings* is the third in a loose "cultural engineering" trilogy, with *Seen and Not Seen* (2015) and *Prisoner of Infinity* (2018). He hosts a regular podcast, *The Liminalist*, at his website, Auticulture.

www.ingramcontent.com/pod-product-compliance
Lightning Source LLC
Chambersburg PA
CBHW050627280326
41932CB00015B/2548